D1743069

Sexual Equality in an Integrated Europe

EUROPE IN TRANSITION: THE NYU
EUROPEAN STUDIES SERIES

The *Marshall Plan: Fifty Years After*
Edited by Martin Schain

Europe at the Polls: The European Elections of 1999
Edited by Pascal Perrineau, Gérard Grunberg, and Colette Ysmal

Unions, Immigration, and Internationalization: New Challenges and Changing Coalitions in the United States and France
By Leah Haus

Shadows Over Europe: The Development and Impact of the Extreme Right in Western Europe
Edited by Martin Schain, Aristide Zolberg, and Patrick Hossay

Defending Europe: The EU, NATO, and the Quest for European Autonomy
Edited by Jolyon Howorth and John T.S. Keeler

The Lega Nord and Contemporary Politics in Italy
By Thomas W. Gold

Germans or Foreigners? Attitudes Toward Ethnic Minorities in Post-Reunification Germany
Edited by Richard Alba and Peter Schmidt

Germany on the Road to "Normalcy": Policies and Politics of the Red-Green Federal Government (1998–2002)
Edited by Werner Reutter

The Politics of Language: Essays on Languages, State and Society
Edited by Tony Judt and Denis Iacorne

Realigning Interests: Crisis and Credibility in European Monetary Integration
By Michele Chang

The Impact of Radical Right-Wing Parties in West European Democracies
By Michelle Hale Williams

European Foreign Policy Making Toward the Mediterranean
By Federica Bicchi

Sexual Equality in an Integrated Europe: Virtual Equality
By R. Amy Elman

Sexual Equality in an Integrated Europe

Virtual Equality

R. Amy Elman

First published in 2007 by
PALGRAVE MACMILLAN™
175 Fifth Avenue, New York, N.Y. 10010 and
Houndmills, Basingstoke, Hampshire, England RG21 6XS
Companies and representatives throughout the world.

PALGRAVE MACMILLAN is the global academic imprint of the Palgrave Macmillan division of St. Martin's Press, LLC and of Palgrave Macmillan Ltd. Macmillan® is a registered trademark in the United States, United Kingdom and other countries. Palgrave is a registered trademark in the European Union and other countries.

ISBN-13: 978–1–4039–8275–9
ISBN-10: 1–4039–8275–9

Library of Congress Cataloging-in-Publication Data

Elman, R. Amy, 1961–
    Sexual equality in an integrated Europe / R. Amy Elman.
      p. cm.
    Includes bibliographical references and index.
    ISBN 1–4039–8275–9 (alk. paper)
      1. Sex discrimination against women—European Union countries.
    2. Women's rights—European Union countries. I. Title.

HQ1237.5.E85E46 2007
305.42094—dc22   2007013671

A catalogue record for this book is available from the British Library.

Design by Newgen Imaging Systems (P) Ltd., Chennai, India.

First edition: December 2007

10 9 8 7 6 5 4 3 2 1

Printed in the United States of America.

Contents

Tables and Figures

Tables

Figures

Cases

Court of Justice

Court of First Instance

European Court of Human Rights

Other Jurisdictions

European Union Legislative Materials

Primary Legislation

Treaty of Rome (not published in the official journal)
Treaty of European Union 1992 (Maastricht) (OJ C 191, 29.07.92)
Treaty of Amsterdam (OJ C 340, 10.11.97)
Treaty of Nice (OJ C 80, 10.03.01)

Regulations

Council Regulation (EC) No 1035/97 of June 2, 1997, establishing a European Monitoring Centre on Racism and Xenophobia (OJ L 151/1, 10.6.97)

Council Regulation (EC) 1081/2006 of the European Parliament and of the Council of July 5, 2006, on the European Social Fund and repealing Regulation (EC) 1784/1999 (OJ L 210/12, 31.7.06)

Directives

Council Directive 1975/117/EEC of February 10, 1975, on the approximation of the laws of the Member States relating to the application of the principle of equal pay for men and women (OJ L 45/19, 19.2.75)

Council Directive 1976/207/EEC of February 9, 1976, on the implementation of the principle of equal treatment for men and women regarding access to employment, vocational training and promotion, and working conditions (OJ L 39/40, 14.2.76)

Council Directive 1979/7/EEC of December 19, 1978, on the progressive implementation of the principle of equal treatment for men and women in matters of social security (OJ L 6/24, 10.1.79)

Council Directive 1986/378/EEC of July 24, 1986, on the implementation of the principle of equal treatment for men and women in occupational social security schemes (OJ L 225/40, 12.8.86)

Council Directive 1986/613/EEC of December 11, 1986, on the application of the principle of equal treatment between men and women engaged in an activity, including agriculture, in a self-employed capacity, and on the protection of self-employed women during pregnancy and motherhood (OJ L 359/56, 19.12.86)

Council Directive 1989/552/EEC of October 3, 1989, on the coordination of certain provisions laid down by Law, Regulation or Administrative Action in Member States concerning the pursuit of television broadcasting activities (OJ L 289/23, 17.10.89)

Council Directive 1992/85/EEC of October 19, 1992, on the introduction of measures to encourage improvements in safety and health at work of pregnant workers and workers who have recently given birth or are breastfeeding (OJ L 348/1, 28.11.92)

Council Directive 1996/34/EC of June 3, 1996, on the framework agreement on parental leave concluded by UNICE, CEEP, and the ETUC (OJ L 145/4, 19.6.96)

Council Directive 1997/80/EC of December 15, 1997, on the burden of proof in cases of discrimination based on sex (OJ L 14/6, 20.1.98)

Council Directive 2000/43/EC of June 29, 2000, implementing the principle of equal treatment between persons irrespective of racial or ethnic origin (OJ L 180/22, 19/07/2000)

Council Directive 2000/78/EC of November 27, 2000, establishing a general framework for equal treatment in employment and occupation (OJ L 303/16, 2.12.00)

Council Directive 2002/73/EC of the European Parliament and of the Council of September 23, 2002, amending Council Directive 76/207/EEC on the implementation of the principle of equal treatment for men and women as regards access to employment, vocational training and promotion, and working conditions (OJ L 269/15, 5.10.02)

Council Directive 2003/9/EC of January 27, 2003, laying down minimum standards for the reception of asylum seekers (OJ L 31/18, 6 2.03) Directive 2004/38/EC of the European Parliament and of the Council of April 29, 2004, on the right of citizens of the Union and their family members to move and reside freely within the territory of the Member States amending Regulation (EEC) No 1612/68 and repealing Directives 64/221/EEC, 68/360/EEC, 72/194/EEC, 73/148/EEC, 75/34/EEC, 75/35/EEC, 90/364/EEC, 90/365/EEC, and 93/96/EEC (text with EEA relevance) (OJ L 158/77, 30.4.2004)

Proposals, Resolutions, and Recommendations

Council Resolution of January 21, 1974, concerning a social action program (OJ C 13/1, 12.2.74)

Council Recommendation 1984/635 EEC of December 13, 1984, on the promotion of positive action for women (OJ L 331/34, 19.12.84)
European Parliament Resolution A2-44/86 of June 11, 1986, on violence against women (OJ C 176/73, 14.7.86)

European Parliament Resolution of April 14, 1989, on the exploitation of prostitution and the traffic in human beings (OJ C 120/352, 16.5.89)

Commission Recommendation 1992/131/EEC of November 27, 1991, on the protection of the dignity of women and men at work (tackling sexual harassment) (OJ L 49/1, 24.2.92)

Council Recommendation 1992/241/EEC of March 31, 1992, on childcare (OJ L 123/16 8.5.92)

European Parliament Resolution A3-0259/93 of December 17, 1993, on pornography (OJ C 20/546, 24.1.94)

European Parliament Resolution A4-0326/95 on trafficking in human beings (OJ C 32/88, 5.2.96)

European Parliament Resolution A3-28/94 of February 8, 1994, on equal rights for homosexuals and lesbians in the European Community (OJ 61/40, 28.2.94)

Proposal for a Council Regulation (EC) establishing a European Monitoring Centre for Racism and Xenophobia (COM (96) 615, 27.11.96)

Council Recommendation 1996/694/EC of December 2, 1996, on the balanced participation of women and men in the decision-making process (OJ L 319/11, 10.12.96)

Communication from the Commission to the Council and the European Parliament of December 9, 1998, for further actions in the fight against trafficking in women COM(1998)726 (not published in the official journal)

Resolution of March 9, 1999, on the report from the Commission to the Council, the European Parliament, the Economic and Social Committee, and the Committee of the Regions on the state of women's health in the European Community (COM(97)0224 - C4-0333/97) (OJ C 175/68, 21.6.99)

European Parliament resolution A5-0060/00 of March 16, 2000, on the Annual Report on International Human Rights and European Union Human Rights Policy (OJ C 377/336, 29.12.00)

Proposal for a Council Directive Establishing a Community Action Programme to Combat Discrimination 2001–2006 COM (99) 567 final (OJ C 116 E/16, 26/04/00)

Communication from the Commission to the Council and the European Parliament, Proposal for a Council Framework Decision on Combating Trafficking in Human Beings and Combating the Sexual Exploitation of Children and Child Pornography COM(2000) 854 final (not published in the official journal)

European Parliament Proposal of February 11, 2002, for a Council Directive on the short-term residence permit issued to victims of action to facilitate illegal immigration or trafficking in human beings who cooperate with the competent authorities, COM (2002) 71 final, 2002/43 (OJ C 126/393, 28.5.02)

Council Framework Decision 2002/629/JHA of July 19, 2002, on combating trafficking in human beings (OJ L 203/1, 1.8.02)

Council Resolution of October 20, 2003, on initiatives to combat trafficking in human beings, in particular women (OJ C 260/4, 29.10.3)

Other Communications

Commission Communication of November 20, 1996, to the Council and the European Parliament on trafficking in women for the purpose of sexual exploitation COM(96) 357 final (not published in the official journal)

Joint Action 1997/154/JHA of February 24, 1997, adopted by the Council on the basis of Article K.3 of the Treaty on European Union concerning action to combat trafficking in human beings and sexual exploitation of children (OJ L 63, 4.3.97)

Commission Decision (203/209/EC) of March 25, 2003, setting up a consultative group, to be known as the "Experts Group on Trafficking in Human Beings" (OJ L 79/25, 26.3.03)

Charter of Fundamental Rights of the European Union 2000/364 (OJ C, 18.12.00)

Communication from the Commission to the Council and the European Parliament, Building Our Common Future: Policy Challenges and Budgetary Means of the Enlarged Union 2007–2013 COM(2004) 101 final (not published in the official journal)

Acknowledgments

This book has taken years to complete and I received support from many kind individuals and impressive institutions along the way. First, I extend my appreciation to Martin Schain and the Centre for European Studies at New York University for encouraging my research on European integration. In addition, several of these chapters began as lectures during my stay as a National Endowment for the Humanities fellow (*sic*) in the Department of Romance Languages at the State University of New York (Potsdam). My gratitude extends especially to my hosts, Mylene Catel, Geoffrey Clark, and Celine Philibert. As well, I am indebted to the Salzburg Seminar (summer of 2005) for the many conversations that informed this writing. Not least, I am appreciative of the support I received from Kalamazoo College, which, in 2005, awarded me its first Beeler Grant to complete this manuscript.

Let me thank profusely Edmund Assante, Lisa Brush, Jonathan Laurans, and Katherine Zippel. They all read various stages of this manuscript with care and offered untold assistance in the form of general editorial comments, specific reading suggestions, and hard-nosed criticism. Above all, I am deeply grateful to my closest colleague and friend, Peter Corrigan. At every turn, he read the entire manuscript and commented on it with exacting care. This book is a record of our reasoned conversations and impassioned debates. There is no one in whose company I have laughed while learning as much. This book is dedicated to Daniela Marie MeiNing Corrigan.

Abbreviations

ASTRA	Central and Eastern European Women's Network for Sexual and Reproductive Heath Rights
CATW	Coalition against Trafficking in Women
CEC	Commission for the European Communities
CEECs	Central and Eastern Europe Countries
CFI	Court of First Instance
COE	Council of Europe
COREPER	Committee of Permanent Representatives of the Council of the European Union
CWR	European Parliament's Committee on Women's Rights
DGs	Directorate-Generals—divisions within the Commission
EC	European Community
ECJ	European Court of Justice
ECHR	European Convention on Human Rights
ECommHR	European Commission of Human Rights
ECR	European Court Reports
ECtHR	European Court of Human Rights
EEC	European Economic Community
EMCC	European Monitoring Centre on Change
EMU	Economic and Monetary Union
ENAR	European Network Against Racism
EOS	European Omnibus Survey
EOU	Equal Opportunities Unit
EP	European Parliament
EPD	Equal Pay Directive
ESF	European Social Funds
ETD	Equal Treatment Directive
EU	European Union
EUMC	European Union Monitoring Centre on Racism and Xenophobia
EWL	European Women's Lobby

GM	gender mainstreaming
GMB	Britain's General Trade Union
IGCs	intergovernmental conferences
ILGA	International Lesbian and Gay Association
ILIS	International Lesbian Information Service
ILO	International Labor Organization
IOM	International Organization for Migration
KARAT	Coalition of Central and Eastern European feminist organizations
LGBT	lesbian, gay, bisexual, and transgendered
MDGs	Millennium Development Goals
MEP	Member of the European Parliament
MS	Member State
NAP	National Action Plan
NEWW/P	Network of East West Women—Polska
NGO	nongovernmental organization
NOW	New Opportunities for Women
OECD	Organisation for Economic Co-operation and Development
OJ	*Official Journal of the European Communities*
OOPEC	Office for Official Publications of the European Communities
OSCE	Organization for Security and Cooperation in Europe
SSD	Social Security Directive
STOP	Sexual Trafficking in Persons
TEU	Treaty on European Union (commonly referred to as "Maastricht Treaty")
USD	United States Dollar
UK	United Kingdom
UN	United Nations

CHAPTER 1

Rhetoric and Reality

For the states that comprise it, European Union (EU) membership has its privileges. Membership signifies sophistication, democratization, civilization, and affluence in an otherwise disorderly world. Projecting this cosmopolitan EU image is no small feat because, in a global market, image matters. Ultimately, political panache provides socioeconomic cohesion and strong reputations are crucial in attracting foreign direct investment, bright people, and public influence. The competition for global acclaim is, thus, fierce (Van Ham 2001).

As a trading block committed to peace and prosperity, the EU has evolved into a formidable transnational actor. Having expanded from fifteen to twenty-five Member States in May of 2004 and to twenty-seven such states in 2007, the EU now boasts of a population of 490 million and a fifth of the world's gross domestic product. Such factors render Europe's integration an exciting and useful lab experiment for students of equality as well as for those wondering whether national interests can be subordinated to transnational welfare.

Gender Equality Has Its Privileges

The EU's professed embrace of gender equality is important to its alluring image, particularly given the challenges of its recent expansion eastward. After decades of significant data revealed that women's rights are "critical to economic development, active civil society and good governance" (Coleman 2004, 80), official efforts to counter sex discrimination have become a prominent indicator of political cachet. Objections to sexual and, to a lesser extent, racial prejudice and other forms of discrimination have become too important for policymakers and politicians to ignore. Indeed, the very states, agencies, transnational institutions, and leaders who may have previously skirted sexual equality as either extraneous to or "too controversial for mainstream foreign policy" increasingly view it as critical to their mandate (80).

Within Europe, rhetorical repudiations of inequality can both enhance and impede concrete acts to promote social justice. Likewise, commissions on the status of women and legislation against and investigations into sex and race inequality can be utilized as springboards for remedy or as substitutes for substantive action. Not all of the EU's efforts to *address* inequality are necessarily designed to *end* it. Addressing inequality is not the same as providing redress, though it may be a first step. Distinguishing between initiatives and rhetoric, on the one hand, and effective steps toward equality, on the other, is challenging. Verbiage is not verb.

Given the dynamic and pervasive nature of discrimination, the unusual character and enlargement of the EU's polity, and the elusive goals of women's movements striving for equality, it is easy to mistake rhetoric for reality. What, for example, is "equality"? How is equality measured? What qualifies as "discrimination" and under what conditions does the EU consider it "positive"?[1] How do progressive Europeans understand and fight "race" discrimination? What counts as "same-sex" discrimination within Europe, and who defines it? These queries suggest that the terms of emancipatory discourse are every bit as important as the policies and programs alleged to alleviate the harms of inequality. In releasing its glossary, *One Hundred Words for Equality*, the European Commission similarly reasoned that promoting equality depends not least on creating a common language (CEC 1998a, 45; see also CEC 2004b).

What role does "Europe" have for Member States, if any, in defining, maintaining, constructing, or remedying sex discrimination? This question guides this book's investigation into the origins, institutions, language, policies, and programs associated with EU equality initiatives. These include, but are not limited to, legislation and programs related to employment as well as an analysis of the EU's recent efforts to stem violence against women, sex trafficking, racism, and heterosexism.

Examining the politics of the EU and the process of integration through a lens of social (in)equality offers an innovative means of addressing central matters of state sovereignty, transnational power, intergovernmental prowess, transparency, and social change. Because the increasing politicization of sexual equality coincides with a period of reconfigured European states, their integration and EU expansion, students of social equality and/or EU politics have an exceptional opportunity to develop a nuanced understanding and appreciation for the borders between and relative influence of social movements, states, and transnational institutions.

Virtual Equality

Controversies about whether Europe's integration entails the erosion of state sovereignty and ascent of supranational institutions typically neglect the newly politicized issues this work addresses. This book seeks to ameliorate this oversight, in part, by demonstrating the key relevance of social inequality for such debates.

If, as supranationalists argue, the power of states to act independently has declined, feminists and minorities interested in social change would be well advised to invest their energies elsewhere—in transnational arenas. If, however, state-centered intergovernmentalists are correct in asserting that the nation-state remains the primary unit for dispensing and protecting rights and privileges, it would be premature at best (or perhaps even illogical) for feminists and others to pursue their aspirations within supranational contexts.

Still, there is another possibility: state sovereignty and union building need not be zero–sum. The increased interdependence and harmonization among Europe's Member States is compatible with national influence, indeed it might even enhance it. In her circumspect study of European immigration policy, Gallya Lahav notes that the dominant debates "tend to polarize unhelpfully around the decline or resilience of nation-states in regulating immigration." Rejecting their claims, she observes, "Increasing interdependence and harmonization at the European level are compatible with growing national influence" (2004, 9). I make a similar assertion with regard to EU equality politics. Furthermore, I suggest that the augmented cooperation (and competition) between these levels of governance makes the boundaries between state and transnational actors more difficult to delineate. While blurred boundaries can pose a problem for those seeking optimal access points for social change, they can also enhance the permeability of states and transnational actors to varied claims.

We need, then, to enhance our understanding of this ever-changing political map. We can either grasp the consequences of multileveled governance and potential remedies for inequality, or risk losing ground as each level of governance (or particular institution) credits itself with the adoption of progressive statements and policies while denying responsibility for the shortcomings that attend their implementation. This work thus provides a consideration of how the shifting boundaries of EU governance and modified rhetoric reinforce and/or undermine gender inequality.

Focusing on numerous European-level equality initiatives to counter discrimination, I contend that the EU confers "virtual equality"—impressive rhetoric that often proves disappointing in practical application. Thus, one can assume that the primary beneficiaries of reforms are neither those who have demanded them nor those who might need them most. Indeed, the greatest beneficiary of the EU's (symbolic) shift toward greater attentiveness to sexism may be the EU itself. This does not mean that we fail to appreciate those inroads that might be made (and have been made), nor does it mean that we regard the EU's reforms and declarations against sexism and other manifestations of discrimination as resulting from deliberate social engineering on the part of European elites and bureaucrats (i.e., "Eurocrats").

Engendering (In)equality

In rhetoric, if not reality, the European Community's (EC) ratification of the 1997 Amsterdam Treaty marked a significant change in equality politics. Ratification signaled European recognition of hitherto unaddressed responsibility to mitigate discrimination. In addition to elevating the status of sex equality to a "fundamental principle" of Community activity, the revised Treaty incorporated a general nondiscrimination clause (OJ C 340, 10.11.97, Article 13). This clause expands the legal community's capacity to intervene against unlawful discrimination based on race or ethnic origin, religion or belief, disability, age, and sexual orientation. Previously the EU had chosen to leave such matters entirely to its Member States to resolve.

While the Amsterdam Treaty explicitly delineates the discrimination it is willing to prohibit, the 2000 Charter of Fundamental Rights offers a list of basic values it declares the Community will uphold when implementing Union law.[2] According to the Charter's Preamble, "social progress and scientific and technological developments" combined to change society in ways that "made it necessary to strengthen the protection of fundamental rights" (2000/364, paragraph 4) by making them more visible.

The Charter details the rights of EU citizens in fifty-four articles and six chapters entitled "dignity," "freedoms," "equality," "solidarity," "citizens' rights," and "justice." The following are several examples of clauses that relate closely to this study:

1. Article 3: Everyone has the right to respect for his or her physical and mental integrity.
2. Article 5: Slavery, forced labor, and trafficking in human beings is prohibited.

3. Article 7: Everyone has a right to respect for his or her private and family life.

4. Article 9: Everyone has a right to marry and the right to found a family shall be guaranteed in accordance with the national laws governing the exercise of these rights.

5. Article 18: The right to asylum is guaranteed with due respect to the Geneva Convention and in accordance with the Treaty establishing the European Community.

6. Article 20: Everyone is equal before the law.

7. Article 21: Any discrimination based on grounds such as sex, race, color, ethnic, or social origin, genetic features, language, religion, or belief, political or any other opinion, membership of a national minority, property, birth, disability, age, or sexual orientation shall be prohibited.

8. Article 23: Equality between men and women must be ensured in all areas, including employment, work, and pay. The principle of equality should not prevent the maintenance or adoption of measures providing for specific advantages in favor of the underrepresented sex.

9. Article 33: The family shall enjoy legal, economic, and social protection. To reconcile family and professional life, everyone shall have the right of protection from dismissal for a reason connected with maternity and the right to paid maternity leave and parental leave following the birth or adoption of a child.

Although these articles restate already agreed to positions in varied legislation (for instance, the Equality Directives discussed in chapter 3), sufficient opposition from some Member States to the Charter prevented its complete inclusion into the 2001 Nice Treaty (OJ C 80, 10.03.01). Incorporation would have rendered the Charter legally binding. Whether one thus regards this document as a rhetorical flourish or a renewed and increased commitment to a catalogue of fundamental rights, many critics and supporters alike regard its adoption as a prelude to a European Constitution.

The EU's now panoramic recognition of rights against discrimination has some scholars wondering whether this development demonstrates a victory for European feminists and other progressives or suggests the declining importance of sex in conceptions of inequality and efforts to counteract it. Sonia Mazey explains, "There is a fear that the greater effort on race, disability, religion, etc. might come at the expense of gender" (2002, 3). Such speculation, though perhaps understandable, implicitly and mistakenly construes equality as a zero–sum game between competing conceptions and claimants of harm. It also insinuates that women (perhaps feminists, especially) are uninterested in and unaffected by discrimination based on disability, race, national origin, religion, and sexual orientation—allegedly because these injustices seem to affect only other *people* (i.e., not women).

The notion that feminists are only interested in women and gender equality instead of in a broader emancipatory project that counters racism, xenophobia, heterosexism, anti-Semitism, and discrimination against the disabled is fundamentally antifeminist. A "feminist" perspective holds that women are oppressed (as a group) by men and notes the connections of this injustice to other forms of injustice that women also experience. It is a viewpoint that recognizes injustice and seeks to challenge it. Methodologically, feminism places women at the center of analysis to discern both their varied privileges and privations. According to U.S. feminist legal theorist Catharine MacKinnon, feminism seeks to "extract the truth of women's commonalities out of the lie that all women are the same" (1983, 639). Feminist efforts notwithstanding, progressives and conservatives alike often persist, if only implicitly, in portraying feminists as apathetic to and/or unaffected by other forms of discrimination beside gender.

Consider, for example, the seemingly obvious, oft-repeated statement that "women and people of color are oppressed." The phrase both implies that women are white and those who are not white are persons by virtue of their color. Alternatively, perhaps, persons of color are men and women of color (like white women in general) are not fully persons. If, by contrast, the phrase "men and people of color" (in any context) is startling, it is because it suggests the preposterous claim that (white) men are not people, an obvious absurdity in a world that is dominated by white men. Of course, men are also oppressed, but they do not occupy this disadvantaged position *as men* but, rather, as exceptions to their gender. Black and Jewish feminists have been especially eloquent in making this point, few more so than Gloria Hull, Patricia Bell Scott, and Barbara Smith in their aptly titled anthology on Black feminism, *All the Women Are White, All the Blacks Are Men, But Some of Us Are Brave: Black Women's Studies* (1982). It is, thus, frustrating that one must reassert this point after twenty-five years.

The conflation of "race" with people of color and "gender" with women implies that to be raced or gendered is something particular to oppressed groups. Although this is obviously untrue, it is common in progressive writings. For example, in the collaborative report by the

European Forum of Left Feminists and others, entitled *Confronting the Fortress: Black and Migrant Women in the European Community*, the authors deliberately decided in their editorial practice that throughout the report "gender" would "mean women" and "race" would "mean Black and minority people" (1993, 2–1). Sadly, works that address "sexual orientation" share this analytic shortcoming. Thus, in its efforts to counter heterosexism, Europe's International Lesbian and Gay Association (ILGA) declares that "LGBT [lesbian, gay, bisexual, and transgendered] *people as well as women*, jews [*sic*] and migrants suffer from discrimination and violence" (Simon 2004, 5; my emphasis).

A 2002 study of public officials charged with promoting gender equality throughout the EU reveals that these bureaucrats are concerned as to whether "priority should be given to equality between women and men, given the other urgent need of other population groups (immigrants, the socially excluded, the disabled and so on)" (OPTEM 2002, 8). In addition to implying inadvertently that women and men are unconnected to "other population groups," such statements marginalize those who are subject to multiple and often overlapping systems of subordination. They generate the common fallacy that women hold no stake in "other population groups"—a perspective echoed through Left organizing, as well as in tensions between feminists in various nationalist, socialist, and progressive movements throughout the late nineteenth and twentieth centuries.

Perilous Ignorance

The above-noted propositions would be ridiculous, or even trivial, were it not true that the consequences of leaving women outside the common conceptions of harm and personhood can be dire. For example, according to the Geneva Convention, a refugee is one who "owing to well-founded fear of being persecuted for reasons of race, religion, nationality, membership of a particular group or political opinion, is outside the country of his nationality and is unable, or owing to such fear, is unwilling to avail himself of the protection of that country" (United Nations 1951, Chapter 1, Article 1). Both the masculine possessive pronoun and the reluctance to see gender as constituting "membership of a . . . group" appear to exclude women from the category of refugee under the Geneva Convention.

The Geneva Convention's failure to recognize explicitly the specific oppression of women and girls has meant that neither have had access to asylum as members of a (gendered) group of persons targeted for persecution, a problem that the EU has only recently addressed. In its 2003 Refugee Directive 2003/9/EC, the Council insists: "Member States shall take into account the specific situation of vulnerable persons . . . who have been subjected to rape or other serious forms of psychological, physical or sexual violence" (OJ L 31, 6.2.03, 23).

While the 2003 Refugee Directive makes it clear that Member States must now consider the vulnerability of women and girls fleeing sexual persecution—involving, for example, death for adultery, forced pregnancies, forced marriages, bride burning, and genital mutilation—it is less certain whether such factors will qualify them for permanent refugee status within Europe. In announcing the proposal for this legislation, then commissioner for Justice and Home Affairs, António Vitorino, explained that while the Commission has established the foundation for a common EU asylum policy, "the ball is now in the court of the Member States" (CEC 2001a, 1).

When, on occasion, women and girls have received temporary refugee status in the past, Member State authorities have tended to regard their cases as exceptional. The current legislation's tone is in keeping with this inclination insofar as it places the potential remedy for sexual abuse under the rubric, "Provisions for persons with special needs." Sadly, then as now, such abuse is not the exception but the rule among women and girls seeking asylum. Moreover, many of these women and girls may remain susceptible to human rights violations once in a host country. A 1997 UNICEF report stated that violence against women "is so deeply embedded in cultures around the world that it is almost invisible" (Bunch 2003). More recently, a prominent political commentator on European affairs, Jane Kramer, observed that the "terror against ordinary women living in what passes in most of the world for peacetime, persecution as theocracy or policy or a kind of mass social psychosis, has been for the most part ignored" (2003, 68).

Were it not for the efforts of feminist activists and analysts who contested the conventional Left/Right, market-oriented emphasis of integration, European political actors and commentators might have continued to regard the sexual subordination and violent abuse of women and girls as economically inconsequential and thus politically irrelevant. In fact, with the notable exception of egregiously gendered pay differentials, the EU has long regarded sexism as unworthy of its intervention, a position that also mirrored the evolution of its Member States.

The inclination to ignore sexism is no less prevalent among human rights organizations and progressive political actors engaged in efforts to end discrimination. When the European Parliament's Committee of

Inquiry into Racism and Xenophobia released its 1990 investigation, for example, it virtually ignored racism's impact on women. Of the seventy-seven recommendations advanced to target racism, only one specifically addressed women. This was especially worrying not only because racist attacks had become more frequent and violent but also because racists had actually targeted women as the potential bearers of "unwanted children" (European Parliament 1991, 1–5). These attacks sometimes resulted in the murders of women. A decade later, the Parliament was again remiss, but not because the sexist dimensions of racism and xeno-phobia had diminished. In its 2000 "Report on Countering Racism and Xenophobia in the European Union," only one of the thirty-three rec-ommendations to counter racism considered the "potential double dis-crimination" women face (European Parliament 2000b, 11). In a 2003 special report on anti-Semitism in the Member States, the authors ignored gender entirely (European Monitoring Centre on Racism and Xenophobia 2003).

There are three reasons, in particular, that help explain why women's inequality receives such short shrift, not least in discussions of discrimi-nation where one would expect enhanced receptivity to women's claims. First, because few advocates focus their attention on the private sphere, they can overlook crucial aspects of sexual and reproductive life fun-ctions that specifically disadvantage women. Second, the tendency to treat underprivileged "minority" groups as (masculine) monoliths means that progressives focus more on the (masculine) differences between and among groups than on the differences within them (Okin 1999). Third, because women are ubiquitous and women's subordination essentialized, problematizing discrimination against them can seem too expensive in terms of political and financial capital.

However, with the growing emphasis within the Member States on EU integration, porous boundaries, and anxiety over national identity, politics can frequently pivot on male access to and control of women's sexuality in ways that even the most mainstream politicians can no longer afford to disregard. Whether through the acrimonious arguments over Polish and Irish identity and antiabortion policy, Turkey's position on "honor killings," or French and German debates over assimilation, religious freedom, and the veil, political actors typically project their positions onto the bodies of women and girls. Writing from France, Kramer holds that for many boys, "transforming a bluejeaned teen-age sister into a docile and observant 'Muslim' virgin was a *rite de passage* into authority, the fast track to becoming a man, and more important, a Muslim man" (2004, 66; see also Amara and Zappi 2006).

Individuals who struggle on behalf of women to bring such matters to the public's attention often do so at risk to their own lives in the hope that their reasoned, nonviolent protest will matter. Consider Ayaan Hirsi Ali, a Somali-born refugee and former member of the Dutch Parliament. Hirsi Ali is living under renewed death threats and police protection following the 2004 release of her eleven-minute documentary "Submission," an exposé of murders, incest, forced marriages, and other forms of abuse that many Muslim men living in Europe perpetrate daily against the women in their lives, often in the name of the Koran. One may wonder if, by portraying naked women's bodies as canvases on which the Koran is inscribed, "Submission" reinforced the objectification of women that it claims is objectionable. The film was nonetheless Hirsi Ali's response to the persistent denials within the Muslim community about these problems. Moreover, it expressed her frustration toward the many Dutch who remain silent out of fear "of causing religious tension, of being called racists" (Simons 2004, A4). Sadly, such fear and denial have not abated, particularly since an infuriated religious fundamentalist murdered the film's controversial director, Theo van Gogh.[3] Indeed, this slaying may further exacerbate the very conditions of terror that inspired "Submission," and women throughout Europe are likely to continue to pay the costs of political paralysis with their lives.

Consider, for example, a young Swedish woman, Fadime Sahindal, whose father shot her to death after she refused to submit to a forced marriage to a Kurdish man. Shortly before her death in 2002, Ms. Sahindal often appeared before the media, and later the Swedish Parliament, in an effort to increase the visibility of her own plight and that of many others.

As "honor killings" generate headlines throughout the EU and some Muslims there openly declare their approval for such murders, feminists from within these communities are struggling "against Islamist oppression of women and its proponents" as well as "against the guilt-ridden tolerance of liberal multiculturalists." Writing from Germany, noted journalist Peter Schneider also explains, "It is women who suffer most from German sensitivity toward Islam" (2005, 69; see also Women Living under Muslim Laws 2001–2007). To be sure, woman-abuse pervades Europe (see chapter 6) and the number of "honor killings" may seem insignificant when compared to the number of murders of non-Muslim women by non-Muslim men but, "honor killings" rarely generate the explicit condemnation of the killers that other murderers receive from their own communities.

Even Tariq Ramadan, a self-proclaimed and widely celebrated "moderate" Muslim scholar, refuses to condemn the practice of stoning women accused of adultery as mandated by Koranic law. When Mr. Sarkozy, France's then minister of interior, asked Ramadan to articulate a "moderate" position on this practice in a televised exchange in 2003, Ramadan called only for a "moratorium" until a "dialogue" could generate consensus among Muslims. This moral equivocation evokes George Orwell's warning about "political language . . . designed to make lies sound truthful and murder respectable, and to give an appearance of solidity to pure wind" (2005, 120).

Kahina Benziane, whose young sister Sohane was doused with gasoline and burnt alive by young men in a Parisian housing project, explains: "In the cités, women have little value. It's easy to kill a girl here. Their lives are not important. Authorities look the other way and just ignore the violence" (in Goodwin 2005, 116). When a reported 20,000 women took to the streets of Paris in March 2003 to denounce the treatment of Muslim women, then prime minister Jean-Pierre Raffarin promised to provide shelters to women seeking to escape the violence against them. However, nearly three years later, a principal organizer of that march insists, "Nothing is being done to prevent gang rapes, reprisal attacks or honor killings that force women and girls underground to survive" (in Goodwin 2005, 118).

Furthermore, matters may be worsening as government officials in France and throughout the EU grant greater power and visibility, through increased subsidies and official posts, to organizations of religious fundamentalists and dubious individuals that actively deny women's rights. In 2005, for example, Prime Minister Tony Blair invited Mr. Ramadan to serve on his thirteen-member panel to root out violence and "extremism" in Britain. Obviously, Ramadan's position on stoning women did not disqualify him from this post. These circumstances, among others, demonstrate that, unless policies ostensibly directed to the needs and claims of racial, ethnic, and cultural minority groups take women's rights seriously, reforms to further the substantive well-being of all the groups' members are hollow.

Novel Contexts and Queries

The feminist insight that women's oppression is profoundly political, economically significant, deeply connected to other injustices and requiring constant intervention continues to drive and distinguish my work on European integration from other analyses of and objections to discrimination (Elman 1998; 1996b). Moreover, because most scholarship on women and/or equality focuses almost exclusively on gender-segregated labor in the market and/or in the family, it extends limited attention to the sexual aspects of subordination in these (and other) places. By contrast, sexual subordination channeled through, for example, violence, sexual abuse, and heterosexism figures prominently in this book.

Over the last decade, the EU has established formal policies and programs to counter sexual abuse and male violence against women. In addition, the EU's expanded definition of illegal discrimination (to include race, ethnicity, disability, and sexual orientation) has generated very important case law, particularly in those instances where prejudice is connected to the sexual orientation of lesbians. By assessing these later developments, this work builds on prior analyses maintaining that women's safety, sexual autonomy, and personhood is central to the welfare of any polity. The EU is no exception.

Now more than ever, in the aftermath of the Amsterdam Treaty, the Charter of Fundamental Rights, enlargement and debates about the proposed European constitution, an analysis of EU sex-equality politics requires a consideration of discrimination's elusive and multidimensional character (Verloo 2006). For example, how do European institutions understand discrimination against lesbians? Is it sex discrimination because their chosen intimates are women, not men? Alternatively, is heterosexist discrimination distinct from sexism? If so, in what ways is it different for women and men? Not least, does the Treaty's added recognition of race, age, sexual orientation, and disability discrimination effectively confront the simultaneous intricacies and intersections of oppression as lived by, for example, Moroccan domestics in Spain or lesbian mothers in Britain and Sweden?

These questions are hardly abstract. In the midst of an increase in the recognition of ostensibly different manifestations of discrimination, it is ironic that the intricacies of and connections between different types of discrimination are routinely ignored. Consider the *Economist's* coverage of Denmark's strict anti-immigration laws: "Danes may tie the knot with *anyone* (*same sex marriages included*), but getting a foreign spouse into the country is harder." The magazine continues, "The pair must have a permanent home (no staying with family) and—the crunch for many brown skinned Danes—be judged to have ties to Denmark exceeding those to any other country" ("Love Bridge to Sweden" 2004, 46; my emphasis). In addition to wrongly assuming that all same-sex partnerships are between (white) Danish nationals, the analysis equates marriage with registered partnerships though Danish law precludes same-sex marriage. Put simply, not every Dane can marry.

Yet, given the manifold dimension(s) of discrimination, the Treaty's more inclusive reach (through Article 13), and the temptation to deemphasize *sex* discrimination in the midst of extensive expansion and institutional transformation, one might ask why we still focus on sex-discrimination policies and programs at all. In answer to this question, it is important to note that Europe has forged its equality law within the crucible of sex inequality and, in part, through the resistance of feminists to male supremacy.[4]

The 1957 Treaty of Rome, which established the EC, also affirmed the principle of sex equality for its six original Member States. Belgium, France, West Germany,[5] Italy, Luxembourg, and the Netherlands were to share membership within a singular economic community and, as stipulated by the Treaty of Rome, any other European state could apply to join them by agreeing to substitute their calamitous rivalries of the past with a common market for goods, services, and workers. By 1995, the Community included fifteen constituent states. After its most ambitious enlargement in 2004, it contained twenty-five and now has twenty-seven (see table 1.1). A united Europe seemed to promise to transcend those national rivalries and parochial loyalties that helped to engender the dictatorships that made past horrors possible.

Sex discrimination at the workplace was the first discrimination that Europe recognized (in Article 119 of the 1957 founding Treaty of Rome); until recently, it was the only one it expressly prohibited. When, for instance, the British Commission on Race Equality and other race-related agencies submitted draft legislation for the Elimination of Racial Discrimination to the European Commission in 1992, it used the 1976 EC Directive on Equal Treatment for Women at Work as their

Table 1.1   Enlargements over time

1958	1973	1981	1986	1995	2004	2007
Belgium	Denmark	Greece	Portugal	Austria	Cyprus	Bulgaria
France	Ireland		Spain	Finland	Czech Republic	Romania
Germany	UK			Sweden	Estonia	
Italy					Hungary	
Luxembourg					Latvia	
Netherlands					Lithuania	
					Malta	
					Poland	
					Slovak Republic	
					Slovenia	

model (see chapters 2 and 3 for more on Article 119 and the 1976 Directive).

Moreover, immigration reforms that successfully challenged the patriarchal bias of descent and citizenship-acquisition throughout Europe rested less on migrant rights discourse than on older legal mechanisms to end sex discrimination. Challenges to sexual-orientation discrimination were likewise connected to condemnations of sex discrimination in general. Indeed, the European Commission's 1991 Code of Practice on sexual harassment offered the first explicit censure of harassment based on sexual orientation within the EU, noting, "Lesbians and women from racial minorities are disproportionately at risk" (OJ L 49, 24.02.92, Introduction, paragraph 5). Prior to this, the EU remained silent on this matter and thus indistinguishable from its constituent states, most of whom offered no protection against such discrimination (see chapters 8 and 9). This fact warrants the question that all chapters address: what precipitated the EU's interest in this matter?

With the EU increasing its opposition to discrimination, now is an ideal time to embark on a historical overview and thorough analysis of women's ongoing struggles against sexism; doing so provides an invaluable roadmap for everyone determined to reach destinations that are more democratic. In addition, for those wanting simply to better understand the politics of European integration, the quest for social justice that animates this study may provide a more interesting, accessible, and pragmatic approach than is typically in more conventional legal and technical accounts of European politics.

Organization of the Book

This book provides a detailed historical analysis of EU equality initiatives and explores the interactions among various political institutions and actors, often within contexts where race, ethnicity, class, and sex converge to create multiple disadvantages for women across Europe. By engaging *interactions* about initiatives at these *intersections*, I emphasize the many complexities that undermine instrumentalist assumptions, however implicit, that policies derive from the enlightened foresight and/or nefarious planning of EU policymakers.

The EU's equality policies and administrative structures may be distinctive and relatively new, but they did not arise from a coherent and deliberate plan. Ongoing struggles and bargaining among Member States about equality leave their mark on EU policies and institutions in the form of improvisational policies and explicit settlements that specify (or even waffle on) the rights and expectations of affected parties. In chapter 2, the historical investigation into the adoption of Article 119 with its promise of equal pay for equal work between women and men underscores this point. In it, I suggest that although European Commissioners, heads of state, EU judges, bureaucrats, and activists are important political actors, they are not the fundamental architects of gender equality, virtual, intersectional, sexual, or otherwise. This assertion is significant. Although one should recognize the initial importance of all these players, I suggest that there is a more tenuous relationship between them, their plans, policies, and outcomes. In this way, one can better discern the difference between rhetoric and reality, national sovereignty and transnational power, as activists and other actors adjust their strategies and expectations accordingly.

The meaning(s) of policies and their consequences are not determined entirely by the intentions of those who create them. There are, in fact, two key factors in the formation of policy to consider. First, those who use, analyze, abandon, or deny others access to policies can affect the policies themselves. Second, the global context of multilevel governance can influence the way that various actors view policies. For instance, activists engaged on behalf of asylum seekers must consider international factors while mobilizing within a Community whose national histories and state provisions for asylum vary. Yet, the EU's attempt to harmonize national immigration policies explains, in part, why these activists often draw on the experience of other EU countries. Thus, the pursuit of social justice is often serendipitous and complicated, with unintended and often confusing and capricious consequences. Nonetheless, this entire nexus of complex influences informs all subsequent policy debates, interventions, and inertia.

Despite the rapid evolution of the EU's polity, along with the relative youth and complexity of its equality policies, programs, and discourse, an astonishing consensus has emerged among scholars. Most agree that equality efforts have enhanced the expectations, the demands, and the power of social movements and EU institutions to redress discrimination. Although most scholars recognize these strides are incomplete and insufficient, criticisms remain measured; the general response has been one of respectful enthusiasm.

Gender equality has its privileges, if only because it may offer those who claim to embrace it a shield from criticism. Still, those less impressed by the self-proclaimed advocates of equality emphasize that previously overt prejudice may be taking increasingly covert forms, implying that praising the EU for its policies to address discrimination is premature, if not potentially counterproductive. In other words, unearned praise may lessen the vigilance needed to secure substantive, progressive social change.

Whether one is critical or complimentary, moving beyond the received wisdom in European politics requires both a concentrated and consistent search for excluded voices and an acceptance of their challenges. Foremost among these challenges is the recognition that rights are extraneous for those who are unaware that they need and/or possess them. According to a 2003 *Eurobarometer* survey, two-third of the Europeans (from the older fifteen Member States) do not know that they have rights against discrimination even though the Amsterdam Treaty of 1997 stipulated them. The survey, however, reveals that "the meaning of discrimination was explained to all respondents as: treating differently, negatively and adversely people on the grounds of their racial or ethnic origin, religion or beliefs, disability, age, and sexual orientation" (CEC 2003, 4).

With sex discrimination omitted from the 2003 survey, one was unable to conclude anything about the respondents and their awareness of or remedies for sex discrimination until a newer (2006) *Eurobarometer* on discrimination included gender. Then 43 percent of women and 36 percent of men from twenty-five Member States were of the opinion that gender discrimination is widespread in their country and 40 percent of them knew that there were rights against it (CEC 2007a, 16, 24). However, when all forms of discrimination (including, for instance, sexual orientation, ethnicity, and disability) were combined, the percentage of respondents who know that they have rights against discrimination dropped to 32 percent, a finding essentially unchanged since the 2003 survey (CEC 2007a, 26).

An analysis and accurate assessment of the significance of the EU's most recent equality investigations and initiatives require a historical exploration of their context. Chapter 2, thus, offers more than just a focused consideration of the EU's earliest equality law (i.e., Article 119 from 1957). Specifically, chapter 2 identifies the key EU institutions within which equality policies emerged and explores the reasons for the EU's stated interest in advancing them. Chapter 3 provides a detailed account of related sex-equality laws, policies, and programs adopted from the 1970s through the end of the 1990s. It also considers the debates that ensued and the strategies employed by those who restricted such reforms. Not least, like chapter 2, chapter 3 accounts for the many factors (including the sometimes-harsh differences between EU institutions) that compelled the Community to privilege certain courses of action over others in its efforts to promote equality. Following this discussion, chapter 4 moves into a synopsis of both the success and shortcomings of equality efforts with a focus on women's earnings and reconciliation (of home and work) policies. A consideration of legal and subsequent developments, including those that specifically target race and discrimination based on sexual orientation, unfolds throughout subsequent chapters with the recognition that the way these issues are framed matters.

In moving from the EU's adoption of its principal equality measures to more recent considerations of their impact, one observes a rhetorical shift away from "women" toward "gender." Whether this suggests that sex equality is more apt to occur through gender neutrality is a matter for further inquiry in chapter 5, which investigates gender mainstreaming with attention to women's presence in formal political decision-making. Also under inquiry are core questions of whether the rhetorical shift has broadened discussions of democratization and enlightened debates over other forms of discrimination that demand redress. For instance, chapter 6 examines the early efforts of feminists within the Member States and EU institutions (in the 1970s and 1980s) to address male violence and sexual abuse. After exploring the reasons for the EU's increased involvement on these matters and its direct support of specific programs to counter male violence and sex trafficking (in the mid-1990s), chapter 7 considers the consequences of these transnational efforts. Chapters 8 and 9 both concentrate on discrimination against lesbians. The first of these emphasizes the Commission's development from a once reluctant authority to apparent advocate of (gay and) lesbian rights. Chapter 9 examines whether other EU institutions share the Commission's professed commitment to these rights and, for those that do, it asks whether such assurances translate into substantive rights for lesbians in the Community. Specifically, it looks at the issue of same-sex marriage.

The book pursues an essentially chronological structure regarding the emergence of the policy debates over sexual equality. Whether the issue is "heterosexism," "male violence," or "sexual exploitation," the EU's ability to frame these matters informs redress (or the absence of it) for lesbians, the victims of male violence and sexual exploitation—whether real or perceived. In sum, we consider how the public's understanding of key terms can simultaneously instruct, obstruct, and facilitate remedy.

What motivated the EU's interest in these issues? More importantly, how does Europe express its opposition to heterosexism and sexual violence? What, if any, are the consequences of its involvement? In answering these questions, we explore the socioeconomic dynamics that inform the EU's response. As well, we reveal the discord among various Member States, EU institutions, and the contradictions characterized by their separate policies.

The contradictory dimensions of sexual equality within the EU become clearer when one notes the way that each level of "integrated Europe" off-loads responsibility onto another level for the promise of fulfilling it. The reader is urged in the following chapters to watch closely as the language and politics of integration increase expectations through equitable rhetoric, while the responsibility for inequality and the implementation of measures to end it are scattered and so elusive that the promise of substantive equality is easily deferred and what is achieved, instead, is virtual equality.

To assist the readers through their journey, chapter 2 maps out the legal terrain of the EC, and the various mechanisms (such as directives and action programs) as well as the institutions and agencies central to its stated pursuit of social justice. More specifically, our consideration of EU "women's policy" that counters sex discrimination necessarily opens with a discussion of the Treaty of Rome and its incorporation of Article 119, the only Article to make explicit mention of women.[6] It does so by reference to "the principle that men and women should receive equal pay for equal work."

CHAPTER 2

Sexual Equality Conceived

Within the EU,[1] sexual (in)equality has been conceived within the parameters of economic considerations because the unification of Europe is foremost an economically inspired plan, one designed by men who believed that a single, cohesive economic region could engender prosperity so as to diminish dissension among once warring states. For these architects of integration, stemming the economic disparities and tensions among states was, thus, their chief concern. Curtailing gender inequality within them was much less important, if important at all.

Women were conspicuously absent from the initial deliberations that established the EC. In fact, its primary policymaking body, the European Commission, was composed entirely of men until 1989. What then compelled the Community to pursue sexual equality, and what policies did it adopt and why? To answer these questions, this chapter commences with a brief introduction to the Community's chief institutions (including, e.g., the Commission). It then describes Article 119 of the 1957 Treaty of Rome and considers its significance for fashioning future interventions, including equality directives, equal opportunity agencies, and action programs—all of which are discussed in detail in chapter 3.

Key EU Institutions

Exploring routes toward sex equality requires a compass to offer direction. Although this book makes no claim to providing an exhaustive survey of the EU, it does offer the essentials so that we may critically explore and comprehend it. The following section provides a general overview of the EU's principal political institutions for this purpose.

The EU is neither a confederation of states nor a federal state but a supranational and international actor that is entirely novel and historically unique. Since its founding, the Community's political system has evolved continuously through a series of treaties—from Rome (in 1957) to those signed years later in Maastricht (in 1992), Amsterdam (in 1997), and Nice (in 2001). These treaties constitute the Community's "primary legislation" and from them derive a vast body of "secondary legislation" (e.g., regulations, directives, and recommendations) that have a direct impact on the daily lives of EU citizens.

In general, EU laws and related policies stem from decisions taken by five key institutions:

- the Council of the European Union (representing the Member States),
- the European Council (the EU's highest-level policymaking body),
- the European Commission (a politically autonomous body that advocates the collective interests of the Community),
- the European Parliament (representing European citizens), and
- the European Court of Justice (the EU's highest judicial body).

The Council of the European Union

The Council of the European Union (or simply "the Council") functions as the Community's main decision-making body and perhaps most powerful, though least scrutinized and understood, institution. Indeed, a 2004 *Eurobarometer* survey revealed that nearly one in three Europeans had never *heard* of the institution.[2] Known formerly as "the Council of the Ministers," the Council comprises the relevant government ministers from all Member States (e.g., foreign affairs, agriculture, and justice).

The Council holds its meetings in secret and one minister from each of the Member States attends each of these gatherings though which ministers attend depends on the agenda. If, for example, education is the subject under consideration, ministers of education will preside. There are currently nine different Council "configurations," covering various policy areas including, but not limited to, the economy, environment, health, and equal opportunities. The preparatory work for the Council Meetings is done by the Permanent Representatives Committee (COREPER), a committee comprising the Member States' ambassadors to the EU, assisted by officials from the national ministries. In sum, COREPER serves as a bridge between Brussels and the Member States.

Its decisions are binding and increasingly taken by a qualified majority vote, although unanimity is still required in several areas. Treaty amendments, taxation, and the admission of new Member States are all decisions for which the decision rule is unanimity. In most other cases, qualified majority suffices. That is, a decision cannot be taken unless a specified minimum number of votes are cast in its favor and the votes of Council Members are weighted according to the size of the nations they represent.

The Council must accept, amend, or reject legislative and budgetary proposals that emanate from the European Commission and (increasingly) the European Parliament. Together these bodies form an "institutional triangle." Given the difficulties in generating a consensus among an expanded membership, the 2001 Treaty of Nice introduced increased political flexibility through "enhanced cooperation." According to this procedure, a minimum of eight states may choose to cooperate in certain areas, if participation is open to all and does not infringe on the rights of other Member States.

The European Council

Conceivably the EU's most visible body, the European Council is often confused with the Council of the European Union.[3] Yet, unlike the above-noted Council, comprising various ministers of policy, this body consists of the Commission president and the leaders of all the Member States, each of whom serves as its president for six months. Prior to the Union's expansion to over twenty Member States, each country's president or prime minister chaired the Council for six months on a strictly alphabetical rotation. The new constitution proposes to replace this rotation by a new president who will serve up to five years. The European Council usually meets in Brussels.

It meets semiannually at highly publicized "summits" (generally in June and December) to pursue strategic decisions about the Union's future. Such was the European Council's function when it convened in Brussels in December of 2003 with leaders from the ten applicant Member States to adopt a constitution designed to influence the identity, scope, and expanding structure of EU institutions.

Despite the often-confidential character of its deliberations, European Council summits usually promote the most visible decisions on European integration and, thus, provide a major impetus in defining the political guidelines for the Council of the European Union. In brief, these summits encourage the Council and other EU institutions, like the Commission, "to work more expeditiously in preparing proposals that . . . contribute to the creation of a single [European] market" (Cameron 1992, 64).

The European Commission

Students of the European Commission often characterize it as the institutional embodiment and "policy engine" of the EU. The Commission both proposes policy and ensures that the provisions of treaties and the decisions of the institutions are implemented properly. Located in Brussels with additional offices in Luxembourg, it consisted of twenty commissioners, all of whom were appointed for a renewable term of five years by their Member State. Larger states (Britain, France, Germany, Italy, and Spain) had an extra delegate until, at Nice, they agreed to relinquish their second commissioner to accommodate enlargement. At present, the Commission contains one commissioner from each Member State (i.e., twenty-seven in all). However, the principle that all countries have one commissioner at all times was abandoned and the size of the Commission will be limited, though likely not for years after the adoption of a new constitution.

Commissioners, like Council Ministers, are expected to pursue the long-term, *common* interests of the EU; nearly thirty distinct divisions (Directorate-Generals or DGs) serve them. To date, the commissioners and their subsidiary staffs of approximately 27,000 make the Commission the EU's largest institution. Each DG pursues a particular policy area. Within the division of Employment, Industrial Relations, and Social Affairs (DG V), the Equal Opportunities Unit (formerly the Women's Bureau) is charged with the development of women's rights policy. By virtue of its ability to initiate action, the Commission plays a vital role in the Union. However, the Council retains the power to reject the proposals from both the Commission and the European Parliament.

The European Parliament

The European Parliament (EP) is the only directly elected body in the EU and the world's only elected international assembly. However, it is not a typical legislative body; it does not make laws. The EP is, instead, an institution comprising 732 representatives[4] who influence budgetary decisions and elaborate on EU policy directions through detailed policy reports, the power of amendment, and veto on select bills.

Because these Members of Parliament (MEPs) are directly elected from their Member States for five-year, renewable terms, European elections have been largely national affairs. However, once elected, MEPs split their time between Strasbourg, Brussels, and Luxembourg and go on to form political rather than national groups based on party affiliations. Thus, the EP's Socialist bloc comprises parties as varied as the British Labour Party, German and Swedish Social Democrats, and French Socialists—a factor likely to inhibit ideological cohesion.

Of the EU's main institutions, the EP is usually regarded as the most democratic and least powerful, yet one must not assume that it is powerless. Since the Treaty of Amsterdam, the Commission sends most of its initial proposals to both the Council and the Parliament for deliberation; however, on proposals involving the EU's Economic and Monetary Union (EMU) and at intergovernmental conferences (IGCs), the Parliament's role is often merely one of an observer. Still, this "co-decision" procedure has increased the Parliament's interactions with both of these key institutional actors.

Indeed, the European Commission must have the Parliament's approval, and even then the EP is empowered to dismiss it. In fact, in 2004, the Commission was in limbo for nearly a month after its president, José Manuel Durão Barroso, was unable to generate support from the Parliament for his new twenty-five-member Commission. The Parliament's civil liberties committee recommended against the appointment of Mr. Rocco Buttiglione (from Italy) as a commissioner for Justice and Home Affairs, suggesting that his views on abortion, women's rights, and homosexuality ran counter to the civil liberties he would be called on to protect. To cite but one reason for their skepticism, this candidate had submitted an amendment to the Community's constitutional convention that proposed the deletion of "sexual orientation" from the list of prohibited grounds for discrimination in the EU's Charter for Fundamental Rights. The EP's success in denying that appointment suggests its growing influence as well as the importance of essential rights for women and gay men.

The European Court of Justice

The European Court of Justice (ECJ) sits in Luxembourg and comprises one judge appointed by each Member State for renewable six-year terms. These judges may deliberate either as a full court or in chambers of three or five. Given the increase in cases, it is rare that all judges preside in one chamber. Although the ECJ can choose to hear cases, it functions essentially as a court of appeals for the Union—taking references from national courts and community institutions (e.g., the Council, Commission, and Parliament). Member States ensure the proper implementation of European law, and the Court intervenes when plaintiffs allege that they have failed. The ECJ is powerful because its verdicts override those of the Member States and of their courts.

Given the growing demands associated with enlargement, the Treaty of Nice increased the role of the Court of First Instance to alleviate the ECJ's caseload. It is now the common law judge for all direct actions, though the ECJ remains the undisputed supreme judicial body on "essential" issues. The ECJ can also entrust the Court of the First Instance with responsibility for preliminary rulings in certain specific matters. To further ease the Court's workload, ECJ judges rely on eight advocate generals. Advocate generals propose legal solutions to the Court by delivering preliminary opinions that, though often followed, are not binding. Rather, the opinions of advocate generals serve primarily as a point of reference for the Court.

The ECJ interprets and upholds EU laws—both primary legislation (from the treaty) and secondary legislation, of which there are three kinds: regulations, directives, and recommendations. Regulations are binding in law and thus national legal systems automatically incorporate them. They require no separate ratification. Directives, though also binding, introduce broad objectives without dictating the means of achieving them. Member States must implement directives, but each in its own way. Because recommendations are not binding, they generally function as advice given to governments, institutions, or sometimes individuals.

Given the often-controversial character of sexual-equality policies and the disparate social systems and standards of the Member States, legislative interventions to diminish discrimination have typically involved either directives or recommendations, not regulations. This "softer" and more "flexible" approach is expected to guarantee the effective adoption of policies because those most affected by them have a direct say in implementing them (Falkner et al. 2005). However, this expectation might prove naïve and the alternative to more binding legislation can also mean that the interventions are ineffectual. Although one could convincingly argue either of these positions in the abstract, this work considers the substantive consequences of these policies and begins with Article 119.

The Treaty of Rome—Article 119

Although the founding treaty of the EC, the 1957 Treaty of Rome, stipulated in Article 119 (now Article 141) that Member States should apply the principle of sexual equality through "equal pay for equal work," historical investigations into the Article's adoption reveal that sexual equality was hardly the object of its intent (Buckley and Anderson 1988, 41; Hoskyns 1996b; Hubert 1998). Indeed, the demand to counter sex-based wage discrimination came less from organized women than from industry within France, one of the original six Member States. Short on labor, France's new constitution of 1946 included an equal-pay provision to encourage women to take on wage work.

France was concerned that other states not undercut its labor costs by employing women at lower rates than men. The wage differential between women and men in France was 10 percent whereas in the five other negotiating states it was three to four times higher (Sullerot 1975, 102). Still, Belgium, Italy, and Germany had reason to take France's concern seriously. They too had earlier ratified the International Labor Organization's (ILO) 1951 Equal Remuneration Convention. Established by the Treaty of Versailles in the aftermath of World War I, the ILO was the first official international organization set up to deal with economic and social issues through the promotion of international labor standards and basic human rights. In 1946, following the demise of the League of Nations, the ILO became the first specialized agency associated with the United Nations (UN).

As signatories to the ILO's 1951 Convention, four of the Member States had already agreed to promote the principle of pay equity and take legislative intervention against wage differentials between men and women. However, as was the case with Article 119, their impetus to act had little to do with direct promotion of women's rights (Berkovitch 1999; Lubin and Winslow 1990). Rather, employers throughout Europe had relied upon "work that was done equally well by women" during World War II and, fearing that employers would reduce men's salaries, trade unionists succeeded in pressuring several states to adopt equal-pay policies (Hubert 1998, 51). Organized labor's fear was hardly irrational. Wages associated with male-dominated jobs often tumbled down the wage hierarchy once women entered them.

By adopting nearly identical wording to the ILO's earlier convention (see figure 2.1), the authors of Article 119 similarly emphasized the value of jobs within the Community, as opposed to distinguishing between the types of employees (i.e., men or women) who performed them (Ellis 1991, 41). The Treaty of Rome was thus neither extreme nor innovative in its approach to equal pay. On the contrary, Article 119's explicit reliance on masculine pronouns suggests that the interests of *male* workers were paramount. Moreover, by restricting equal pay to only identical jobs (rather than similar jobs), Article 119 provides little

---

The International Labor Organization, 1951

The Equal Remuneration Convention, Article 100

Each Member shall, by means appropriate to the methods in operation for determining rates of remuneration, promote and, in so far as is consistent with such methods, ensure the application to all workers of the principle of equal remuneration for men and women workers for work of equal value.
For the purpose of this Convention:

(a) The term "remuneration" includes the ordinary, basic or minimum wage or salary and any additional emoluments whatsoever payable directly or indirectly, whether in cash or in kind, by the employer to the worker and arising out of the worker's employment;
(b) The term "equal remuneration for men and women workers for work of equal value" refers to rates of remuneration established without discrimination based on sex.

The European Economic Community, 1957

The Treaty of Rome, Article 119

Each Member State shall during the first stage ensure and subsequently maintain the application of the principle that men and women should receive equal pay for equal work.
For the purpose of this Article, "pay" means the ordinary basic or minimum wage or salary and any other consideration, whether in cash or in kind, which the worker receives, directly or indirectly, in respect of his employment from his employer.
Equal pay without discrimination based on sex means:

(a) that pay for the same work at piece rates shall be calculated on the basis of the same unit of measurement;
(b) that pay for work at time rates shall be the same for the same job.

Figure 2.1   Comparing equal-pay texts.

relief from pay discrimination for women in gender-segregated labor markets. The significance of Article 119 and its implementation may be less in bridging the socioeconomic gap between women and men than in establishing the acceptable and enduring bounds of public policy and political discourse concerning discrimination, one that privileges the market's efficiency over gender equality.

Litigating Article 119

Less than a decade after the Treaty of Rome, women recognized and then challenged various organizations, conventions, and treaties for their failure to deliver on their promises of sexual equality. However, it would be misleading to credit autonomous women's movements with this first burst of activism. Unlike organized labor, these movements were initially reluctant to engage in European-level politics and knew little about its transnational institutions. Nonetheless, groups of women dedicated to social change did emerge, especially within Belgium (Ellina 2003, chapter 2). Their mobilization and subsequent protests had inspirational consequences.

When, for example, nearly 3,000 women at a Belgian munitions factory in Herstal struck, in 1966, demanding improved working conditions and equal pay, their banners at a Brussels demonstration exclaimed, "Give us Article 119" (Hoskyns 1996b, 16). Belgium had not yet taken measures to incorporate Article 119 into its national legislation. These persistent protesters garnered favorable media and public support that helped rescue the Article from its largely symbolic significance. Within months, Belgium's government revised its labor law, allowing equal-pay cases to be referred to the EU's highest court and final legal authority, the ECJ.[5]

Two Belgian lawyers, Eliane Vogel-Polsky and Marie-Thérèse Cuvelliez, quickly seized the opportunity to litigate before the ECJ. Vogel-Polsky had watched the Herstal women from the sidelines and, in 1967, authored a groundbreaking legal commentary suggesting that women employ Article 119 to demand pay equity (Hoskyns 1996b, 69–70; Vogel-Polsky 1967). She was searching for a solid test-case and, in Cuvelliez, Vogel-Polsky found a reliable ally. Cuvelliez had been working with women flight attendants angered by their union's refusal to take up sex discrimination. It is not surprising that this duo was the first to insist on formal European remedies against sex discrimination. Relative to their other European counterparts, both had greater access to Brussels and more knowledge about Community law and institutions.

In 1971, Vogel-Polsky and Cuvelliez appeared before the ECJ on behalf of flight attendant Gabrielle Defrenne and invoked Article 119 against the Belgian airlines, Sabena. The case seemed promising. Although male and female flight attendants held identical job responsibilities for Sabena, male employees received higher wages until 1966. Thereafter, men still maintained access to special pension plans that enabled them to retire at fifty-five with annuities comparable to their full salary. By contrast, the company forced women into retirement fifteen years earlier because it reasoned that its presumably male traveler wished "to have his whisky served by an attractive woman" (quoted in Hoskyns 1996b, 70). For older women flight attendants, this preference meant lost pay, reduced pensions, and a new job search at a vulnerable age. Because Sabena had already forced Ms. Defrenne into retirement at forty, the case focused specifically on her exclusion from the more generous pension schemes extended to male flight crews.

The Court ruled that though states are required to ensure equal pay for equal work, pensions paid through state social security schemes did not constitute pay under Article 119. Only those private pension plans paid into by employers, in return for employment, *might* count as wages. Because Sabena's system was largely state administered, the Court insisted that it was beyond its reach (*Defrenne v Belgium*, Case 80/70 [1971] ECR 445). According to one of the ruling judges, "an audacious Court might have ruled that retirement age and pensions are part of deferred pay, but we were not ready to take that decision" (quoted in Hoskyns 1996b, 74). Clearly, the Court was apprehensive; hence, its judgment implied that while some private pensions might constitute "pay," states could legally maintain gendered differentials despite the redress that Article 119 appeared to offer.

A persistent Vogel-Polsky and Cuvelliez pressed the Court to reconsider *Defrenne I*, which it did in 1976. In *Defrenne II*, pensions were not directly at issue (*Defrenne v Sabena*, Case 43/75 [1976] ECR 455). Instead, the claimant sought compensation for sex-based wage differentials. This time the Court ruled that though Article 119 covered neither the pension schemes of Member States nor certain conditions of employment that might have financial consequences, like special age-limits, it did directly cover wages. The Court's comments in this case concerning the "double" function of Article 119 expose its rationale.

> Article 119 pursues a double aim. First, in the light of the different stages of the development of social legislation in the various member states, the aim of article 119 is to avoid a situation in which undertakings established in states which have actually implemented the principle of equal pay suffer a competitive disadvantage in intra-community competition as compared with undertakings established in states which have not yet eliminated discrimination against women workers as regards pay.
>
> Secondly, this provision forms part of the social objectives of the Community, which is not merely an economic union, but is at the same time intended, by common action, to ensure social progress and seek the constant improvement of the living and working conditions of their peoples, as is emphasised by the preamble to the Treaty. (Case 43/75 [1976] ECR 455, paragraphs 8–10)

For the Court, then, Article 119's primary purpose was to promote the market's efficiency for the benefit of the Member States. Countering sex-based wage discrimination falls within this scope.

This second ruling also made clear that a Member State (like Belgium) could no longer claim that European law lacked standing simply because it had failed to incorporate (i.e., transpose) Article 119 into national law. Article 119 thus became foundational for equal-pay claims within national courts. There was, however, an exception. The Court insisted that its judgment not support new claims relating to pay periods *prior* to this decision. This "exceptional approach" resulted from the Court's fear that a large number of claims for backdated pay could otherwise be submitted, resulting in cluttered courts and financial ruin for businesses throughout the Community (Weatherill and Beaumont 1995, 308–09). Still, the decision offered redress for claimants to come.

In their haste to credit the judges with an enlightened position, few EU commentators account for the Court's apparent conversion on the matter of its reach. A prominent analyst, by contrast, quotes a former ECJ judge who concedes the Court is composed of "impressionable people" and argues that the ECJ "was responding to political activism among women" (Hoskyns 1996b, 91). That feminists are to be credited with influencing EU policymakers is argued persuasively by Catherine Hoskyns, but this emphasis neglects a consideration of the Court's own agenda and the global context within which it functions. Feminist influence and institutional dynamics are not mutually exclusive, but neither are they interchangeable.

In 1976, the Court asserted its expertise over a burgeoning policy area that was gaining significance as women mobilized throughout Europe, and indeed the world, for equal rights. In 1972, for example, the UN's Commission on the Status of Women succeeded in having its General Assembly designate 1975 International Women's Year.[6] In 1975, the UN's first World Conference on Women convened in Mexico City. Over 133 member countries attended this keystone event, 113 of them represented by women delegates. The subsequent visibility extended to women's issues (including equal pay) compelled the governments of these states to seek favorable coverage, despite the often-symbolic character of the proposals they proffered.[7]

The EC was no exception; the Commission adopted its first directive on equal pay "to coincide with the 1975 United Nation's Year of the Woman" (Ellina 2003, 39–40). This legislative measure (detailed in chapter 3) served to reinforce Article 119's promise of equal pay for equal work. Given this transnational context, it is hardly surprising that the Court agreed to reconsider and change its ruling in *Defrenne I*. Through a more interventionalist posture in *Defrenne II*, the Court enhanced its prestige and relevance.

Conclusion

In *Defrenne II*, the Court made equal pay directly binding on Member States; however, it took no action against sex-based social security schemes or retirement ages. The ECJ thus drew sharply constrained boundaries around its own power over commerce and wages in Member States. Concomitantly, it enhanced its image *vis-à-vis* equality without seriously challenging national sovereignty, a tactic the ECJ would use again on other matters of sexual inequality. *Defrenne II* exposed a complicated interplay between Member State sovereignty and transnational influence.

This ruling on Article 119 was pivotal in fostering a legal framework for equality claims, one apparently beneficial to everyone involved. First, the Court established its own competence regarding equality legislation, keeping pace with the Commission, which had already adopted equal-pay legislation the year before. Second, Member States retained considerable independence to ignore and/or enact legislation that transcended the parameters of "equality" so narrowly conceived. Last, the Court provided women some redress as "member governments and private organizations alike realized they could no longer simply ignore Article 119" (Mazey 1988, 68).

However, throughout the Community, problems of enforcement persisted. Legislative action was necessary to ensure compliance with the Court's about-face and the vast sea change in global consciousness relating to women's rights. Though it refrained from adopting a single "hard law" promoting women's rights, the Community adopted three key Equality Directives in the 1970s that clarified Article 119. In addition, it established bureaucratic agencies and funded several action programs. These early efforts and some that followed later (in the 1980s and 1990s) are the focus of chapter 3.

CHAPTER 3

Fashioning Interventions

The Court's emerging concern for women's workforce participation paralleled other Community developments in the early 1970s, not least the reappearance of women's movements across all six Member States. By challenging "persistent inequalities in the workplace, restricted access of women to various professions and institutions, restrictive abortion laws, and hypocrisy . . . in matters of sexuality," these movements came into conflict with their states and civil society (Rucht 2003, 260). Whether in public settings like demonstrations and speak-outs or the relatively more intimate contexts of small consciousness-raising groups, the importance of women's personal testimonies discredited the received wisdom of "experts." Paradoxically, such skepticism may have goaded authorities into action against sex discrimination. Whatever the reason, the matter of sexual inequality was firmly on the public agenda and the Community took note.

When, in 1972, the leaders from nine states launched their Paris Summit to undertake preparations for an enlarged Community that would soon include Britain, Denmark, and Ireland, they were keen to enhance their strength as a political community on an international stage. To this end, these statesmen pursued new fields of Community action (including, e.g., regional, environmental, energy, and social policies) and reaffirmed their commitment to economic and monetary union. The leading legal theorist J.H.H. Weiler insists that this summit marked the first step in a "brick by brick demolition of the wall circumscribing Community competencies" (1991, 2448–49).

Promoting popular support for this larger more politically engaged and economically integrated Community necessitated greater emphasis on social reform and, thus, equal opportunities. Support for the Community had never been particularly strong, but it was, at this time, at an all time low. The Community needed to "show a human face and give the lie to those who said it was simply an industrialists' club with no interest in social conditions or the plight of the weak and disadvantaged" (Vallance and Davies 1986, 75).

When the Council of Ministers called on the European Commission to develop an initiative to reflect its changing agenda, the latter responded with its 1974 Social Action Program. It contained a section on women that urged states to increase access to employment, vocational training, and advancement. Not least, that program called for improved working conditions, including pay (Council Resolution, OJ C 13/1, 12.2.74).

This chapter provides a detailed account of the Community's first equal-opportunity laws, related pronouncements, equality agencies, and action programs that followed from this request. Furthermore, like chapter 2, it accounts for those factors that compelled the Community to pursue the reforms that it did.

A Trio of Equality Directives

Although the Commission took no action to establish entirely binding and directly applicable legislation guaranteeing equality, it proposed three Equality Directives. These signaled the expectation that Member States nonetheless adopt common policy goals toward that end that each would implement in its own way (figure 3.1).

In 1975, the Council of Ministers adopted the first Equality Directive, the Equal Pay Directive (EPD) (1975/117/EEC). It introduced the

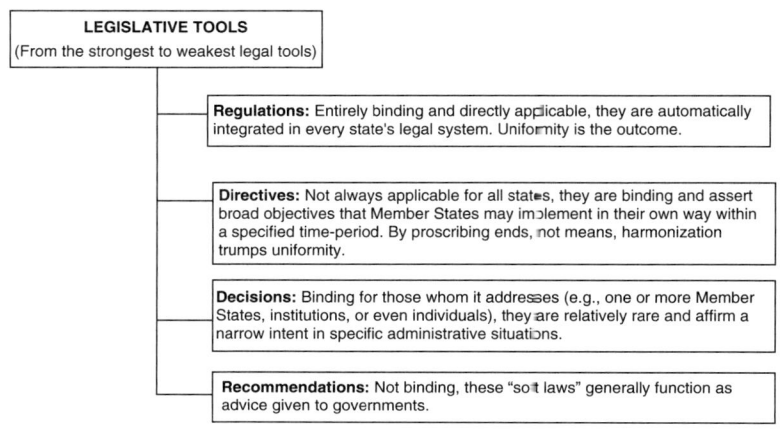

LEGISLATIVE TOOLS
(From the strongest to weakest legal tools)

Regulations: Entirely binding and directly applicable, they are automatically integrated in every state's legal system. Uniformity is the outcome.

Directives: Not always applicable for all states, they are binding and assert broad objectives that Member States may implement in their own way within a specified time-period. By proscribing ends, not means, harmonization trumps uniformity.

Decisions: Binding for those whom it addresses (e.g., one or more Member States, institutions, or even individuals), they are relatively rare and affirm a narrow intent in specific administrative situations.

Recommendations: Not binding, these "soft laws" generally function as advice given to governments.

Figure 3.1   Legislative chart.

principle of equal pay for "work of an equal value" and thus recognized that pay equity requires eliminating the practice of paying women less than men for work that requires *comparable* skill, effort, responsibility, and working conditions. Prior to this reform, one could construe Article 119 to mean equal pay for the *same* work, a formalistic equality perspective that overlooked indirect discrimination manifest in, among other factors, apparently neutral provisions or practices that disproportionately and unjustifiably affected the members of one sex. For example, the Community had long ignored national laws that authorized lower pay, fewer statutory protections, and lower (or no) social security contributions for part-time workers, although the imposition of these seemingly gender-neutral laws on this segment of the workforce had an adverse and disparate impact on women, who made up a majority of part-timers. The principle of "comparable worth" embraced in this first Directive mirrors the ILO's 1951 Convention and, more importantly, enlarged the possibilities for redress. In consequence, even those economies that preserved extensive occupational segregation (a crucial factor in the wage gap) could be held accountable.

The second Directive, adopted the following year, concerned equal treatment (76/207/EEC). Both Article 119 and the EPD cover women once they enter the wage-labor market; the Equal Treatment Directive (ETD) encourages women's entrance into the market by discouraging obstacles that can precede their participation. The Directive, thus, focused on ending discrimination in vocational training, hiring, and promotion practices. As well, it called for improved working conditions, which soon raised the issue of childcare because, without it, many women could not access employment-related opportunities (e.g., vocational training). By contrast, the Commission was slow to recognize the centrality of sexual harassment to hostile working conditions. Indeed, it was not until 2002 that the Commission modified the ETD to recognize sexual harassment as unlawful sex discrimination (Council Directive 2002/73/EC).[1]

The third Equality Directive of the 1970s involved social security, prohibiting sex discrimination with regard to health and retirement benefits (1979/7/EEC). This 1978 Social Security Directive (SSD) recognizes that many women neither wish nor want to rely on the institution of marriage for fiscal security. Despite a general decline in marriage rates, divorce rates were climbing throughout the Community[2] and women needed to become more fiscally independent. A more equitable set of employment-related benefits provided an added incentive for women to join the wage-labor market. Moreover, the SSD helped harmonize the

Community's diverse array of social security schemes, facilitating the free movement of workers across borders.

In the midst of this legislative output, the Community took administrative steps to institutionalize its reforms. In 1976, the Commission appointed a small Women's Bureau to monitor and implement the ETD. Four years later the Bureau established a larger network to ensure the effectiveness of all three directives. Then, as the 1980s closed, the Commission extended funding to the European Women's Lobby to represent women throughout the Community. Both the Bureau (now the Equal Opportunities Unit) and the Lobby still exist. It is to their establishment and evolving agenda that we now turn.

Equality Agencies and Networking

Situated within the division of Employment, Industrial Relations, and Social Affairs (DG V), the Women's Bureau was charged with resolving problems pertaining to women's paid labor. Yet, the Bureau's charge was constrained in large measure because the EPD did not come under its remit. Rather, equal pay remained under the control of another department, the wage policies division. To be effective, the parameters of its responsibilities would have to expand. The Bureau thus kept abreast of numerous developments, including social security and other matters that also fell outside its formal jurisdiction. In this way, it slowly established authority beyond its original purview.

Within four years after its inception, the Bureau helped generate a European-wide network among the newly established equal-opportunity offices from within the Community. This network's final objective was to augment the existing Equality Directives. When it convened in 1980 at a conference in Manchester, UK, those in attendance desired more effective connections with one another and with the Commission. The year before, Margaret Thatcher had become Britain's first woman prime minister, and the country veered sharply to the Right. Perhaps this explains why attendees stayed within the acceptable bounds of "equality" discourse. Future EC policy was to "be based on the individualisation of benefits, positive action to desegregate the labour market, the provision of a wide variety of child-care facilities, and the development of 'appropriate' leave arrangements" (Hoskyns 1996b, 125).

Childcare policies, unlike other gender policies, offered the Women's Bureau and its network leverage in the struggle for equality because such issues were unlikely to alienate the Community's powerful establishment (e.g., the all-male Commission of the early 1980s). Although autonomous feminist movements have long been ambivalent about motherhood, they have also understood its importance to many women. The above policy prescription may have eventually bridged the political divide between the EU's establishment and women's movements, however, the political advantages of pursuing sex-equality claims within "family-friendly" or "maternal" contexts are less effective than one might think. At best, this tactic ignores women who may not wish to restrict their identities and political aspirations to home and hearth. All mothers are women, but not all women are mothers. That motherhood has implications for equal rights that cannot (and should not) be neglected does not mean that motherhood is (or should be) a feminist movement's main concern.

Ironically, the call for childcare and leave arrangements may have contradicted the very equality platform that the Bureau insisted it would enhance. Three reasons are noteworthy. First, childcare provisions may facilitate many women's entrance into the labor market, an outcome that appears to coincide well with the objectives of the ETD. However, parental leaves and other benefits for "heads of households" might inevitably involve compensating workers for the number of their (alleged) dependents and not solely for their work as the equal-pay provision insists. Such a practice of awarding benefits and flexible schedules based on one's household or reproductive status rather than the quality and quantity of one's work is discriminatory. Second, it is erroneous to assume that no one is especially disadvantaged by the privileges extended to parents because everyone has (or wants) children. Last, the Bureau's pursuit of childcare provisions in order to desegregate the wage-labor market often perpetuates the problem the reforms were designed to ameliorate. After all, childcare is, at present, one of the most sex-segregated and poorly paid professions in Europe and women constitute the overwhelming majority of these workers. Although the absence of a common definition of "childcare workers" complicates efforts to obtain consistent comparative data, the European Monitoring Centre on Change estimates that throughout most of the EU, less than 10 percent of the childcare workforce is male (European Monitoring Centre on Change (EMCC) 2006).

A year after the Manchester conference, the European Commission duplicated the Bureau's efforts by extending an invitation to the various equality agencies throughout Europe to work more closely to improve the formulation and implementation of European equality legislation. By the end of 1981, this ad hoc group became the Advisory Committee on Equal Opportunities for Women and Men. The name itself reveals a great deal about the politics of "equality" in the EU. Under the guise of promoting sexual equality, the Commission obscured the existence of women's subordination. It simply placed women alongside men, together in search for equal opportunities as if one sex held no power over the other. This shift in idiom was not the Commission's alone. A change in discourse was taking place throughout Europe.

With embattled women's movements on the wane throughout the 1980s (Banaszak et al. 2003; Fouque 1992, 57–58; Hoskyns 1996b, 129; Katzenstein and Mueller 1987), states that were previously unresponsive to these autonomous movements were better positioned to insist that they were women-friendly, nonetheless, through the equality agencies that they established. Without an organized grassroots opposition to contradict them, states could monopolize public discourse and authoritatively render "women's policy issues" and related institutions gender-neutral in the official language they used to describe them. "Women's oppression" and "women's rights" became déclassé. Replaced by considerations of "gender equality" and "equality between women and men," even the EU's Women's Bureau renamed itself the Equal Opportunities Unit (EOU) in 1994. Four years later, the Parliament's committee on women's rights was forced to do the same and renamed itself the Committee on Women's Rights *and Equal Opportunities*, "signifying the shift from focusing on women's rights to including men in its scope" (Stratigaki 2005, 177). The Committee has more recently been changed to the Committee on Women's Rights and Gender Equality. Lee Ann Banaszak, Karen Beckwith, and Dieter Rucht explain, "While the state's focus on gender appears to be a success of the women's movement and an opportunity for further activity, it also reflects the limits of and political constraints on women's movements" (Banaszak et al. 2003, 26). This insight extends to transnational institutions and actors as well.

The bureaucratic structure of state equal-opportunity offices, with clearly identifiable personnel necessarily deferential to authority, echoed the EU's own structures and political culture. Consider Odile Quintin, a long-time Eurocrat who served the Commission in external affairs before heading the Women's Bureau from 1982 to 1990. Quintin described herself as "not militant but interested in women's issues" (in Hoskyns 1996b, 144). During her tenure, the Bureau organized a seminar on "Migrant Women in Employment." Following this 1987 event, the Bureau was advised against raising "sensitive issues" that might question the Commission's competence and told to concentrate on the concerns of all women, not "partial interests and special needs." Hoskyns argues that this warning helps to explain the "tentative" way that the Bureau (and later EOU) addressed issues of race and gender (1996b, 49). Maria

Stratigaki explains, "Odile Quintin was known in the Commission to be ambitious and able to reframe EU policies as requested by her political hierarchy" (2005, 174). For the Commission, these traits likely made Quintin the ideal candidate to oversee the drafting of the Fourth Action Program (1996–2000), the first to make explicit mention of gender mainstreaming (see later).

By contrast, grassroots women's movements and feminist nongovernmental organizations (NGOs) pose a greater challenge for Eurocrats intent on claiming to represent the women of Europe. Their enduring preference for relative autonomy from formal state and transnational institutions means movements in general and feminists in particular are less amenable to control. However, this independence also often casts feminists and their movements as "militant" and thus outside of the influential loop of policymaking (Vallance and Davies 1986).[3]

Women MEPs began meeting in 1980 as an informal group, worried that with few women in senior positions within Community institutions, and insufficient mechanisms of enforcement, equality law would remain a rhetorical claim, not an authentic goal, let alone an actual achievement. Although this group had wide support to begin with, it soon ceased to draw women across the political spectrum. For many Conservative women, in particular, the group was dominated by the political polemics of their Socialist peers (Vallance and Davies 1986, 82–85). Still others (including women from the Left) resented the expectation that they represent "women's interests." As the prominent British Labour MEP Barbara Castle once remarked, "I've always thought of myself as an MP, not as a female MP. Being a woman here is something I'm not even conscious of. I never had any conscience determination not to take up women's issues in the European Parliament—I have just not been particularly interested in them" (quoted in Vallance and Davies 1986, 69). These and other misgivings aside, by 1984 an unofficial group of women MEPs evolved into a permanent committee, the European Parliament Committee on Women's Rights (CWR, now the Committee on Women's Rights and Gender Equality). The CWR sometimes joined forces with the Women's Bureau and the Advisory Committee on Equal Opportunities. Together they lobbied the Council of Ministers to take further action to promote women's rights, which it did in the form of action programs.

As the 1980s closed, several women's advocates, with the encouragement of the Parliament, also convinced the Commission that it had to do more than maintain a connection to the equality agencies of its constituent states. With women historically less supportive of European integration than men (Nelsen and Guth 2000), the Commission needed to establish direct contact with women's movements and related NGOs, particularly if it wished to claim an authoritative enunciation of "women's interests." A new strategy was needed to increase the receptivity of women's movements and feminist NGOs to "Europe." Women would have to sense that they not only needed the Community, but they would benefit from greater access to its institutions.

In 1987, a group of prominent women's advocates founded the European Women's Lobby (EWL) and within two years, it received Commission funding to ". . . inform, link and raise awareness of women's organizations about European issues, and to ensure that women's needs and perspectives become an equal and integral part of European policies" (Stratigaki 2000, 35). To fulfill this mission, the Lobby established a Bureau and a permanent Secretariat in Brussels that developed close contact with the CWR and with every political party at the European level. The EWL bases its current membership on women's organizations from within the Member States. Each Member State, however, retains a single national membership organization that devises its own means of selecting voting representatives to the Lobby's General Assembly, which meets annually to establish the organization's policy agenda and priorities.[4] Like the Bureau, the Lobby's priorities likely coincide with those of the Commission. It is, after all, no secret that the Commission manipulates discourse within civil society by financing organizations that "directly promote political messages congenial to the commission" (Charlemagne 2004b). According to the EWL's former general secretary Barbara Helfferich, the Lobby is almost entirely dependent on the Commission for its budget, and "its survival and effectiveness depend on 'friendly individuals' inside the Parliament and the Commission" (Helfferich and Kolb 2001, 148). In its efforts to ensure that these and other EU institutions consider women's needs and perspectives, it is unlikely the EWL will adopt a critical stance against its allies.

Augmenting Equality—Action Programs

Convinced by the emergence of the above-mentioned networks of the need for greater vigilance in pursuing equality, the Council adopted four sequential action programs between the early 1980s and 2000. Such programs represent the use of "political power to supersede, supplement or modify operations of the economic system in order to achieve results which the economic system would not achieve on its own" (Marshall 1975, 15). All four of these programs sought to increase women's presence in the wage-labor market and strengthen the force of existing equality legislation.

Coordinated by the Women's Bureau (and then the "European Equal Opportunities Unit") within the European Commission, the programs were funded through a budget-line that the CWR helped fashion. As the British feminist historian Claire Duchen explains: "Much work carried out on behalf of women in the EC is in the context of the Action Programme" (1992, 18).

First Action Program (1982–1985)

The goal of the First Community Action Program on the Promotion of Equal Opportunities for Women (1982–1985) was to consolidate women's employment rights through positive action (a.k.a. "positive discrimination" in Europe, "affirmative action" in the United States). The program proposed two additional directives to bolster the ETD; one extended the application of the principle of equal treatment to occupational pensions (86/378/EEC); the other broadened the principle of equal treatment to self-employed women (including pregnant women) whose occupational status and ensuing pay and benefits were unclear (86/613/EEC).

In contrast to the initial equal-treatment approach that emphasized equality of access, positive action involved "creating conditions more likely to result in equality of outcome" (Rees 1998, 34). This meant funding non-traditional educational and job-training programs intended to desegregate the labor market. Mindful that national leaders are particularly averse to proposals that require domestic spending, Joyce Marie Mushaben writes: "The initial reactions from the national governments were 'predictably cool' and internal assessments unabashedly pessimistic." Indeed, an interim report from January 1984 placed blame at the feet of employers for their general reluctance to initiate special training programs for women (1994, 267).

Some men responded with litigation, as in the case of *Hofmann v Barmer Ersatzkasse*, filed in 1984 by a German who objected to his Member State's grant of additional paid parental leaves to mothers, but not fathers (Case 184/83 [1984] ECR 3047). Germany extended the statutory period of eight weeks of maternity leave from employment following childbirth until the child reaches the age of six months. The plaintiff, Mr. Hofmann, argued that because these optional leaves were adopted for the ostensible benefit of the child, they should be available to fathers as well. Until then, he reasoned that his country's restriction of parental leave to mothers constituted a violation of the ETD. The Court rebuffed Hofmann's position and insisted that the ETD could accommodate a sex difference (e.g., pregnancy) without being inequitable.

Confident in its ability to distinguish between invidious and benign discrimination, the Court rejected the father's position that he was a victim of discrimination. Nonetheless, its elaboration revealed a key discrepancy. It found Germany's position in keeping with the Directive because Member States have a legitimate stake in protecting the "special relationship between a woman and her child . . . by preventing that relationship from being disturbed by the multiple burdens which would result from the simultaneous pursuit of employment" (Case 184/83 [1984] ECR 3047 at 3075). The ECJ also held, however, that the same Directive never intended to "settle questions concerned with the organization of the family, or to alter the division of responsibility between parents" (Case 184/83 [1984] ECR 3047 at 3075).

According to British legal scholars Tamara Hervey and Jo Shaw, the Court's 1984 position in *Hofmann* furthers the view that women are different (i.e., mothers) in a manner that promotes them as stereotypical caregivers. The case "offers the archetypal statement of the perpetuation of 'separate spheres' ideology in EC case law, and the acceptance of the private sphere as beyond the reach of (EC) law" (1998, 50).[5] Finally, this case also cautions against facile conclusions—particularly in those instances like maternity leave that appear favorable to women. Indeed, a further exploration of the policies and programs that comprise the EU's equality initiatives suggests that while Eurocrats and others have legitimized some women's concerns (e.g., those pertaining to motherhood), they have undermined the possibility for a more radical agenda. That is, reforms that might transcend the public/private dichotomy and the liberal understanding of equality as sameness are forfeited, replaced by far more modest rulings (e.g., *Hofmann v Barmer*) that leave male power and related sex roles largely intact. Having legitimized a special treatment approach to motherhood, the Court (however unintentionally) perpetuated the notion that children should remain the principal responsibility of women.

Second Action Program (1986–1990)

Shortly after the ECJ insisted (in *Hofmann*) that the ETD never meant to settle family matters such as the division of parental responsibilities, the Second Medium-Term Community Program for Women (1986–1990) recognized that without substantial progress toward "reconciling" working life and family responsibilities, there would be no sexual equality. It thus established, as part of its initiative, the European Commission Childcare Network in 1986. The Network (later renamed the Network on Childcare) comprised a representative from each of the then twelve Member States and a coordinator. It emphasized parental leave programs and support for childcare facilities to help parents "combine roles" related to work and family. In particular, it urged the Commission to adopt a specific directive on childcare that would have required the Member States to develop publicly funded services for children up to at least ten years of age. Instead, the action program developed the above-mentioned directive, which expanded equal treatment to self-employed women, including those who were pregnant (Council Directive 86/613/EEC).[6] The adoption of any new legislation that might require funding was out of the question. These were hard times. Unemployment and recession showed no signs of abating.

Efforts to integrate women into the Community's wage-labor market continued under the rhetoric of equal treatment, though by the program's conclusion it was clear that women were not always the beneficiaries of the ETD. In *Barber v Guardian Royal Exchange Assurance Group* (Case 262/88 [1990] ECR 1889), for example, male employees in Britain successfully challenged their employer's policy of basing deductions for early retirement on a compulsory retirement age, which was usually fifty-five for men and fifty for women.

In the 1990 *Barber* decision, the Court emphasized that the principle of equal pay applies to all types of remuneration, including occupational pensions. Nonetheless, fearing disastrous economic consequences for national security systems, the Court limited *Barber's* effects to cover occupational social security schemes in the future. In 1992, the Treaty on European Union (TEU), more commonly referred to as the "Maastricht Treaty," codified the Court's position with an amendment to Article 141 (previously Article 119). It declared that it would not consider pension schemes as pay prior to May 17, 1990, the date of the decision.

Leveling occupational pension entitlements between women and men "produced short-term gains for men and long-term losses for both men and women" (Beveridge et al. 2000, 142). Fifteen years after *Barber*, the British government proposed raising the age at which both female and male state employees can receive their state pensions to sixty-seven by the year 2020. Germany is also likely to raise its retirement to sixty-seven, and the Danish government has already agreed to increase the pension age from sixty-five to sixty-seven between 2024 and 2027. The Court's decision, together with current circumstances (e.g., an aging baby-boomer generation), serves as a warning to all that benefits can be gained, expanded, and even reduced under the rubric of sexual equality.

When, at last, the program broached the subject of paternity leave, it acknowledged men's avoidance of parental responsibilities. The Council later responded (in 1992) with the Recommendation on Childcare that "encouraged" men to increase their participation in the care of children (92/241/EEC, OJ L 123/16 8.5.92). This was the first explicit equality measure, albeit a weak one, to target male behavior. It was not to be the last.

Although both action programs addressed obstacles hampering women's access to the labor market, they ignored the deeply gendered quandaries (such as sexual harassment) that women encountered once there. This oversight helps explain, at least in part, why the numerous investments in childcare and non-traditional occupational programs for women throughout the EU did little to remedy the high degree of sex segregation in the community's wage-labor market. Women may have acquired the time and skills necessary for traditional male jobs, but once hired many quickly opted out; for scores of these women the inverse connection between sexual harassment and occupational segregation by sex was obvious. Establishing a causal link between harassment and sex discrimination through law was another matter. Proponents of legal reform within France and the Netherlands regarded the EU as an ideal venue to push for measures their governments were reluctant to adopt (Zippel 2006, 92). However, it was only in 1983 after the U.K. Industrial Tribunal concluded that sexual harassment constitutes unlawful sex discrimination, that the Parliament's CWR was able to request (in 1986) an assessment of existing remedies available to women sexually harassed at work (Collins 1996, 26).

The Committee's demand for an inquiry into sexual harassment bridged the EU's treaty-bound emphasis on the workplace with women's movements' radical determination to politicize sexual abuse. Upon receiving the request, the Council asked the Commission to conduct an investigation. The Commission, in turn, contacted Michael Rubenstein, a legal expert on industrial relations, to author a report. In 1988, the Commission released Rubenstein's Community-wide report on sexual harassment. Entitled "The Dignity of Women at Work," it offered an overview of the problem throughout the Member States and the initiatives each had taken to end the abuse (Rubenstein 1988). Although it corroborated the need for a directive to counter sexual harassment, the Commission insisted that the 1976 ETD offered adequate protection (Carter 1992).[7]

With the second action program about to conclude and Ireland holding the presidency of the Council, the Irish government called on the Commission to take additional action. More specifically, it requested the adoption of a Code of Practice, guidelines to help establish effective ways of mitigating sexual harassment throughout the Member States. In general, Member States welcomed the reform, "the significance of which was more symbolic than legal." Evelyn Collins, a former official from Northern Ireland's Equal Opportunities Commission, explains, the resolution "appeared attractive to governments and employers/trade unions who wished to be seen as taking the issue seriously, especially as the costs associated with implementing this measure were likely to be minimal" (1996, 27–28). While pensions and other matters more directly tied to earnings proved costly, on the matter of sexual harassment, a broad-based, influential constituency emerged that questioned the Commission's assertion that existing legislation (namely the 1976 ETD) offered adequate redress to women at work.

Under pressure to adopt some measure, the Commission passed the Recommendation on the Protection of the Dignity of Women and Men at Work and appended the Code of Practice to it (92/131/EEC). The recommendation's goal was two-fold: to define sexual harassment and to promote awareness that it conflicts with equal treatment as provided in the ETD. The Commission defined sexual harassment as "unwanted conduct of a sexual nature, or other conduct based on sex affecting the *dignity* of women and men at work" (92/131/EEC, Section 2; my emphasis). In addition, it emphasized the recipient's perspective of unwanted, offensive behaviors that could stem from employers and employees alike. In consequence, the recommendation recognized that a work environment in which employees feel sexually intimidated (e.g., through the public display of pornographic material) is as violative as when colleagues and/or employers implicitly or explicitly threaten women with material retribution for not performing sexually.[8] According to the German legal scholar Susanne Baer, this "was the first time that the Community acted, however ineffectively, to counter an overtly sexualized form of sex discrimination" (1996, 57).[9] Following the Commission's lead, states found it difficult to ignore the recommendation completely, even if (as a discretionary measure) it did not require them to act.

Third Action Program (1991–1995)

During the Third Medium-Term Action Program on Equal Opportunities for Women *and Men* (1991–1995),[10] the momentum for efforts against sexual harassment slowed. The program contained no explicit mention of the abuse and, for the first time, the Commission inserted the concept of "gender-mainstreaming" into the discussion. Calling for the systematic incorporation of equal opportunities into all Community policies, but nowhere providing the means to do this, the Commission instead committed nearly one-third of the program's budget to encouraging women's presence in decision-making. Having established Women in Decision-Making, a new network that issued comparative research on women and politics, the Commission helped inform the strategies of women wishing to enter the European Parliament (in 1994). This particular objective was a high priority for the new head of the EOU (1992–1996), Agnès Hubert. More importantly, women's political presence was considered an important indicator of democracy, one that coincided with more general efforts (taken at Maastricht in 1992) to emphasize "European citizenship" and augment the Parliament's power through co-decision.[11]

Although gender-neutral in name, the third program clearly affirmed positive action on behalf of women. In fact, the Commission's recommendation was explicit: "An employer with a choice between equally qualified candidates should give preference to women" (CEC 1993, 6).[12] To enhance the qualifications of women already in the workforce and reduce the mounting unemployment of still others, the Commission made the job training initiative NOW (New Opportunities for Women) an integral part of its third action program. Commissioners believed that their "positive action strategy" (i.e., "positive discrimination") was expressly provided in the ETD (Article 2(4)), as a temporary measure that would complement existing prohibitions on unlawful direct and indirect discrimination. In accordance with this goal, Member States implemented various positive action programs for women and those objecting to such efforts pursued legal challenges as they had done in the past.

Debate over the legality of "positive discrimination" reached a fevered pitch in 1995 when the ECJ released its ruling in *Kalanke v Freie Hansestadt Bremen* (Case C-450/93 [1995] ECR 3069). The case involved a regulation adopted by the German city-state of Bremen regarding appointments and promotions to administrative posts in sectors where women had been underrepresented. Under the presumption that women should make up at least half of the staff, the municipality's equal-treatment law declared that when women and men with the same qualifications apply for the same position or promotion, the city-state should give women priority in predominantly male sectors. Bremen's Park Service applied the regulation when seeking a department manager and Mr. Kalanke, a horticulturist, sued when an *equally qualified* woman horticulturist applied for and received the position he sought. In turn, Germany's Supreme Labor Court requested the ECJ's assistance in determining whether Bremen's law conformed to the ETD.

The Court ruled in Mr. Kalanke's favor, finding that Bremen's automatic guarantee of appointments and promotions to women over equally qualified men constituted *impermissible discrimination*. The decision read: "A national rule which guarantees women absolute and unconditional priority for appointment or promotion . . . goes beyond promoting equal opportunities and substitutes for it the result of 'equality of representation' which is only to be arrived at by providing such equality" (Case C-450/93 [1995] ECR 3069, Summary). This reasoning implies that positive action constitutes "reverse discrimination" and that equality can be reached by simply treating everyone the same, as if equality between men and women had already been achieved. The fact that granting women formal equality with men has proven an insufficient means to achieving material equality is ignored. As Patrizia Longo pointedly suggests, "The way rights are conceptualized seems to maintain, to affirm and sometimes even to increase the relative power relations between the sexes" (2001, 273).

The Court found Bremen's approach to affirmative action excessive, but it offered little guidance for establishing what initiatives would be permissible. Moreover, *Kalanke* could be read to contradict the spirit of the recently adopted 1992 Treaty on European Union (a.k.a. the Maastricht Treaty). Under the Social Protocol, the Treaty insists that the Union "shall not prevent any Member State from maintaining or adopting measures providing for specific advantages in order to make it easier for women to pursue a vocational activity or prevent or compensate for disadvantages in their professional careers" (OJ C 191, 29.07.92).

A frustrated Commission reacted immediately and interpreted the *Kalanke* judgment narrowly to reduce its impact. It was thus able to still the more indignant responses from varied women's organizations such as the EWL, the Parliament's CWR, and the European Women Lawyers' Association. The Commission claimed, "Quota systems which fall short of the degree of rigidity and automaticity provided for by the Bremen law have not been touched by the Court's judgment" (CEC 1996a, 9). In short, the Commission insisted that the Court rejected only rigid applications of affirmative action. Nonetheless, confusion persisted among national courts with calls for further clarification.

In what was clearly a political response (Stratigaki 2000, 41), the Court substantiated the Commission's call for a narrow reading of *Kalanke* two years later in *Marschall v Land Nordrhein-Westfalen* (Case C-409/95 [1997] ECR 6363). In yet another German case, reminiscent of *Kalanke*, a tenured male secondary school teacher (Mr. Marschall from the state of North Rhine Westphalia) was denied a promotion that went, instead, to a woman. Upon learning that he was *as qualified* as the successful female candidate, but that the region's regulation favored her application in an effort to achieve gender balance, Mr. Marschall challenged the law, which maintains:

> Where, in the sector of the authority responsible for promotion, there are fewer women than men in the particular higher grade post in the career bracket, women are to be given priority for promotion in the event of equal suitability, competence and professional performance, *unless reasons specific to an individual [male] candidate tilt the balance in his favour.* (Case C-409/95 [1997] ECR 6363, paragraph 3; my emphasis)

By emphasizing this last clause ("the savings clause"), the Court distinguished *Marschall* from *Kalanke*. It stressed that the state does not guarantee women absolute and unconditional priority for appointment or promotion. Indeed, administrations can still "tilt the balance" in men's favor.

If in *Kalanke* the Court implied that granting women the same rights and opportunities as men could be a sufficient guarantor of equality, then in *Marschall* it recognized that this is not always the case. "Even where male and female candidates are equally qualified, male candidates tend to be promoted in preference to female candidates." This happens "because of prejudices and stereotypes concerning the role and capacities of women in working life and the fear, for example, that women will interrupt their careers more frequently" (Case C-409/95 [1997] ECR I-6363, paragraph 3). After conceding that men "tend to be promoted," the Court implicitly attributed this circumstance to women's roles as mothers and caretakers.

In emphasizing wide-ranging prejudice and employers' "fears" about whether women are reliable workers, the Court evaded the possibility that some men may simply resent and/or fear competition from women over appointments and pay. Throughout the *Marschall* decision, men were conspicuously absent in their own roles as potential employers and coworkers responsible for the hiring and promotional decisions that might adversely affect women's lives. This is curious, especially as the (above-mentioned) litigants who militated against sex-discrimination reforms have all been men, not women.

Fourth Action Program (1996–2000)

Drafted in the aftermath of the UN's Fourth World Conference on Women, held in Beijing in 1995, amid conflict over "positive discrimination" and with limited input from the EOU, the Fourth Medium-Term Community Action Program on Equal Opportunities for Women and Men (1996–2000) endeavored to "mainstream" (i.e., integrate) sexual equality into all activities and program areas. Although the Commission first formally acknowledged gender mainstreaming (GM) in its previous action plan, it failed to define GM until its 1996 Communication on the matter (CEC 1996e).

Unlike earlier approaches that may have restricted efforts to promote equality to the implementation of specific measures to help women, GM mobilizes "all general policies and measures specifically for the purpose of achieving equality by actively and openly taking into account at the planning stage their possible effects on the respective situation of men and women (gender perspective)" (CEC 1996e, 2). Utilizing a procedure known as "gender auditing," GM calls for the systematic examination of measures and policies to account for the possible consequences of their definition and implementation. A GM "tool kit" suggests that auditors ask, "In what ways are policies and their associated resource allocations likely to reduce or increase gender inequalities" (CEC 2004a, 103)? The program's ambition has been "to make sure that discriminatory effects are neutralized and that gender equality is promoted" (CEC 2001b, 17).

According to policy analysts Christine Booth and Cinnamon Bennett, GM "fully acknowledges for the first time in the Union's history, the relevance of men's lives to the equality debate." Indeed, they assert this policy shift was a political response to men's "feelings of resentment and alienation" over positive action measures (2002, 438), an assertion since substantiated by evidence of its initial use to eliminate positive action (Woodward 2003). In addition, Stratigaki (2005) provides textual evidence from various Commission reports and notes that NOW (New Opportunities for Women), an employment training program once specific to women, was replaced by a more general program to combat discrimination (EQUAL) that no longer referred to women as a group targeted for discrimination.

The increased emphasis on men was not, however, without benefit to some women. For example, the passage of the 1996 Parental Leave Directive seeks to redefine the gendered division of labor by encouraging greater male participation in domestic responsibilities (96/34/EC). Accordingly, it establishes a three-month minimum leave (though not necessarily paid) *for each parent*, to be taken during the first eight years of his or her child's life.

For the first time, European law extended the right to parental leave to fathers, thus indicating that childcare need not be the exclusive responsibility of mothers, a position that women's movements had argued for decades prior. Yet, without a provision for a minimum standard of remuneration for workers during their period of absence, the Directive fails to address the ways that gendered salary scales severely constrain choices within the family about who can and cannot afford to stay at home with children. That is, it is unlikely that dual-career families with higher earning fathers can afford paternity leaves, despite their personal desire for egalitarian parenting.

After reflecting on the circumscribed character of the Parental Leave Directive and the various communications leading up to it, scholars suggest that the EU's interest in "family" policy stems less from the desire to redress gendered imbalances within the domestic sphere than from anxiety over decreasing birth rates and the problem that this presents for the wage-labor market (Guerrina 2002, 52; McGlynn 2000). While this concern had been around for years, GM—with its emphasis on deeply gendered matters such as childcare—offered a novel context within which to raise the matter once again.

One of the most ominous aspects of GM is not that it focused attention on men but that it put all gender-equality mechanisms into question, a particularly ironic consequence as many women from within the EU's equal-opportunities network initiated the demand for GM. Following her promotion in 1995 to Director of Employment (DG V), Odile Quintin, the once deferential head of the Women's Bureau, was charged with equality policy and, in turn, assigned the task of drafting the Commission's position on GM to two male officials, neither of whom had prior experience with equality issues. If, in the Weberian sense, any neutral individual might function as a bureaucratic expert, these men were better qualified than women's advocates whose political commitment to social justice undermined the appearance of their objectivity.

Not only did these male officials reject the input from the recently renamed Women's Bureau (now EOU), they insinuated that the unit represented a "women's ghetto" (Stratigaki 2005, 175). The suggestion that the EOU was no longer suitable in the era of GM coincided with the 1996 dismissal of that unit's head, Agnès Hubert, and the discontinuation of an expert group that she helped start, Women in Decision-Making. Given this climate, it is hardly surprising that others adopted a similar hostility toward offices associated with women's issues. The following year, the very existence of the Committee on Women's Rights was challenged from within the European Parliament. Indeed, when the Swedish MEP, Hadar Cars, proposed its elimination, the matter generated international headlines ("New Steps Proposed in Equality Dance" 1997).

Concerned that their opponents could further employ GM to dilute equality offices, instruments, and arguments, women's advocates (from CWR, EWL, and the EOU) convinced the Commission of the need for a "dual strategy." This approach recognizes that persistent inequalities require *both* positive action measures and GM. The Commission's 1998 follow-up report, prepared in part by the EOU, reads, "Programmes, positive action measures and budget lines/budgetary allocations specifically targeted to equal opportunities should complement the mainstreaming approach" (CEC 1998e, 7).

The Treaty of Amsterdam

The 1997 Treaty of Amsterdam presaged the two-pronged approach to GM in two important ways. First, the treaty granted mainstreaming legal standing by stipulating, "the Community shall aim to eliminate inequalities, and promote equality between men and women" in all its activities (Article 3(2)). Second, it expressly permitted Member States to maintain positive measures for the underrepresented sex (most often women), insisting this does not conflict with the principle of equal treatment (Article 3(2)). Women's advocates welcomed this clarification, especially in the aftermath of the Court's resistance (in *Kalanke* and *Marschall*) to positive action measures.

In addition, the treaty encouraged Member States to develop coordinated employment strategies to promote gender equality. To this end, the Commission initiated annual employment guidelines that Member States consider in the National Action Plans (NAPs) they develop for both the Commission and Council. Ultimately, however, the Commission determines whether states are sufficiently addressing equal opportunities. If this suggests the diminished role of states (however slight) in defining national employment and equality policies, stagnant expectations could undermine the Commission's strength. The Commission's first common issue was childcare and a special section of its 1999 guidelines called for "reconciling work and family" in ways that brought to mind the Community's Second Action Program (1986–1990). Nonetheless, other changes are noteworthy.

Prior to Amsterdam, the promotion of equality between men and women was largely restricted in scope since it related only to equal pay in Article 141 (ex Article 119) of the EC Treaty. While the nonbinding equality provisions of this treaty ultimately rested on the political will of the constituent states, they broadened the scope of Article 119 (Shaw 2002). Article 13 of the Amsterdam treaty allowed that the Community "may" take action to combat race, ethnic, disability, and sexual orientation discrimination.

Amsterdam did not create legally enforceable rights, but it did expand the opportunity-structure for social justice advocates, a move that coincided with the Commission's adoption of an additional directive on sex discrimination the same year. The 1997 Directive on the Burden of Proof in sex-discrimination cases shifted some of the onus away from those alleging violation(s) to those that stand accused of them (97/80/EC). For example, after an employee shows a prima facie case of direct or indirect discrimination, the burden shifts to the employer to prove that no violation occurred. In essence, plaintiffs enter courts under the legal presumption that they have endured discrimination.

In light of these reforms and others, the Community insists that its "legislation has been key to making progress in equality between women and men" (CEC 2006b, 3), but the question remains: have women gained more than just the added *potential* to counter discrimination? Answering this question is the task of chapter 4. I conclude this chapter with the reasons why the Community selected to pursue gender equality in the first place.

Conclusion

That the EU should be interested in promoting "women's interests" at all is politically significant. The Community's economic liberalism has long functioned as a key incentive for its social initiatives (Majone 1993), and efforts to counter sexual inequality at work have been chief among them. When, for example, the leaders of nine of the Member States met at the Paris Summit to enlarge the Community, they initiated the 1974 Action Program to both respond to worker unrest and legitimize their efforts. In addition to calling for the upward harmonization of labor standards, the program called for measures to increase women's access to and advancement within the labor market.

While access to the labor market may prove beneficial to women, the Union's access to women's relatively inexpensive and well-disciplined labor advances the interests of capital across Member States and, not least, the men living within them (Leghorn and Parker 1981, 78–79). Thus, "women's equality" meant more skilled labor to offset labor shortages, a more efficient use of human capital, extra incomes to tax, a reduction in occupational pension benefits (through *Barber*), and, perhaps, greater support for the political systems of the Member States and the larger Community.

If it is tempting to credit Community's elite with the adoption of policies that they anticipated would redound to their own benefit, several factors compromise the image of their confident planning. First, by adopting equal-pay legislation to offset a possible decline in male wages, the architects of Europe's integration actually increased expectations among women to fulfill its promise of equal pay. Second, reforms often entailed the adoption of several other measures to implement them. For example, the initial guarantee of equal pay led to a pledge of equal treatment, which, in turn, brought calls for improved work conditions and, by extension, an end to sexual harassment in the workplace. Third, subsequent struggles within the Community over the adoption and implementation of various initiatives inspired the formation of equality networks and women's increased presence in conventional politics. Last, women's resulting public visibility led to public discourse about men and the increased expectation that they take on their fair share of parental and other household responsibilities.

Women's advocates also met with unanticipated challenges, several of which likely stemmed from their political success. For instance, when advocates of GM demanded a thorough and rigorous incorporation of equal opportunities into public policies and EU institutions, they had not fully anticipated the ways that their opponents would employ the logic of mainstreaming to undermine women's rights agencies. Considering the proliferation of gender-equality policies and programs, today's Community is vastly different from decades ago. Nonetheless, this change may result less from the specific intentions of the EU's political actors than to factors over which they have had limited control.

That the Community regards itself as a leader in efforts to combat gender inequality is indisputable. In 2006, the Commission's report on equality between women and men avers both that "the EU has been at the forefront of gender equality from the outset," and that it "has contributed to gender equality beyond its borders" (CEC 2006b, 9).

Our historically grounded analysis of gender equality efforts nonetheless reveals a significantly more modest role for the Community than is suggested by the material it often publishes on itself. Indeed, the EU is less a leader than a follower of gender equality reform. Consider, for example, the Community's first Equality Directive. The Community introduced this 1975 EPD to coincide with the UN's first World Conference on Women, a meeting that women working within the UN fought hard to convene. The Directive may have formally introduced the principle of equal pay for "work of an equal value" into the Community, but the ILO's Equal Remuneration Convention had already promoted this "comparable worth" principle back in 1951. Moreover, although several of the Member States had signed it, the Treaty of Rome in 1957 neglected to include it. This was not the only time the Community rebuffed progressive insights and actions before enthusiastically embracing them later as if they were its own.

Consider the Parliament's Committee on Women's Rights and its 1986 request that the Commission adopt a directive to counter sexual harassment, a problem the U.S. government had already chosen to counteract six years prior. After first insisting that its 1976 ETD offered adequate protection, the Commission at last adopted a directive on the matter in 2002, after overcoming resistance from several Member States (such as the United Kingdom, Sweden, Ireland, and Austria) (Zippel 2006, 118). Such examples testify to the incremental character of consensus surrounding progressive policy innovations as well as the ways that differing preferences among varied EU institutions and Member States can foment confusion. Not least, struggles within the Community over "positive discrimination" expose sometimes-bitter differences between institutions (e.g., the Court and the Commission), and confusion persists.

It would be wrong to assume that the incremental character of EU policy makes it ineffective. On the contrary, the Community may benefit from the eventual adoption of policies and programs that have been implemented elsewhere, policies it can thus improve upon. Then again, perhaps women's achievements and the EU's ostensible support for equality might obscure gender discrimination altogether. In fact, some successes, like the increased presence of women in the labor market, might raise doubt about the need for continued vigilance. For this reason, realizing equality requires more than a chronological tallying of related reforms—it necessitates a willingness to consider their consequences with candor. Chapter 4 turns to this task.

CHAPTER 4

Assessing Material Reforms

Clearly, the EU's approach to equal opportunities moved from a narrow focus on equal pay and equal treatment in the workplace, to a gradual acceptance of specific, positive actions and even the increased expectation that men take on their just share of household tasks and family obligations. However, the extent to which this transformation contributed substantially to changing the lives of women throughout Europe is, at present, unclear.

Chapters 2 and 3 emphasized the reasons for and incremental development of the various gender-equality initiatives that the Community chose to adopt in the first four decades of its existence; this chapter provides a general synopsis of their successes and shortcomings. To achieve this goal, its chief focus is on women's lives in the decade since 1996 when the EU reaffirmed its full commitment to gender equality by initiating efforts to mainstream it throughout the Community.

We begin with an analysis of women's earnings and then move to legal redress for pay discrimination. We conclude with a consideration of the impact of measures such as childcare to reconcile the demands of work and family life as progress toward sexual equality necessitates a clear understanding of the connections between public policies and seemingly private choices.

On Earnings

Despite the increased recognition of gender inequality and an expanding arsenal of Community reforms to combat it, wage equity has not accompanied women's increased presence in (see table 4.1) and preparedness for the labor market (Rubery et al. 1999, 90). Instead, women have continued to earn considerably lesser than men in every occupation (see figure 4.1), throughout the EU (see figure 4.2).

Table 4.1   Employment rates by gender

Total employment rate by gender in the EU-25 (%)

	1997	1999	2001	2003	2005
Total	60.6	61.9	62.8	62.9	63.8
Women	51.1	52.9	54.3	55.0	56.3
Men	70.2	71.0	71.3	70.8	71.3

Data source: Eurostat. Data covers the 15–64 years age group.

A 2005 Commission study of employment trends revealed that in 1995 women working full-time earned, on average, 75 percent of the male gross hourly wage, a gender gap that decreased by 2 percent in 2002 when women increased their earnings to 77 percent of men's (CEC 2005b, Chapter 4, 178).[1] Nonetheless, the Commission also estimates that controlling for gender differences in educational attainment and training would have likely widened the gap by an additional percent in 2002 (CEC 2002a).[2] That is, women with comparable education to their male counterparts still earn less, and women with lesser education than their male counterparts earn significantly less.

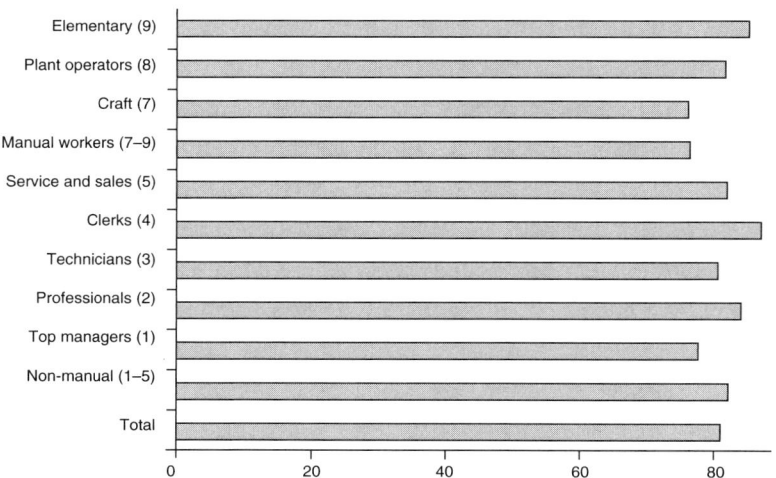

Source: SES 2002; ISCO categories; manual (ISCO 7-9) and non-manual (ISCO 1 to 5) categories are aggregates

Figure 4.1   Women's hourly wages as percentage of men's, by occupation.

Source: *Employment in Europe 2005: Recent Trends and Prospects*, © European Communities, 2005b, http://ec.europa.eu/employment_social/employment_analysis/eie/eie2005_chap1_en.pdf.

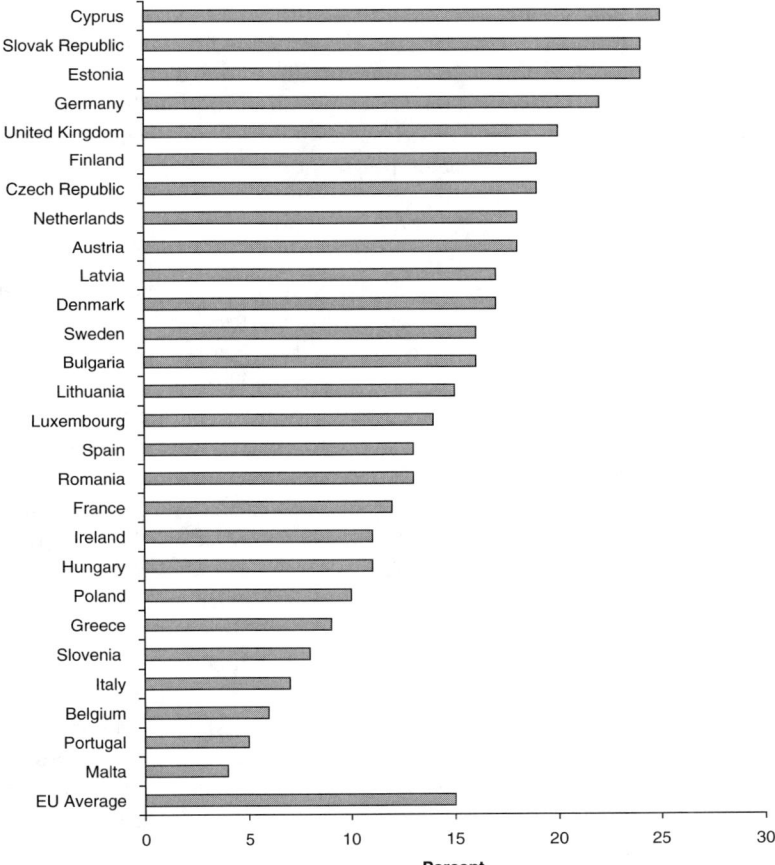

Pay gap between women and men in unadjusted form in EU Member States—2005

(Difference between men and women's hourly earnings as percentage of men's average gross hourly earnings)

Figure 4.2 Pay gap throughout all Member States.

Data source: Report from the Commission to the Council, the European Parliament, the European Economic and Social Committee and the Committee of the Regions on Equality between Women and Men, COM (2007) 49 final, 7.2.07, © European Communities, 2007, http://eur-lex.europa.eu/LexUriServ/site/en/com/2007/com2007_0049en01.pdf.

While a narrowing wage gap, however slight, suggests progress toward gender equality, the continued exclusion of part-timers (most of whom are low-paid women) from such data is misleading. To cite but one example, in 1996 the British Labour Force Survey underrepresented the gendered pay gap by excluding part-time workers in its official figures on gendered pay ratios. The survey reported women's earnings to be at 78.9 percent of men's, but including part-time workers would have increased the gap by nearly 5 percent (i.e., women earn 74.1 percent of men's earnings) (Rubery et al. 1999, 230). This disparity is not Britain's alone. The Organisation for Economic Co-operation and Development (OECD) finds that the hourly wage rate for part-time workers has been, on average, 10 percent lower than for those in full-time employment (1999).[3]

Since the 1980s, part-time employment has been an increasing feature of the EU labor market, offering employers a means of circumventing regulatory constraints and reducing costly benefits. In 2005, roughly 33 percent of women held part-time jobs, less than a third of them voluntarily (CEC 2005b, 100). Earnings for part-time work are not commensurate with full-time scales, which explains, in part, why many workers find it unappealing (CEC 2005b, 186).

According to Eurostat, only 7.4 percent of men worked part-time in 2004, compared to 32.6 percent of women (CEC 2006b, 11). It is, however, worth noting that the percentage of women working part-time varies between states. Thus, while in Greece, the Slovak Republic, Hungary, and Lithuania less than one in ten women works part-time, 40 percent of women work part-time in Luxembourg, Germany, Belgium, and the United Kingdom. In the Netherlands, nearly 75 percent of women are working part-time (CEC 2006b, 11).

That large numbers of women may choose reduced hours when they have children is impossible to deny,[4] but attributing an increase of part-time employment to women's preference for it is misleading. Despite the absence of fully comparable data on maternal employment rates for all the Member States, mothers are having fewer children and fewer women are becoming mothers (see figure 4.3). Thus, whereas nearly a third of women working part-time attribute their working hours to family or personal responsibilities, over 15 percent state that they are working part-time because they are unable to secure full-time employment (CEC 2005b, 103).

Having linked women's increased presence in the wage-labor market with women's empowerment, the EU credits its equality policies with both. Indeed, after acknowledging that women have filled 75 percent of the new jobs created within the EU over the last five years

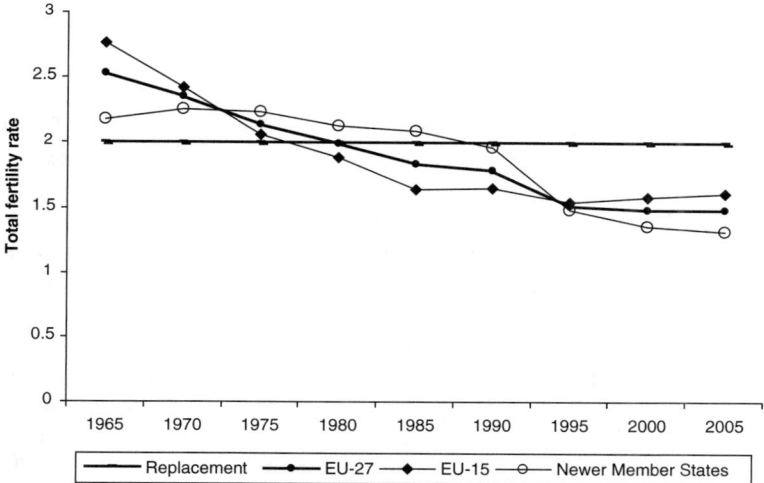

Figure 4.3 Trends in fertility rates in the EU, 1965–2005.

Data sources: Council of Europe, *Recent Demographic Trends in Europe 2004* and Eurostat, *A Statistical Illustration of Women and Men in the EU-27*.

(CEC 2006b, 3), the Commission remarks this "favourable trend in female employment has led to a narrowing of the gender gaps in employment and unemployment" (CEC 2006b, 5). Against this favorable backdrop, suggesting that Europe's integration has simply increased the demand for low wage, part-time, and temporary workers, most of whom are women, might seem uncouth. However, this recognition helps to explain the persistent gap in wages between men and women.

The influx of women into the labor market constitutes only half the story; the other half involves their peripheral location. In its 2006 annual report on equality between women and men, the Commission acknowledged that throughout the EU's largest business enterprises, women account for only 10 percent of board members and only 3 percent of CEOs (CEC 2006b, 6). In a survey of several hundred top business organizations throughout Europe (seventy-five in each of the "big five EU countries"—France, Germany, Italy, Spain, and the United Kingdom), researchers Marta Dassu of the Aspen Institute Italia and Daniel Franken of The Economists' Intelligence Unit found only two of the seventy-five business organizations were headed by women. It was the same in Spain. In Germany, only one woman made it to the top, and the findings were equally dismal in France. Italy, by contrast, was without a single woman leader. "Add all this up and it is clear that decades of rapid social change and all the years of stepped-up European integration have yet to be reflected in the hiring of the most senior executives in Europe" (Dassu and Franklin 2005).[5]

The Commission has conceded, "The main areas of growth for female employment continued to be concentrated in activities and occupations already predominately feminine." In fact, it concludes, "this has reinforced segregation in the labor market" (CEC 2006b, 5). More than four in ten women (as compared to two in ten men) work in public administration, education, health, or social services. What is more, women are also overrepresented in the temporary employment sector and informal economy (through, e.g., domestic work).[6] Last, women's increased susceptibility to unemployment is particularly troubling given that their activity (or participation) rates still lag 15 percent behind those of men (CEC 2005b, 27). According to Eurostat, the unemployment rates for 2004 were 8.1 percent for men and 10.2 percent for women (CEC 2005b, 24).

Perhaps unexpectedly, a 2005 Commission report on employment trends found that women's earnings are highest in Bulgaria, the Slovak Republic, Slovenia, Romania, Belgium, Denmark, Greece, Italy, Luxembourg, and Portugal. Women in the transitional economies, it reasoned, "have a significantly better earnings position owing to the fact that the transition period itself brings an increase in the demand for those skills held predominantly by women, and exemplified by the high proportion of women working in the services sector" (CEC 2005b, 176).

Whatever the explanation, it is ironic that several of the states that may have been least influenced by the Community's equality policies were those best able to provide for wages that are more equitable. Furthermore, these newer Member States expressed less interest in achieving pay equality than in reducing unemployment (CEC 2004d).[7] While more in-depth research is needed to determine effective remedies for gendered pay differentials, activity rates and even poverty throughout the Community, this is no easy task. The literature on gender gaps is replete with analyses that consider the methodological quandaries of comparison.

Scholars often attribute their limited capacity to render definitive assessments of EU equality policies to the absence of consistent and comparable employment-related data over time.[8] These limitations increase the appeal of more circumscribed impact-analyses that link qualitative approaches with quantitative analysis within only one or two Member

States. Nonetheless, even these modest case studies fail to generate a consensus regarding the consequences of EU initiatives for women.

Reflecting on Germany and Ireland, Hoskyns suggests that the first Equality Directives often helped tip the legal balance in women's favor, placing equal pay firmly on the political agenda. She notes, for instance, that when the German Federal Labour Court in Kassel considered the matter of overtime allowances paid exclusively to men, it ruled that the Community's equality provisions went beyond basic pay rates to include such allowances (1996b, 122–24).

Christina Bergqvist and Ann-Cathrine Jungar reach similar conclusions about Sweden. "The impact of EU legislation on national legal practice in Sweden has been to require adaptation and *leveling up* of the existing Swedish equal opportunities act" (2000, 176; my emphasis). They note that when Sweden entered into the Community, it strengthened its regulations on wage discrimination, clarified its position on "equal work," and introduced efforts to end sexual harassment. Their finding defies conventional wisdom and especially challenges the egalitarian view that Swedes have of themselves. Because "this country considers itself to be ahead . . . the usefulness of Community action is perceived as more applicable to other European countries," although, again, a careful sifting through the data suggests otherwise (OPTEM 2002, 13).[9]

Political analyst Myra Marx Ferree, writing exclusively on Germany, is less enthusiastic. She argues that without meaningful penalties, these directives held "no immediate practical effect" (1995, 99). Not one to confine insights to articles, Ferree posts a photograph on her website: it shows an advertisement in a German drugstore window specifically seeking male employees for its shop near the parliament, in a high traffic area. She concludes, "In Germany, anti-discrimination law is still controversial and rarely enforced" (see http://www.ssc.wisc.edu/~mferree/GenderPictures.htm), a conclusion shared by many other scholars, including those who nonetheless credit the EU with the passage of such legislation (e.g., Zippel 2006).

Writing from Ireland, Ailbhe Smyth (1993), a founder of Irish women's studies, remarks that Irish feminists and the state's mainstream First Council for the Status of Women had forcefully articulated claims for employment equality prior to the adoption of the first directives. Indeed, she notes that their implementation has required constant vigilance from the women's movement and trade union women. From Spain, Emanuela Lombardo likewise describes a conscientious women's movement that was up against an intransigent government. Spain's negligence in its incorporation ("transposition") and implementation of these laws appears most clearly evidenced in the persistent refusal of its courts and legal practitioners to learn about them (Lombardo 2003). Although Britain's Equal Pay Task Force also found that its employment tribunals lacked sufficient expertise to resolve the complexities of equal-pay cases, it chose to underscore the difficulties that these board members faced in determining pay (Equal Pay Task Force 2001, 46–47).

On Legal Redress

Whether one argues that women often successfully negotiated policies against discrimination both prior to and even despite the existence of Equality Directives and inexperienced hearing bodies, or one insists the legislation increased awareness of sexual discrimination and enhanced the willingness of Member States to confront the problem (e.g., Alter and Vargas 2000; Collins 1996; Mazur 1996),[10] equality claims have cluttered courts and tribunals throughout the Community since their adoption. In 1976 and 1977 in the United Kingdom alone, industrial tribunals heard nearly 3,000 such claims (Mazey 1988, 70). Given the sheer volume of cases, an exhaustive and precise analysis is impossible to provide. Still, if conditions in Britain offer any insight, there is little reason for optimism. Records from that state's Equal Opportunities Commission reveal that almost half of the nearly 13,000 equal pay cases from 1976 through 1999 were withdrawn and fewer than 5 percent resulted in a victory for the claimant (Equal Pay Task Force 2001, 54).[11]

Analyzing directives through case law, though important, may exaggerate the reach of directives by referring principally to those few actually engaged in litigation about them. In consequence, scholars frequently ignore several important issues.[12] First, employees often remain ignorant of the potential relief directives provide. A 1996 Eurobarometer found that 60 percent of Europeans lacked knowledge about the EU's policies against discrimination (CEC 1996b). Four years later, in the aftermath of both the Amsterdam Treaty and the Burden of Proof Directive, that percentage remained essentially unchanged (CEC 2002b). Second, even those trained in labor law may not adequately understand the directives and related case law,[13] a factor that might explain the revised ETD of 2002 and its emphasis on the provision of a "more effective" level of legal protection against discrimination (2002/73/EC, paragraph 20).

The Commission itself acknowledges that the impact of ECJ case law is "frequently not understood by the persons responsible for EO [equal opportunities] in the Member States" (CEC 1998b, paragraph 20). Research in Great Britain supports this conclusion (e.g., Corcoran 1988) and, as suggested earlier, research on the Spanish courts found that legal practitioners were "ignorant about EC gender law and scarcely or incorrectly apply it," thus *de facto* reducing the potential for remedy (Lombardo 2003, 169). Moreover, Gisela Lange, the woman responsible for enlargement in the Commission's Equal Opportunities Unit, suggests that matters may be even worse in the newest member states (in Ellina 2003, 143–44).

As the EU's ultimate legal authority, the Court bears some responsibility for much of the confusion. Whether in its initial rulings on equal pay (in *Defrenne*) or later decisions on "positive discrimination" (in *Kalanke* and later *Marschall*), the Court has been reserved, if not largely ambivalent about what gender equality is and how best to achieve it.[14] More recent rulings resonate with this complicated past.

In 2006, for instance, the Court came under fire for its ruling in *Cadman v Health and Safety Executive* (Case C17/05 [2006]).[15] The case involved a British health and safety inspector, Bernadette Cadman. After five years on the job, she learned that her annual earnings were about 9,000 GBPs less than four male colleagues of the same rank. Ms. Cadman had been promoted faster than her male colleagues, yet she was paid substantially lesser. Her employer attributed the difference in wages to her shorter service and Ms. Cadman (and her public services union, Prospect) argued that the pay structure indirectly discriminates against women who are more likely than men to have had career breaks that prevent them from accruing similar seniority. Persuaded by Cadman's position, the advocate general found that employers should be required to justify using length of service as a determinant of pay *if* it results in women earning lesser pay than men receive. The Court, however, sided with the employer and agreed that, generally, the "length of service is appropriate to attain the legitimate objective of *rewarding experience* acquired which *enables the worker to perform his duties better*" (Case C17/05 [2006], paragraph 38; my emphasis).

The Court's emphasis on rewarding seniority in *Cadman*, though understandable, also requires justification from employers *only* when aggrieved employees provide "evidence capable of raising serious doubts" (Case C17/05 [2006], paragraph 40), an expectation that undermines the 1997 Burden of Proof Directive (97/80/EC). That legislation reversed the burden of proof in cases of indirect discrimination by placing the onus on employers to prove that they are not discriminating in cases of gendered pay disparities. Reference to that legislation is conspicuously absent from the Court's decision as is its earlier position on the gendered character of seniority, presented in *Marschall*. In *Marschall*, the

Court conceded that "traditional promotion criteria," like seniority, might seem neutral in theory, but "in practice [these] put women at a disadvantage" Case C-409/95 [1997] ECR 6363, paragraph 4). Yet, the Court's judgment in *Cadman* does more than reverse its earlier decision and invalidate the 1997 Directive. According to an *Irish Times* editorial, it "goes against the spirit of a number of EU directives seeking to end discrimination against women, including those protecting part-time workers and workers with broken service, on the basis that women are more likely to . . . take time out for family duties than men" ("A Retrograde Decision" 2006).

For those with a legitimate claim and legal awareness about the formal remedies the EU may offer, resources remain an issue. Obtaining legal counsel proves time-consuming and costly. Until the Commission's adoption of the 2000 Framework Directive (2000/78/EC),[16] which obliged member governments to ensure some support and representation for claimants, few states had provided assistance to those that confronted employers who likely had more power and resources. However even thereafter, the expectation of legal assistance was disappointed because only three of the fifteen Member States had transposed the directive by the 2003 deadline. A year later, the Commission initiated infringement proceedings against Austria, Belgium, Finland, Germany, Greece, and Luxembourg for their failure to respect their obligations to follow EU law. This was, however, only part of the problem.

Despite efforts to protect claimants from vengeful employers, employees have been especially reluctant to initiate grievances for fear of retaliation. High unemployment exacerbates this anxiety, particularly for women. These obstacles once led a former legal advisor to Britain's Equal Opportunities Commission to conclude that "the political will to provide effective means for enforcing the principles contained in Directives is absent: lip-service is paid but no real support is given" (Corcoran 1988, 68). In sum, most forms of discrimination go unchallenged; few cases are likely to reach the attention of local authorities much less a court.

The absence of redress is especially troublesome given that, in the words of the Commission, "the pay gap between women and men remains at unacceptably high levels and shows no significant signs of being closed" (CEC 2006b, 6). The Court's stance in *Cadman* will likely complicate efforts to diminish this gap by warranting higher pay to employees with seniority, a criterion that almost invariably financially penalizes women for the time they take off for pregnancies and various caring responsibilities. Moreover, this position is at odds with the

Commission's stated equality efforts to "reconcile paid work and family life" whereby women are bound neither by family/household obligations that prevent them from entering paid labor nor by waged work that precludes them from fulfilling various family responsibilities (i.e., reproductive tasks, including childcare and parent-care).

On Reconciling Home and Work

By emphasizing childcare provision and encouraging men to take on a greater share of domestic tasks to decrease women's "double burden," the EU endeavored to facilitate women's choice to enter motherhood while, at the same time, it encouraged women's participation in the wage-labor market. Now that we considered women's presence in and policies pertaining explicitly to the labor market, it is time to reflect on men's presence in and policies pertaining to the household in general and childcare-related tasks more specifically.

As in the case of women's earnings and legal redress, evidence of substantive progress relating to the reconciliation of work and home life is slim. Although fathers are able, by law, to take parental leave, few do. Men comprise less than 5 percent of those taking parental leave in both Spain (Valiente 2000, 155) and France (Lanquetin et al. 2000, 87). One of the main reasons is that, in most cases, men's higher earnings lead cohabiting parents to "choose" for the mother to stay home, a point parental leave legislation fails to address. Moreover, in those few cases where a somewhat higher percentage of fathers do take leaves, disaggregating the data on parental leaves shows only minor changes.

Consider the oft-cited example of Sweden. In 1974, it was the first Member State to introduce parental leave that included fathers. That year, 7 percent of fathers took advantage of parental leave. By 1996, the year the EU's Parental Leave Directive was adopted, 30 percent did so. This increase might appear to be good evidence for the efficacy of the legislation. However, if one examines the number of parental days taken by fathers, the figures are less impressive. In 1974, these men took 2 percent of parental-leave days; by 1996, the numbers had only increased to 12 percent (Bergqvist and Jungar 2000). Figures from 2003 reveal that Swedish fathers take as little as 15 percent of all available parental days ("Forced Fatherhood" 2004, 46). Not only do men in Sweden not take long continuous periods of leave; it is common to jest about the possible correlation between leave days and recreational events, such as soccer and moose hunting. If, as these data suggest, Sweden's "woman-friendly" image results largely from an early adoption of parental leaves, and less from their modest effect, we might wish to focus less on formal rights and more on policy implementation.

The reach of the EU's Parental Leave Directive and the realities of its implementation suggest the largely symbolic, and thus limited, significance of such reforms—and not merely in Sweden. First, all the Nordic states (i.e., Denmark, Finland, and Sweden) already had parental leaves well before the legislation passed. Moreover, by the end of 1997, eleven of the fifteen Member States had leave arrangements similar to those within the Directive.[17] This was two years before its implementation deadline. In their comparative study of the fifteen Member States (together with the Czech Republic and Poland), Marlene Lohkamp-Himmighofen and Christiane Dienel suggest that only Ireland and the Mediterranean states might not have otherwise created policies to coincide with the Directive. Ironically, they also found that the greatest strides toward equal sharing of parenting usually occurred outside an EU context, largely because of independent "family-friendly" policies (2000, 66–67). While the Parental Leave Directive entailed only a minor policy shift in reconciliation measures for a majority of states, it is nonetheless important to consider the direction that shift took.

After comparing a wide range of public provision policies pertaining to childcare across fifteen Member States, Vicky Randall concludes, "Different traditions of state intervention in social provision, specific exigencies of the labour market, and population concerns have all contributed to contrasting policy outcomes" (2000, 352). Several factors nonetheless complicate an analysis of these variations and chief among them is that, prior to the establishment (in 1986) of the Commission's Childcare Network, there was no systematic collection of data throughout the Community for these policies.[18] Thereafter, the different starting dates for compulsory schooling as well as inadequate information about the extent and forms of private provision complicate the data. A state whose mandated starting date for school is seven (such as Denmark) would represent a greater and longer demand for childcare than those states whose compulsory schooling starts at five (such as Luxembourg and the United Kingdom).

Some states (e.g., Denmark and Finland) have a common and centralized approach to childcare, covering everything from the social and pedagogical objectives of particular programs and their cost to parents to operational hours and staffing. For other states (e.g., Britain and Greece), fragmentation remains the norm. Whereas the private provision of childcare remains scarce in Scandinavia, one finds that private facilities are expanding in Belgium and Portugal. Moreover, the governments of the Netherlands, Germany, the United Kingdom, and Luxembourg are encouraging individual employers to play a more active part in the cost of childcare provision. Together, such trends raise questions about the quality of public provision and state regulation.

If there is an overall policy convergence to discern over the last two decades, it is not in the substance of childcare policies but in the rhetoric related to them. More specifically, Vicky Randall observes a shift from parental needs toward an increased emphasis throughout the Member States on "choice, " "diversity," and "flexibility" in relation to childcare (2000, 361). She is especially circumspect about these terms as they relate to the provision of childcare itself.

As noted earlier, the assumption that "choice" means the development of public measures that enable parents to decide for themselves between paid employment and staying at home to care for their children is false. According to Randall, Member States that identify "choice" as a central objective of childcare policy often seek to divest the state from an obligation to provide it. She quotes a British Conservative MEP who insists that parents who "go out to work" choose for themselves "how best to care for their children" (2000, 366).

Similarly, while "diverse" public services for children might suggest multiple and equally desirable options, "diversity" can mask the extreme fragmentation that results from inadequate connections between welfare, childcare, and educational programs. Randall argues that the segmentation of these public services impairs their quality and creates an undue burden for parents (usually mothers) left to stitch together needed measures. This task is particularly onerous for those with limited time. "Flexible" hours for women are unlikely to compensate for the inconvenience.

Last, emphasizing "flexibility" as independence from more restrictive work schedules may merely conceal the longer hours that women work. Recent studies reveal that as companies strive to meet the challenges of increased competition on the global market, working conditions appear to be deteriorating. Researchers from the European Foundation for the Improvement of Living and Working Conditions, an EU-affiliated think tank, found that whereas working time has, on average, decreased over the last decade, work intensification has increased. In consequence, the time one spends at work is more stressful, fast-paced, highly supervised, and under tighter deadlines (Broughton 2001).

A more balanced share of caring activities and housework between cohabiting women and men has not accompanied women's increased presence in the wage-labor market. Italians refer to this condition as "the partial emancipation of women." In other words, women who are "free" to work for wages are still then expected to bring up their children, look after their other relatives, and do the housework. According to Eurostat, partial emancipation is pervasive—with women throughout the EU doing two-third of all unpaid domestic work (2004, 44–45),[19] a fact that helps explain why, on an average day, men spend more time in the labor market but have nearly thirty minutes more of free time than do women (2004, 87).[20]

Conclusion

Although the number of women entering the Community's wage-labor market has significantly increased so that gender gaps in employment and unemployment have narrowed, women are so often employed as auxiliary, marginal, or part-time workers that they are deprived of fair wages and full work benefits, and their chances of promotion are reduced or even eradicated. When women and men work in wage-labor markets segregated by sex, equal pay for equal work means little.

Not only have over four decades of reform failed to alter "women's work," the Commission concedes that recent growth in women's employment continues in precisely these areas of the market where women are most likely to be employed and vulnerable—a factor that exacerbates gender segregation. This trend might help explain why women have thus far achieved greater income equality in states least influenced by the EU's market liberalization and related equality initiatives. Put somewhat cynically, one of the EU's greatest assets may be its cheap, disciplined, readily available, and flexible female labor force.

That the Commission has recently acknowledged the persistence of gender segregation and yet failed to consider the role played by sexual harassment in women's alienation from the labor market is at once curious and yet consistent, given its somewhat capricious approach to policymaking. After all, less than a decade ago, it acknowledged that this abuse functions to reinforce the desirability of menial, part-time labor for women while keeping them out of male-dominated job sectors (e.g., CEC 1998c, 28). Moreover, after earlier EU initiatives against sexual harassment (e.g., the Recommendation on the Protection of the Dignity of Women and Men at Work) proved wanting, the then new Commissioner for Employment, Social Affairs and Equal Opportunities, Anna Diamantopoulou, persuaded the Commission to pass a revised ETD (2002/73/EC), forcing Member States to take the matter more seriously (Zippel 2006, 82). In addition to requiring that they establish official bodies to prevent and enforce laws against sex discrimination in general, the Directive specifically required Member States to adopt or modify their laws against sexual harassment by October 2005. With the exception of Greece and Latvia, all claimed to have done so by June of 2004 (Irish Government 2004). That such claims might mask the inadequacy of these efforts is rarely addressed, though readily excused.

As Kathrin Zippel suggests, "Raising awareness around sexual harassment and bringing the issue onto the national agenda in many countries is currently tempered with the harsh economic and social context throughout Europe" (2007). However, as chapter 5 reveals, such conditions have also encouraged the adoption of reforms that appear to foster the democratization of the EU and its Member States. It is to a consideration of women in political decision-making and GM that we now turn.

CHAPTER 5

Assessing Political Equality and Mainstreaming

As chapter 4 reveals, EU employment and reconciliation policies have fallen shy of their stated objectives of achieving equality between women and men, yet the EU repeatedly holds these as essential tools for achieving social justice—a contradiction that either implies acceptance of the continued chasm between rhetoric and reality or attributes these policy shortcomings to problems in execution. This good-policy/bad-implementation dynamic might explain the increased resources spent on fostering women's voices within the very states and transnational entities that previously denied, ignored, or even permitted the violation of their rights. Still, what, if anything, have decision-making reforms and GM accomplished?

On Decision-Making

Recall that the Community's stated interest in equality between women and men has long focused on women's market-oriented participation, but it was not until the early 1990s and the Commission's adoption of the Third (1991–1995) and Fourth (1996–2000) Action Programs that it recognized the importance of women's active participation in political decision-making. With growing concerns over chronic unemployment, the collapse of communism in Eastern Europe, and the renewed assertion of national identities throughout the continent, political actors within the EU came to appreciate that emphasizing only the material benefits of integration would not guarantee a continued commitment to the process.

The Community's initial emphasis on political rights was most readily apparent in the Maastricht Treaty's call for a more expansive and inter-ventionist government, one that required greater legitimacy in order to establish a European Central Bank and a single currency by 1999. To this end, it formally introduced "European citizenship" in Article 8 whereby "Every citizen holding the nationality of a member state shall be a citizen of the Union," entitled to free movement within all Member States. Two factors point to the largely redundant character of this status. First, the guarantee of free movement to Member State nationals for economic pur-poses dates from the Community's inception. Second, Member State nationals are already citizens within Europe, a matter that underscores the largely symbolic character of this offer. Indeed, according to the Commission, the "purpose" of European citizenship is "to deepen European citizens' *sense* of belonging to the European Union and make that sense more tangible by conferring on them the rights associated with it" (CEC 1995a, 21; my emphasis). Knowing that the only novel applica-tion of this "right" is the ability of any (Member State) citizen to vote and stand for office outside of one's own Member State in local and EP elec-tions accounts for the tepid enthusiasm with which most Europeans received EU citizenship.[1]

As the ink dried in Maastricht in February of 1992, the EU descended into one of its worst economic recessions and women soon achieved prominence in referenda campaigns challenging the Community's fur-ther integration. In June of 1992, Danish voters rebuffed the Maastricht Treaty, only later accepting the modified Edinburgh Treaty. Swedish voters supported a consultative referendum to join the EU by a mere 52 percent in November of 1994, though two weeks later Norwegians opposed EU entrance by the same percentage. Of particu-lar concern in each of these campaigns was the Treaty's requirement that Member States have deficits below 3 percent of GDP and outstanding debts below 60 percent before joining the single currency. Member States consistently challenged this policy in practice and it was officially relaxed in 2004 for six of the ten new entrants to the EU. Yet almost from the start, women rightly feared these targets (or "convergence cri-teria") would lead to cuts in the very public sectors that employed them.[2]

In November of 1992, Agnès Hubert, then head of the Equal Opportunities Unit, met with women leaders from throughout the Community at a summit in Greece and there issued the Athens Declaration calling for equal political representation (Hubert 1998, Appendix 2).

Having been convinced that the persistent underrepresentation of women in political decision-making constitutes a "democratic deficit," the Commission prescribed women's increased participation as an antidote for the EU's crisis of legitimacy.

According to Hubert, the Athens Declaration provided ammunition to those working for gender equality in the Member States and gave momentum to initiatives to improve women's representation within EU institutions as well. Consider the subsequent adoption of the Charter of Rome in May of 1996 by the EU Ministers for Women's Affairs from the fifteen Member States. It declares, "A *renewal* of politics and society will be realized with the joint contribution and balanced participation of women and men." Moreover, it advised that women's political involvement will "increase citizen confidence" throughout Europe (in Lovenduski and Stephenson 1999, 3; my emphasis), a challenging task given that a month earlier a Eurobarometer survey revealed that only 39 percent of women, as against 51 percent of men, favored increased European integration (CEC 1996b).

By the close of 1996, the issue of gender balance in decision-making processes entered into the mainstream and the Council of the European Union followed with a Recommendation (96/694/EC), in December, that called on the Member States to develop suitable measures to correct the underrepresentation of women in decision-making positions at the national level. As well, the text recommended that European public authorities adopt a comprehensive integrated strategy to promote a gender balance within their own institutions. Although in legal terms the recommendation was not binding, it did offer a source of reference and inspiration to women as they mobilized to gain access to institutions that once seemed entirely off limits (Hubert 1998).

Within the upper reaches of the EU, women were conspicuously absent from the first decades of "Europe's" construction and thereafter have had only limited access to its most powerful institutions. As mentioned earlier, the European Commission had no women commissioners during the first thirty years of its operation. Then, from 1994 to 1999 and again from 1999 to 2004, five of twenty commissioners were women. With a newly enlarged commission of twenty-seven since 2007, eight commissioners are now women.

The ECJ, which began in 1952 as a court for the European Coal and Steel Community, contained no women members until France appointed Simone Rozès, its first woman advocate general to the Court in 1981. Eighteen more years elapsed before Ireland appointed the first woman justice to the Court, Judge Fidelma Macken. As of 2007, six of the thirty-three members of the Court are women; however, only three are justices and the other three are advocate generals. All of the women are recent arrivals; the two most senior members were appointed in 2003, three arrived in 2006, and one has been with the Court only since 2007.

Visibility in certain arenas can distract our attention from shortcomings in others. This may be obvious when it comes to women on the Court, yet a similar caution is necessary when considering the increase in number of women commissioners. While their numbers are impressive, a 2004 audit of senior and middle management posts within the Commission reveals that women comprise only 12 percent and 17 percent of these staffs, respectively. The audit's author, Administration Commissioner Siim Kallas, also found that after "an appreciable improvement between 1995–2000, when the percentage of women in senior management rose from 4% to 10.7%, there has been a distinct slowdown in recent years" (King 2005).[3] Such figures reveal that, despite the increased number of its women commissioners, this body is far from achieving gender balance in its staffing and whatever gains once attained are vulnerable to reversal.

Similar criticisms can be made of the EP where, in 2007, women constitute nearly a third of all representatives but hold only six of the institution's twenty-four chairs that oversee important committee work (e.g., the Committee on Women's Rights and Gender Equality). Nonetheless, as the worlds' only democratically elected international assembly, the EP has often been both catalytic for and receptive to women's increased political presence. The percentage of women MEPs has gone from 16 percent in 1979 to 25 percent in 1994 and to 30 percent in 1999 and 2004 (see figure 5.1), accounting for more women representatives at the EU level than nearly all the national legislatures throughout the EU. On average, women hold 23 percent of all national seats (see figure 5.2).

While the number of women MEPs has increased, voter turnout has dropped in every ballot year since the EP held its first direct elections in 1979 (figure 5.1). That year 63 percent of the electorate voted and, by 1994, the percentage fell to 56.8 percent. In 1999, less than half of the European electorate (49.4 percent) turned out and, in 2004, only 45.6 percent bothered to vote. Perhaps surprisingly, the lowest turnout came from the ten new members where only 26 percent of the voters cast a ballot. Some, like the outgoing EP president Pat Cox, rebuked the new members for not encouraging voter participation. Others pointed to a disenchanted public both skeptical about the effectiveness of political parties to evoke change following the demise of communism and

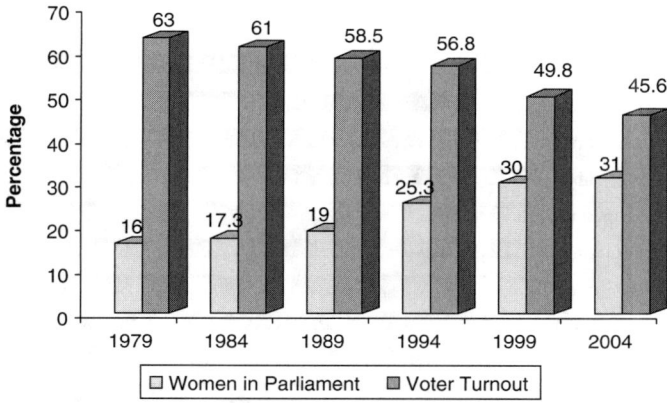

Figure 5.1 European Parliament elections.
Data source: European Parliament—EOS Gallup Europe.

discouraged by, among other matters, press reports of MEPs exploiting generous compensation and travel reimbursements.[4]

Whatever the reasons for lower voter turnout, women's increased presence within the EP has coincided with this decline, and while correlation is not causation, it does invite speculation. As the EU's least powerful and most democratic institution, the Parliament has long been seen as a playground for political amateurs. Yet whether the institution's lower status encouraged women's greater access to it or women's increased presence hastened voter apathy, we cannot know. Nonetheless, this condition is riddled with contradiction, because although women's enhanced presence is suggestive of the Parliament's (if not the EU's) democratization, its low voter-turnout evokes the fragility of its legitimacy.

The Commission's Third and Fourth Action Programs reached beyond the democratization of EU political institutions to encourage women's participation in decision-making at the national level as well. To accomplish this, both programs funded numerous projects and studies to provide information about women's political achievements and shortcomings within the Member States. Recall, for instance, that the first program funded the establishment of the Expert Network on Women in Decision-Making. This short-lived network gathered and distributed valuable statistics on women in national political decision-making throughout the then twelve Member States. Nonetheless, by 1999 (under the second program), political scientists called for further

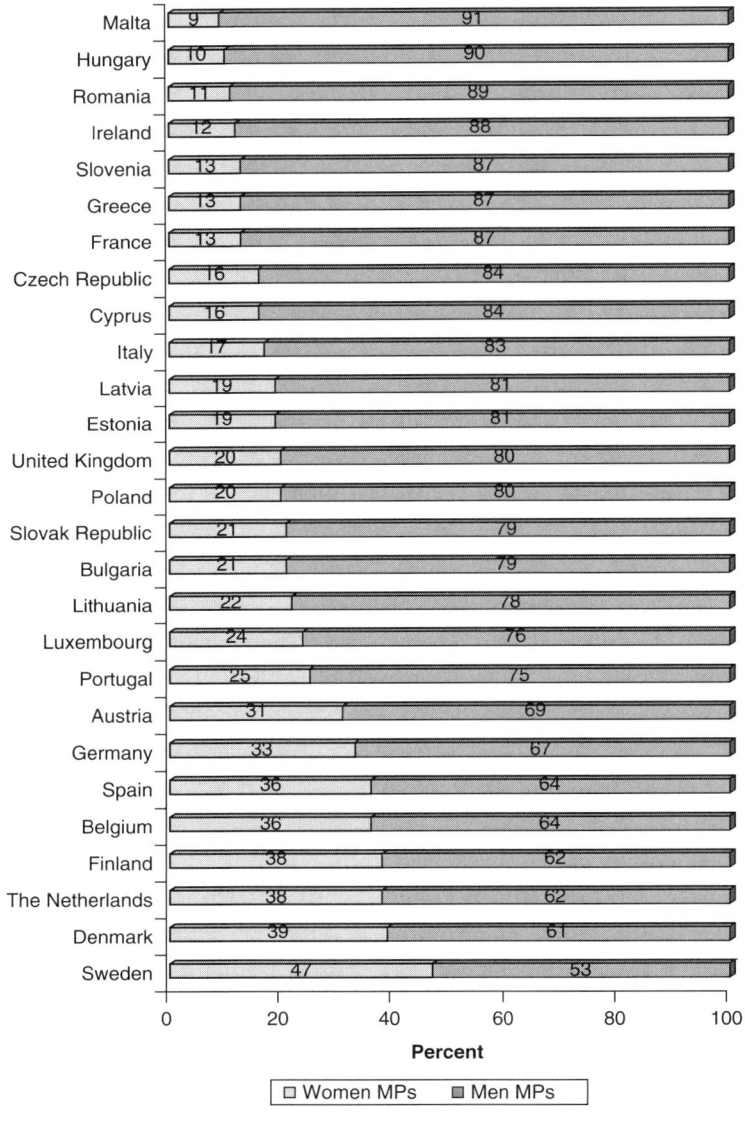

Figure 5.2 Gender imbalances in national parliaments (2006).

Source: European Commission, DG Employment, Database on women and men in decision-making.

research, stating basic data were nowhere comprehensive. They found that research so focused on the presence of women in formal politics that it neglected to account for women's actual role in decision-making. Not least, these scholars found comparative assessments hampered by "the absence of a uniform protocol for official statistics on women in decision-making" (Lovenduski and Stephenson 1999, 9)—a finding as apt for today's enlarged EU of twenty-seven Member States with considerable variations between them.

At present, some Member States such as Sweden and Denmark have as many as four times the number of women representatives in their national parliaments as others (e.g., Malta and Hungary); but what, if anything, do such numbers suggest about women's power or the lack thereof? Consider Sweden and Denmark again. Like their non–Member State Nordic neighbors, the parliaments of these two states have long had more women representatives, a matter that has led researchers to explore the politics of these parliaments and the women in them closely (e.g., Bergqvist and Nordiska ministerrådet 1999). After completing the first large-scale comparative study of the Nordic countries in the mid-1980s, scholars found that politics was still a man's domain and that, with a few exceptions, the percentage of women decreases the closer one gets to the pinnacle of power (Hernes and Hanninen-Salmelin 1985). Over twenty years have passed since the completion of that study, yet its chief conclusion appears as applicable today for the EU's other Member States as it did back then for just the Nordic ones.

The era of all-male group photos of national politicians may be over, but current research also suggests that as Nordic women gained greater access to national parliaments, power shifted both to the EU level and to corporate structures at the national level, with women losing in the process (Borchorst in Lovenduski and Stephenson 1999, 36).[5] These corporate structures function as advisory boards that work alongside governments and they are especially influential in formulating economic, political, and social policy. Because male-dominated labor unions and employers' associations occupy most of the seats within these bodies (and women's organizations are rarely represented), women's perspectives are often overlooked despite their growing political presence elsewhere. Given the vital importance of corporate structures to policy development in other states as well (such as Belgium, Germany, and Austria), one must not overlook the Commission's 2004 audit of fifty-six European employer and trade union organizations. It found that only 8 percent of women headed these bodies (CEC 2006a, 7).

Table 5.1 Percentage of women MEPs in twelve Member States

	1990	2000	2006
Belgium	8.5	23.3	34.7
Denmark	30.7	37.4	36.9
France	6.9	10.9	12.2
Germany	20.5	30.9	31.8
Greece	6.7	6.3	13
Ireland	7.8	12	13.3
Italy	12.9	11.1	11.5
Luxembourg	13.3	16.7	23.3
The Netherlands	21.3	36	36.7
Portugal	7.6	18.7	21.3
Spain	14.6	21.6	36
UK	6.3	18.4	19.7

Data source: UN site for the Millennium Development Goals (MDG) indicators.

A 2006 Commission report, *Women and Men in Decision-Making—A Question of Balance*, notes that less than a quarter of all senior ministers and junior ministers in the Member States were women (CEC 2006a, 4). In addition, only Finland, Ireland, and Latvia had a woman president and Germany alone could boast of a woman prime minister, Dr. Angela Merkel: that state's first. The Commission concludes, "Women at the top are few and far between, but they can be counted" (CEC 2006a, 2). Indeed. A tally of women MPs reveals a consistent increase in the percentage of women within the lower houses of all national parliaments since the EU began its first efforts (in 1991) to promote women in decision-making.

As women continue to increase their numbers within elected institutions at both the EU level and throughout the Member States, the lessons learned from Nordic women are worth considering, in part because Europeans are witnessing an augmentation of supranational (EU) power precisely at a time when women have increased their political presence within their Member States. (See table 5.1.) That women are more visible within EU institutions (such as the Commission and the Parliament) may reduce some anxiety about the consequences of this shift or it might increase expectations for a more "women-friendly" integrated Europe. Regardless, the next chapters suggest that without women's increased political mobilization at both the national and supranational levels, it is unlikely that issues that are crucial to women's lives (like male violence against women) would have ever been featured in the political agenda.

Gender Mainstreaming

Women wanted more than just access to political office, and following the Beijing World Conference on Women in 1995, the Commission acknowledged the need to "focus on the full and equal participation of women *in all spheres of society*" (CEC 1995b; my emphasis).[6] The Commission accomplished this, in part, through the formal adoption of GM (gender mainstreaming) for its Fourth Action Program (1996–2000). According to the Commission, mainstreaming is a policy to "promote equality between men and women in all activities and policies at all levels," a goal that was subsequently reaffirmed by all Member States in their ratification of the 1997 Treaty of Amsterdam. Article 3(2) of the Treaty calls on Member States to "eliminate inequalities and promote equality between women and men *in all the activities of the Union*" (CEC 1997b, 12; my emphasis). The notion that actions to promote the principle of gender equality must be integrated and implemented throughout all Member State and EU institutions rather than just within offices established (at each of these levels) to promote equal opportunities meant that the pursuit of gender equality would become everyone's task.

If in theory GM involves a systematic examination of policies "to see whether they will affect women and men differently, with a view to adapting . . . proposals to make sure that discriminatory effects are neutralized and that gender equality is promoted" (CEC 1996e, 21), in practice it was first used as "an alibi for neutralizing positive action" for women (Stratigaki 2005, 165). In education, for example, projects closely connected with the Equal Opportunities Unit and aimed at challenging gender stereotypes for boys and girls were discontinued in 1996 whereas other programs (such as SOCRATES—then a new higher education program) received funding with the argument that they had mainstreamed gender equality. Recall, as well, how programs that once served women (such as NOW—a job-training program) were dismantled, replaced by allegedly gender-neutral ones (such as EQUAL) that target "socially excluded" people—as if to imply that women, as a group, are not disadvantaged.

Only after the Commission forcefully countered the Court's initial resistance to positive action measures (in *Kalanke*) and the Amsterdam Treaty passed did it become clear that GM would *complement*, and not replace, previous equality policies (like equal treatment). Only then was the threat that GM posed to dismantling EU equality policies meaningfully impeded.

Thereafter, as the potential grew to integrate gender-equality policies within other policy objectives and priorities, the EU's social funding programs became a central venue for pursuing social change. European Social Funds (ESFs) are the investments that the EU makes in people by the transfer of substantial funds to Member States through programs that support the creation of more and better jobs. For its 2000–2006 funding cycle, the Council pursued a dual-track equality strategy and, in 2006, strengthened it through the adoption of a regulation that explicitly calls for "a gender mainstreaming approach [to] be combined with specific action to increase the sustainable participation and progress of women in employment" (Council Regulation No 1081/2006, paragraph 16).

Prior to these initiatives, the gendered character of the ESF was often ignored and, in an effort to alter the basis of analysis and the processes for measuring the design and impact of social funds, the EWL worked hard to transform the consciousness of the Community about this matter. In its 2004 pamphlet, the organization promotes "gender budgeting" as a means to assess and improve expenditures for their contribution to gender equality (Hugendubel 2004), a position in keeping with the Treaty's promise of mainstreaming equal opportunities.

In addition to raising the general consciousness of political actors about the differential impact budgets may have for women and men, the Lobby suggests that analysts divide expenditures into three categories to facilitate an understanding of their effect. First, "gender targeted expenditures" concern the *specific* needs of women and men but do not necessarily involve the promotion of gender equality. Gender-sensitive health programs that address sexually transmitted diseases like HIV/AIDS and other sexual and reproductive health matters may typify targeted expenditures. Second, "equal opportunity programs" that explicitly *aim to achieve equality* (like advancing women in decision-making) may have varied success.

However, the third "mainstream" expenditure, which consists of the majority of total state expenditures, is so often seen as gender-neutral (i.e., equally available to the entire community) that gender-related injustices are repeatedly overlooked. For example, transportation policies that privilege road construction over expenditures for public transit reinforce existing gender inequalities relating to time constraints. Not only do women have less access to private cars, they are frequent users of public transport—often with children in tow. Moreover, women are underrepresented among those making decisions on transportation despite their standing the most to gain from improvements in this sector. After finding that 63 percent of men hold drivers licenses whereas only

46 percent of women do, the Irish government developed its National Development Plan (for 2000–2006) to promote gender equity by, in part, bolstering women's presence on government bodies pertaining to transportation. To this end, it received over €5 million from the ESF (Irish Government 2006).

Sonia Mazey describes GM as the "latest stage in the incremental 'broadening' of EU gender policies. In contrast to earlier 'equal treatment' and 'positive action' EU equality strategies, which, respectively, treated women the same as men and helped women adjust to the (gender blind) male norm, mainstreaming is based upon the recognition of gender differences between men and women" (2002, 1). Though such descriptions are undoubtedly meant to facilitate our understanding of sex discrimination and GM, one is unlikely to find analogous assertions about other forms of discrimination and efforts to mainstream, for example, race- or class-based considerations. According to Brush, "the exercise of power in race relations and class conflict is much more obvious than in the case of men and women, where the roles are treated as complementary" (2003, 42).

The stress on "gender," as opposed to "power," differences concerns feminists (Hubert, interview, 2003). Indeed, a 2002 survey containing interviews with 327 equal opportunity officials from all Member States revealed that, among "female officials who took a constructive part in the feminist struggle over the past twenty years and are still active," there is concern that efforts on behalf of women are being "watered down" (OPTEM 2002, 8).

For example, Vogel-Polsky, the first attorney to argue and win a sex-discrimination case before the ECJ (in *Defrenne II*), suspects that the accommodation made for gender roles (i.e., "differences") is hardly benign (2000). Feminists worry that this emphasis might reinscribe the very rigidity and content of (gender) roles to which women's movements have long objected, an understandable concern considering the Court's reasoning about women and their "special relationship" with their children (in *Hofman v Barmer*).[7] In sum, GM risks becoming essentialist when it is both limited to certain features of many women's lives (e.g., motherhood or care giving) and fails to emphasize that these aspects may similarly be connected to subordination or suspect power (Brush 2003, 45).

The skepticism and reserve of these initial assessments parallel several of the EU's own observations and likely inspired some of its later reforms. For example, in a Committee on Women's Rights report on the role of mainstreaming in humanitarian aid, former commissioner Emma Bonino remarks, "gender is given a low priority in situations where there is an urgent need for humanitarian aid." This paradox is exemplified by a single example: "In July 1998 humanitarian aid to Afghanistan was suspended *due to continuing intolerable discrimination against women.*" It is as if the insufferable discrimination against women is reason enough to cease humanitarian intervention. However, the Commissioner insists, "in emergency situations special attention is given to female-headed households and to reproductive health issues as an essential aspect of the protection of women and children" (European Parliament 1998a, 2; my emphasis). This elaboration recommends that the most effective way for women to access "protection" is not through the assertion of their humanity *as women* but through ostensibly "family-friendly" (or "maternal") contexts.

In its "Special Report on the Implementation of the Equal Opportunities Program 1996–2000," released in 1998, the Court of Auditors reached some harsh conclusions about initiatives undertaken to promote mainstreaming (CEC 1998b). First, it observed no comprehensive data on the total annual spending specific to equal opportunities. Second, it could find no overall strategy related to reaching objectives. For example, there were insufficient details on the employment levels or those people that the programs wished to target. Nonetheless, the audit revealed that European officials and related "experts" engaged in "gender" analyses received equal-opportunity contracts to perform duties for which "they were paid gross amounts, unsupported by an invoice or other satisfactory evidence for the work performed" (CEC 1998b, paragraph 61). Moreover, some of these professionals were scarcely "experts" at all.[8] For example, in France and the Netherlands, "the project promoters audited were largely unaware of the type of the assistance that their national or regional support agency could provide, preferring to address themselves directly to their own contact organizations abroad" (CEC 1998b, paragraph 44).

Although problems of accountability, government waste, and elitism are hardly unusual in politics, equal-opportunity programs tend to occasion heightened expectations of ethical conduct and a greater commitment to follow-through. No doubt aware of this, the Commission's response to the report was quick and, at times, apologetic. The Commission immediately ensured the adoption of improved procedures concerning contract payments. That done, the Commission acknowledged that other problems would take more time to resolve. Key among them is the need to clarify what mainstreaming is and identify priorities so that an effective accounting can be implemented and a necessary course of action taken. Thus, in 2005, the Commission distributed a lengthy guide on GM for those involved in EQUAL initiatives (CEC

2005a) and released a "Roadmap for Equality between women and men 2006–2010" (CEC 2006c).

Having reaffirmed its commitment to both GM and equal opportunities, the Commission's equality roadmap provides for the establishment of the European Institute for Gender Equality. The Commission has charged the institute with raising awareness among Europeans regarding EU gender-equality policies. In addition to gathering, analyzing, and disseminating reliable data pertaining to them, the new agency will be developing tools for supporting the integration of gender equality into all Community policies. Nonetheless, the Commission's roadmap outlines several priority areas for EU action. These include, but are not limited to, all of the areas we have thus far explored—equal economic independence for women and men; reconciliation of private and professional life; and equal representation in decision-making. Last, this program calls for the eradication of all forms of gender-based violence. This last priority is the focus of chapter 6—but let us consider first some of the lessons we have learned in this one.

Conclusion

Whereas some commentators portray GM as "broad and shallow," suggesting that with equality as "everyone's responsibility" it is "no one's job" (Hubert 2004; Lombardo 2003, 163), others endorse it as a "broadening" of EU equality policies (Pollack and Hafner-Burton 2000; Mazey 2000; Rees 1998). Despite differing assessments, most agree that mainstreaming has not lived up to its potential (e.g., Pollack and Hafner-Burton 2007).

Perhaps most telling, the Commission's 2006 annual report on equal opportunities found that its "strategy for growth and employment acknowledges that gender equality is essential for progress, yet the National Reform Programmes presented by the Member States this year showed reduced visibility and a loss of momentum of gender issues" (CEC 2006b, 6). The same year, the Commission's Advisory Committee on Equal Opportunities between Women and Men warned of the possible pitfalls for GM in general by considering men's roles in particular. These include "the danger of shifting focus in gender equality work away from the experience and situation of women to that of men." As well, they note the "risk" of "merely empowering men to maintain a status quo characterised by the persistent and significant inequalities by women." Not least, they cite the "dangers of this work (on men) competing for the scarce resources currently available for gender equality work" (Advisory Committee on Equal Opportunities Between Women and Men 2006, 9).

By acknowledging these and other concerns, the Commission believes it can ensure that work on gender equality is not diminished by the need to both examine programmatic shortcomings and include a focus on men as well. It is, however, also worth remembering that equality-opportunity officers voiced many of the above noted concerns four years earlier when they worried that GM would dilute efforts to promote gender equality. Clearly, these troubled outcomes are not what proponents of mainstreaming had in mind in suggesting that GM would offer greater legitimacy to women's issues and organizations. Yet, by 2005, the European Commission designated 2007 as the "European Year of Equal Opportunities for All" as if discrimination targets no one in particular.

One of the great ironies of GM is that despite its supporters' intentions to integrate the principle of gender equality into all Community policies, one finds instead that some of the most outspoken opponents of gender equality are advancing their politics not from outside of women's organizations but, instead, from *within* them. Consider the Committee on Women's Rights and its composition.

In 2004, the newly elected Committee member, British MEP Godfrey Bloom, captured headlines after announcing his opposition to maternity rights. His goal was to persuade his new colleagues (and others) that small businesses should not hire women of childbearing age (Charlemagne 2004a). If Bloom's argument seemed anomalous coming from within the Committee on Women's Rights, it was soon evident that the Committee itself had been transformed, particularly after the Christian Democrats proposed Anna Zaborska as its chair. Zaborska, a Slovakian Christian Democratic MEP, had long been active against abortion rights and had recommended that schools ban homosexual teachers from classrooms. She was able to assume the position of Committee chair only after considerable controversy over the course of which several members abstained from voting. Following her successful election, several long-standing members of the CWR expressed concern that Ms. Zaborska's positions were in direct conflict with the group's spirit and political agenda ("Controversial MEP Elected to Chair Womens' Committee" 2004). While this may be so, one should not overlook the Committee's evolution and current composition, factors that made the election of so strong an antifeminist possible.

In a similar vein, the EWL, with its troubling yet influential affiliates, is also of concern. The organization enjoys a title identifying it as *the* umbrella organization for women's NGOs throughout the EU, but with an estimated 4,000 affiliates ranging from the Vatican and conservative Catholic women's organizations to feminist abortion-rights groups, the flipside of widespread symbolic support can be ideological infirmity.[9]

This background prepares the reader to understand better the often incongruous and seemingly peculiar positions taken by the EWL, the EP's Women's Rights Committee, and various EU institutions on the matter of male violence against women, which is the focus of chapters 6 and 7.

CHAPTER 6

Politicizing Male Violence

At a time when terrorism is at or near the top of the EU's political agenda (e.g., CEC 2005c; CEC 2006d, 5),[1] the greatest challenges to peace, prosperity, and security for many women come less from rival global powers, rogue nation-states, or foreign nationals than from men they know personally. According to the Council of Europe, male violence against women is the major cause of death and disability for women in the age group 16–44, accounting for more death and ill health than cancer or traffic accidents (Council of Europe 2000). Paradoxically, the severity of the violence is often the strongest reason for a woman's decision to stay with her assailant—women rightly fear what men will do if they attempt to leave.[2]

The Commission estimates that 20 percent of women in the EU are the victims of male violence; for them terror is a fact, not a threat. When one considers that a quarter of all reported violent crimes throughout Europe involve male assaults on female partners (CEC 2000), it is hardly hyperbole to insist that male violence is a primary obstacle to the egalitarian and peaceful Europe that bestselling authors such as Jeremy Rifkin (2004), T.R. Reid (2004), and Robert Kagan (2003) describe. Indeed, Kagan's critical treatise on Europe and the United States repeatedly insists that Europeans live in a Kantian world of "perpetual peace" (2003, 57). This pleasant portrait is unfamiliar to many women.

In combing through two decade's worth of research, one finds that despite the differences in population, methodologies, definitions, and timeframes, patterns emerge. For example, a national survey completed in Sweden in 2000 revealed that 22 percent of women, in the age group 18–24, had been subjected to male violence in *a single year* (Lundgren et al. 2001, 8–9; my emphasis). Research indicates that roughly one in four women in the United Kingdom (Mirlees-Black 1999, 18) and the Netherlands (Römkens 1997) reports having experienced domestic violence from a male partner at *some point in their lives*. A similar percentage (25 percent) of young German women in the age group 17–20 had unwanted sexual contact that met the country's criminal offense criteria for rape (Hagemann-White 2001, 751). National research on sexual violence in Ireland revealed that 20 percent of women were sexually abused by men as adults (McGee et al. 2002). Conventional crime surveys yield a substantially lower level of reported abuse throughout these states because though many women have come to view their treatment at the hands of men as abusive, many more are reluctant to regard it officially as a crime (Walby and Myhill 2001). Given the historic indifference of state authorities to women's suffering, women's hesitance to come forward is understandable.

Less than two decades ago, both battered and sexually abused women were without laws to protect them. Ireland was exceptional for its 1976 law enabling women to exclude their abusive husbands from the household—largely because that state constitutionally prohibited women from divorcing until 1995. One must be similarly circumspect about laws pertaining to rape. The serious penalties associated with it derive less from a concern for women than with the preservation and protection of patrimonial property. Women were male chattel, a point that helps us understand why marital rape was legally excused and/or unrecognized as a crime throughout the Community until just twenty years ago. Indeed, in 1999, the EP sought to rectify this with a resolution on women's health (OJ C 175/68, 21.6.99) that repeated, in part, a resolution it had adopted in 1986 (OJ C 176/73, 14.7.86). Both call upon Member States to make rape in marriage a criminal offense. Though such statements and related efforts may now impress us as essential to the workings of a just society, they also serve as a reminder that the problems that they are designed to address persist and that past remedies have been ineffective.

With male violence so deeply personal, pervasive, and even normal in the lives of so many Europeans, why should the EU claim to care, particularly after nearly forty years of relative apathy? This chapter addresses the question of what may have motivated the EU's recent interest, especially given the Commission's claim in the early 1990s that (as an allegedly non-market matter) the Community held no legal competence to address the matter (Gradin, interview, 1999). After this chapter considers the ways that violence against women has been politicized, the next details two recent initiatives (STOP and DAPHNE) undertaken by the EU and concludes with a consideration of the consequences.

There is little evidence from the 1980s and early 1990s to suggest much interest among Eurocrats in addressing the issue of male violence.

On the contrary, during this time, the Commission typically labored at significant remove from the more brutal aspects of women's subordination, focusing instead on the intricacies of existing legal remedies (e.g., Equality Directives) for problems they recognized as directly related to equal pay and equal treatment throughout Europe.

Analogously, women's advocates for abused women were not focused on Europe but rather on establishing women's centers, rape crisis hotlines, self-defense classes, and maintaining refuge for battered women within their immediate communities. Without such resources, especially shelters, many battered women would have otherwise faced homelessness if not death. Women constitute, on average, between one-fifth and one-third of the homeless throughout Europe; experts believe that a significant percentage of these are fleeing male violence at home (Harvey 1999, 60; Malos and Hague 1997).

Despite feminism's idealistic embrace of women worldwide, the goals of most activists have long been domestic, not least because few have had the resources needed to think and act more globally. For feminists, no less than women generally, the future of an integrated Europe was too distant, the EU institutions byzantine and still emerging. This is not to deny the existence of some European networking, but most activists stayed closer to home. Their contacts were (and often still are) regional at most (Delphy 1996, 149).[3]

Movements in Member States

The 1970s and 1980s

A decade after several European shelter and anti-rape movements began in the mid-1970s (e.g., in Belgium, Denmark, France, Germany, Greece, Ireland, the Netherlands, and the United Kingdom), their success in reaching abused women through volunteer staffing and private donations had the ironic, unintended consequence of making self-reliance less feasible. As more women became willing to leave abusive partners, activists were obliged to expand their services. However, they soon discovered that the needs of abused women far exceeded movement resources. This recognition typically followed reduced government social service expenditures that, in turn, made feminist services all the more urgent, especially for poor women.

As worldwide recession settled over Europe from 1973 to 1975 and again from 1980 to 1982, discussions about the appropriate responsibility of governments to citizens abounded. In considering whether governments could continue to provide a broad safety net, several Member States took particular note of battered women's movements. When Britain, for example, held its first national hearings on battered women in 1975, shelters received considerable praise from the Parliamentary Select Committee for their volunteerism, self-help principles, and "the provision of needed services with little financial assistance from local or national government" (Dobash and Dobash 1992, 122).

Emphasizing the accomplishments and potential of feminist initiatives provided the ideological scaffolding from which states could off-load their responsibility for the provision of these public services (such as housing and safety) more generally (Brush 1987). By the decade's end, Britain's ascending right-wing government ardently embraced the movement's desire for autonomy and the market's rhetoric of private provision and self-reliance. How could it and later other governments not? Shelters, in particular, provided cost effective and creative solutions to a bewildering array of social problems including, though clearly not limited to, female homelessness, child abuse, and male violence.

In contrast to the movements they observed, governments had long insisted on deferring action beneficial to women because of the expense (Ashworth 1993). Some women's movements challenged this position with greater effect than others; the Dutch did so in 1982, when they hosted a conference on violence against women, initiated by the then secretary of state for Equal Opportunities, Hedy d'Ancona. Following "the lead of the more radical sections of the women's movement," she argued: "Violence against women is a structural problem against which government should take action as part of its equal opportunities policy" (Grunell 1999, 343). Such assertions later became standard fare for myriad governments, NGOs, and transnational organizations alike but this took time. For instance, both Amnesty International and the UN's Convention on the Elimination of All Forms of Discrimination Against Women (CEDAW) ignored the matter of male violence until the early 1990s.

While violence against women was hardly novel to feminists, femocrats like d'Ancona helped place the matter on a new agenda, that of formal politics. This was exceptional because, at that time, and to some extent still, many politicians and scholars of "equality" kept a considerable distance between policies pertaining to sexual abuse and violence against women and those regarding equality at work and in the family.[4] The unwillingness to address the crucial connections between these matters is especially ironic considering that most violence is intra-familial and has significant economic and potentially dire consequences (Brush 2002).

The Community Responds

The 1980s

In 1984, the EP joined the chorus of outrage against male violence and after two years, its Committee on Women's Rights issued a parliamentary resolution (OJ C 176/73) and report (European Parliament 1986). The report, drafted by d'Ancona (who had joined the EP in 1984), recognized the deep connections between male violence, sexual oppression, and economic inequality. Her report emphasized the importance of shelters and encouraged Member States to take legislative action to assess and heighten the protection available to physically abused and sexually harassed women. Not surprisingly, the report's recommendations paralleled positions taken up in the Netherlands years earlier.

The Parliament's subsequent 1986 resolution on violence was quite comprehensive and sought to combat violence against women and girls as crucial to achieving equality between the sexes. Besides calling for the legal recognition of rape within marriage (a position it reiterated in 1999), it sought the establishment of progressive investigatory procedures and underscored the need for specially trained female police officers and interpreters to work with women from minority communities. The resolution also requested systematic data-gathering and the adoption of "measures in the field of planning, housing and public transport" to "increase general safety and thus benefit women and the elderly in particular" (OJ C 176/73, 14.7.86, paragraph 17).

The resolution's explicit recognition of prostitution and pornography as elements of male violence placed women in the sex industry alongside other abused women, a position antithetical to established thinking. By regarding a prostituted woman as one "whose experience of sexual exploitation is consonant with that of all women's experience of sexual exploitation," the Parliament's position was not only feminist (Barry 1995, 9), it positioned the Parliament in opposition to more powerful EU institutions, such as the Council and the ECJ.

By 1979, the Court had already reinforced pornography's presence as a legitimate commodity on the open market in *Regina v Maurice Donald Henn and John Frederick Ernest Darby* (Case 34/79 [1979] ECR 3795). This case involved two men (Henn and Darby) convicted by the United Kingdom of importing Danish pornography into the country from Rotterdam. Both appealed their conviction, claiming that the United Kingdom had no consistent policies pertaining to the importation of "indecent" and "obscene" materials and that the restriction on Danish pornography violated the Treaty's promise of free trade. The British government, in turn, referred the matter to the ECJ. The Court ruled that states could justify the prohibition of certain goods (e.g., pornography) on "moral" grounds as each state, in principle, determines the requirement of public morality within its given territory. However, in 1986, the Court decided in *Conegate Limited v HM Customs and Excise* (Case 121/85 [1986] ECR 1007) that a state cannot prohibit the importation of pornography and other "erotic" goods if it does not itself ban their production within its own territory. This second case involved British customs and its seizure of imported inflatable sex dolls and other "erotic articles" sent from Germany by the company Conegate. Conegate submitted that while the Court had already recognized (in *Henn and Darby*) that states *could* prohibit such articles, it persuaded the Court that such prohibitions constitute "arbitrary discrimination" and even a disguised restriction on free trade unless the same restrictions exist in the Member State concerned. For Baer, the Court "implies [in the first case] that equality is a culturally relative claim and [by the second case] that Europe, as a whole, should not then act against pornography" (1996, 59).

In the midst of its decisions on pornography, the Court depicted prostitution in 1982 as a matter of "personal conduct" in two cases joined before it. In *Adoui and Cornuaille v Belgian State* (Cases 115 and 16/81 [1982] ECR 1665), the Court admonished the Belgian government for its refusal to tender residence permits to two French women (Rezguia Adoui and Dominique Cornuaille) because they had a history of prostitution when, in fact, Belgium had no laws against it. The Court reasoned that in the absence of "genuine or effective measures intended to combat such conduct" for local nationals, other EU nationals have a right to reside in Belgium and exercise the same behaviors as their hosts (Cases 115 and 16/81 [1982] ECR 1665, paragraphs 8–9). The Court extended similar reasoning four years later in *Conegate* when it informed states that they must move first to combat pornography within their own territories before erecting barriers against its importation from others.

While the ECJ's objection to Belgium's bias against women with a history of prostitution is understandable (as is its implicit recognition of that state's hypocrisy), its reasoning that prostitution is nothing more than "personal conduct" contradicted the Parliament's position (in 1986) that it was a social problem. Moreover, the Court's ruling set a worrisome precedent that traffickers and the pro-prostitution lobby have since been able to exploit. By refusing to recognize the sexual exploitation and violence implicit in the sex trade, the Court could reason: "The private life of individuals is, as a matter of principle, not to be interfered with by the State" (Cases 115 and 16/81 [1982] ECR 1665, 648).

Interestingly, several Member States adopted a similar reckoning in an effort to reject feminist claims for state intervention against wife-beaters in the home. In Britain, Courts were particularly reluctant to issue eviction orders; one judge declared, "I find it difficult to believe that it could ever be fair, save in most exceptional circumstances, to keep a man out of *his* flat or house for more than a few months" (quoted in Dobash and Dobash 1992, 187). Scottish courts were equally resistant, insisting that such orders be used only as a "last resort" (Dobash and Dobash 1992, 188). When Sweden, at last, adopted restraining orders in 1988, the legislation specifically discouraged their use by women battered by the men with whom they live (Elman 1996a). These factors help us to understand the reasons why, in most Member States, arrest was not a preferred strategy of intervention against batterers until the early 1990s.

Whether or not the Court so intended, its emphasis in *Adoui and Cornuaille* on private individuals gave the green light to pimps, procurers, and customers of prostitution, all of whom could then engage women in "personal conduct" under the subterfuge of free will. In short, the Court's analysis in 1982 perpetuated the myth that prostitution is a personal choice and just a job (i.e., "sex work"),[5] amenable to a powerful multibillion euro sex industry, affiliated NGOs, and Member States such as the Netherlands.

The Parliament, by contrast, persisted in its position that prostitution is a manifestation of violence against women, despite opposition from the Greens, and in 1989 it adopted the Resolution on the Exploitation of Prostitution and the Traffic in Human Beings (OJ C 120/352).[6] According to Dorchen Leidholdt, director of the Coalition against Trafficking in Women (CATW), this resolution recognized that "the practice of prostitution involves the violation of certain fundamental human rights and freedoms, especially the rights to privacy, liberty and the integrity of the human person." The Parliament's pronouncement urged the development of "a genuine common policy adopted by all the Member States in order to combat prostitution and eliminate the traffic in persons" (Leidholdt 1996, 91). The document recommended specific legal remedies including, but not limited to, increased penalties against pimps, procurers, and traffickers. The Parliament also suggested the creation of a special police division, staffed by women, to receive victims' complaints and provide them with social services.

The Parliament's woman-centered approach to prostitution, pornography, and trafficking may have derived from its more human-rights oriented cast as the EU's only democratically elected EU institution (Goodey 2004, 30), but its progressive reports and resolutions were hardly a direct basis for concrete measures against male violence. On the contrary, the EU's relatively more powerful institutions chose to ignore the Parliament's positions, an easy choice given this body's political constraints.

The Court was not the only EU institution to disregard the parliamentary stance on violence against women. The Council's adoption of the 1989 Broadcasting Directive (89/552/EEC) proved a boon to pornographers. Before this guideline, also known as the Television without Frontiers Directive, Member States such as Germany and the United Kingdom were able to curtail the importation of much pornography freely available in other EU countries. The 1989 Directive removed these earlier restrictions by stating that any program approved by one Member State is automatically legal in all others. Its promise that Member States "ensure that broadcasts do not contain any incitement to hatred on the grounds of race, sex, religion or nationality" (89/552/EEC; Article 22), has in no way slowed down the distribution of pornography. Instead, pornographers such as Britain's Mark Garner have been swift to profit from the Directive by having their movies first approved in the Netherlands (a Member State notorious for its promotion of legal prostitution and pornography), then reaching viewers in other countries by satellite. Within two years of the law's passage, Garner's "Red Hot Dutch" subscription service reached 22,000 subscribers across the United Kingdom. He explains, "I simply saw that there is a lot of money to be made from this [Directive] . . . Sex sells" (Phillips 1993).

The increased traffic of pornographic goods and sexual services proved profitable to some but problematic for others and the EU's rhetorical commitment to women's rights became more difficult to maintain as activists continued to mobilize within their Member States to reveal those costs. In an effort to capture the attention of those in power, women's movements on the wane by the late 1980s began pursuing strategies that stressed the economic consequences of inequality (e.g., homelessness, lowered productivity, increased absenteeism, and costly medical interventions due to injuries caused by batterers). Their success came, in part, through the consensus they began generating within the United Nations.

Beyond the Community

The 1990s to the Present

In addition to recognizing that violence against women "is pervasive and cuts across lines of income, class and culture," the UN's Economic and

Social Council called upon governments in 1990 to take immediate and decisive steps to eradicate it. The UN Council reasoned that failure to act would slow economic and social development and reduce progress for society as a whole (in Penn and Nardos 2003, 8). Two years later the UN's Committee on the Elimination of Discrimination against Women rectified its earlier omission of male violence in its 1979 Convention on the Elimination of All Forms of Discrimination Against Women. By June 1993, the UN's World Conference on Human Rights in Vienna stressed the importance of violence against women as a human rights violation and that December the General Assembly adopted the first international human rights instrument designed solely to deal with such abuse, the UN Declaration on the Elimination of Violence against Women (Penn and Nardos 2003, 9).

Though not legally binding, the UN's positions increased pressure within the Member States and thus the EU to develop a more unified stance against male violence though, for the EU, this expectation proved more challenging. Not only was the EU without any explicit legal competence in the early 1990s to pursue the matter, the Community's adoption of the 1992 Maastricht Treaty complicated its power by explicitly recognizing the principle of subsidiarity.[7] Subsidiarity may be summarized as the notion that wherever there is discretion, government tasks should be taken as close to EU citizens as possible. As the EU's special Social Rights Committee (Comité des Sages) notes, subsidiarity requires that "the leading role in social matters should belong to the Member States" (CEC 1996c, 42). In this sense, the EU was able to delegate responsibility for male violence to the national level though, in principle, subsidiarity also implies an obligation on the part of the EU to intervene in those instances where states fail to uphold basic rights.

Determining the most appropriate level for intervention on behalf of battered women is often more complicated than it may seem. One of the major issues confronting battered women's shelters throughout Europe has been how best to meet the needs of abused women whose legal status is insecure (Brückner 2001, 773; Nordic Council of Ministers 1998).

This group may include daughters of migrants fleeing from forced marriages and women from all over the world who are newly arrived immigrants legally married to EU citizens who abuse them for pleasure and/or profit. To escape these men, many women run from their homes and, in consequence, risk statelessness. Their precarious status, in turn, can intensify their dependence on (other) traffickers and sex-industry pimps (Leidholdt 1996, 84). As the feminist activist Aurora Javate de Dios explains, restrictive migration policies can enhance conditions that make immigrant women "powerless and vulnerable to traffickers, fake marriage bureaus, and other shady intermediaries such as underworld syndicates . . . which have traditionally controlled migrant labor and entertainment industries." She concludes, "The pressure to go underground will increase, as will the dependence of women of color on European men who are not subject to these restrictions" (quoted in Leidholdt 1996, 85).

Often unable to return to their homelands, many of these women have faced a situation in which they cannot stay in Member States unless they remain married for a specified number of years so that they can establish, to the state's satisfaction, a commitment to national residence. In the Netherlands, for example, women are forced to reside with their partners for at least five years and in Sweden, they must remain with them for two years. In Britain, women were required to stay with their husbands for at least one year or return to their country of origin. Should a third-country national decide to leave her EU citizen husband, she would have to leave "his" country. However unintentionally, women were expected to endure abuse for the privilege of legal residence—a condition that shelters throughout the Community have worked to mitigate for years.

In its initial efforts to address the residential status of third-country nationals, the ECJ's decision in *Diatta v Land Berlin* exacerbated the original injustices suffered by the victims of male violence by reinforcing their problematic legal position (Case 267/83 [1985] ECR 567).[8] This 1985 case concerned a Member State husband separated (though not formally divorced) from his third-country national wife. The Court ruled that the woman was entitled to the protections of Community law only until the marriage was formally annulled. Tamara K. Hervey notes, "The effect of the ruling . . . was to give the EUN [European Union National] husband control over [the] expulsion of his wife: on divorce she would cease to be a member of the family for purposes of Community law" (1995, 106).

As the EU struggled to balance the principle of subsidiarity with increased pressure to develop a more unified stance against male violence, several Member States alleviated the hardships of stateless existence for abused women by decreasing residence requirements. It is likely that these efforts intensified pressure on the Community to intervene, thus piquing EU interest in violence against women. In 1997, a dozen years after the Court's ruling in *Diatta v Land Berlin*, a High Level Panel on Free Movement rebuked the earlier position of the judges as unacceptable. More specifically, the Panel recommended that the Community extend residence rights for divorced spouses, who are third-country nationals (High Level Panel 1997).

Still, in the absence of any explicit legal basis in the Treaty, the EU was hesitant to promote a uniform approach regarding divorced non-EU citizens (Gradin, interview, 1999). It was, thus, not until 2004 that the Parliament and Council adopted a revised directive on freedom of movement consistent with the High Panel's position and the movements that helped inspire it. This legislation acknowledges that "in certain conditions to guard against abuse," measures should be taken to ensure that those "already residing in the territory of the host Member State retain their right of residence" (2004/38/EC, 82). A year later, the EWL emphasized the precarious situation of third-country nationals and requested that Member States grant women migrants not only an autonomous right of residence but also work permits, enabling them to live independently (European Women's Lobby 1995).

Emphasizing the significant costs of violence against women may have helped pique EU interest and initiate government reforms across previously indifferent Member States; however, those in power exaggerated their responsiveness to abused women, often in ways that undermined the very movements that first compelled them to act. For example, while the Swedish government generated considerable enthusiasm for its 1998 Violence Against Women Act (enabling prosecutors to redress the repeated abuse of women without requiring separate proceedings for each incident of abuse),[9] it ignored pleas from battered women and shelters to withdraw its 1995 Child Contact Act, which grants abusive fathers access to those whom they previously terrorized. Under the 1995 law, the state can withdraw child custody from mothers who do not *actively* support their child's contact with the father. Furthermore, some Swedish shelters lost public funding and others are under threat if they do not comply with the Child Contact Act, although such compliance places the women they serve at risk (Elman 2001). Similar problems exist for battered women in the United Kingdom and Denmark, to name just two other Member States (Eriksson and Hester 2001; Hester and Radford 1996).

Politics have unintended consequences and it is unlikely that those (including feminists) determined to exact greater paternal involvement in children's lives considered fully the risk to battered women in making this claim. In consequence, battered EU nationals are also left in legal limbo because, in fleeing with their children from abusive partners, they end up violating child contact or custody orders that often denied or ignored the fundamental right of these mothers to live in safety.

Nonetheless, the increased awareness that many women throughout the EU are unsafe helped inspire two prominent programs to counter this crisis—STOP (Sexual Trafficking in Persons, incorporated into the now defunct AGIS program) and DAPHNE. STOP began in 1996 and was the Commission's first initiative to combat the transport of third-country nationals for sexual exploitation. It extended funding for this purpose to criminal justice officials and social workers throughout the EU. The following year, the Commission adopted the DAPHNE Program to complement its anti-trafficking program by providing financial assistance to the voluntary sector for efforts against male violence more generally. According to the Commission, "the two programmes therefore together include all the major actors involved in the fight against violence" (CEC 1998d, 8). Chapter 7 explores the establishment and consequences of these two initiatives in detail; we end this chapter by elaborating further on the context within which many of these "major actors" began to mobilize.

Conclusion

Whether the EU was more willing to confront violence against women in the 1990s because, like its Member States, it faced growing economic uncertainty or because it wished to diminish its democratic deficit[10] and increase its responsiveness to women, we will never know. Ascertaining motives is always a speculative venture but implying that the EU's recent interest male violence is consistent with or part of a *long-standing policy* to confront human rights abuses is misleading, insofar as most human rights oriented efforts have largely been—and remain—within the jurisdiction of the sovereign Member States.[11]

By the time that the EU ventured into the discussion of male violence, most of the Member States had addressed the issue on their own and their citizens had clearly come to expect the EU's involvement as well. By 1999, a Eurobarometer survey revealed that 67 percent agreed that the EU should "definitely" be involved in countering male violence while only 5 percent suggested a non-interventionist approach is appropriate (CEC 1999, 103). Although this finding would have been unfathomable had women's movements not worked for two decades to politicize this issue, there are several other factors to consider.

First, Brussels' insiders help us to understand the reasons why the EU has become more sensitive to the demands of its citizens in general. Barbara Helfferich stresses that one not overlook the growing sense of alarm among Community elites in the early 1990s. Helfferich, secretary general for the EWL from 1991 to 1999, holds that because the Commission was so troubled by conflicts over the adoption of the 1992 Maastricht Treaty and surveys showing that women's attitudes toward integration were negative, it was more willing to confront other issues pertaining to sexual inequality (Helfferich and Kolb 2001).[12]

Second, Mark Pollack has suggested that the EU may have been keen to take action in 1996 following a political scandal involving sexual abuse, trafficking, and the serial murder of young women and girls throughout Belgium that same year (1999).[13] The man who confessed to these crimes (Marc Dutroux) was joined by a well-known executive (Michel Nihoul) who admitted to having organized numerous sexual "parties" for prominent male judges, senior politicians, lawyers, police officers, and even a former European commissioner. Extending funding to combat male violence may have appealed to the Commission's desire to stand above the appearance of impropriety, but it is impossible to overlook the changing composition of the Commission itself—changes wrought by the EU's northern enlargement.

Sweden's entrance into the Community in 1995 is a third element to consider, especially given the country's stellar reputation for sexual equality and the belief that its entrance would serve as a catalyst for the rights of women in other Member States (Gould 2001; Helfferich and Kolb 2001, 146; Pollack 1999). Whether this is true (particularly as regards sexual abuse and violence)[14] matters less than the expectation that because Sweden enjoys this reputation it is expected to act accordingly.

In an effort not to disappoint, Sweden's commissioner Anita Gradin was more willing and able than most to take a broader view of equality when she assumed the portfolio for Justice and Home Affairs from 1995 to 1999. Commissioner Gradin and her colleagues enjoyed a more hospitable climate than their predecessors when they embarked on efforts to address male violence, a momentum made possible not only by the Belgian scandal and UN declarations but by women's movements that had been organizing for decades, a factor few Eurocrats have chosen to appreciate, including Gradin.

Speaking before the first EU organized conference on "domestic" violence against women in Cologne in 1999, Gradin offered the following narrative. "All the way from the Rome Treaty and its article on equal pay for equal work, equal opportunities have been on the agenda of the European Union" (1999, 2). After crediting the Member States with legal reform, she mentioned women's "organizations" once, noting that they had "been very instrumental in pointing to the necessity for legislation for the protection of women's rights" (Gradin 1999, 8). The fact that feminists throughout Europe have long been ambivalent and divided about engaging some of the very authorities that may have been indifferent to or abusive to women was nowhere noted. When politicians only acknowledge women's movements in connection with their own legislative agenda, they deny the other aspirations of these movements and inflate the protection that the law, Member States, and EU institutions can offer.

The EU's essentially economic character, as expressed in the Treaty of Rome and related Equality Directives, initially precluded its interest in fundamental human rights and thus violence against women. The absence of any specific and detailed articles concerning human rights and male violence also made it easier for the EU to evade action in this area. In contrast to Gradin's claim, it is extraordinary that the EU has grown particularly interested in this women's rights issue. However, just as activists had earlier convinced politicians and others that "there was an economic need for women to be involved in the labor market," they began to argue that the effects of violence spilled over into the workplace, at considerable loss to the economy (Griffin 1995, 7). Throughout Europe, feminists politicized the public nature of this ostensibly private abuse by emphasizing the problems battered women encounter at work (e.g., poor concentration, tardiness, and sick leaves). Politicians and businesses responded—often times for reasons tied to health, safety, liability, legitimacy, and the bottom line (Ostner 2000).[15]

A last factor to consider involves the EU's geographic shift eastward and the structural changes related to it. With the fall of the Berlin Wall, the emergence of newly independent Central and Eastern Europe Countries (CEECs), and desperately impoverished women seeking work, the Commission could no longer ignore the sexual exploitation of women—the trafficking of whom it said involved international organized crime (CEC 1996d, 3). Nor could the Commission ignore the public health threat posed by the spread of numerous sexually transmitted diseases such as HIV/AIDS that accompany the sex trade (CEC 1996d, 18). Yet, more was at stake than the physical well being of women and others within the Community.

The EU's interest in mitigating trafficking and even HIV/AIDS may portend progressive efforts against prostitution, the protection of women's health, and even promotion of their rights. However, when one considers the Court's affirmation of prostitution as work, the continuing increase in trafficking within an enlarged polity, and so much death and money at stake, some reservation and healthy skepticism are in order,[16] perhaps not least when we contemplate the substance and outcomes of both the STOP and DAPHNE initiatives.

CHAPTER 7

The Programs—Stop and Daphne

When the UN issued a Declaration on the Elimination of Violence against Women in 1993, it was the first international human rights instrument designed exclusively to address this issue. Two years later, it held its Fourth World Conference on Women in Beijing, the largest conference the UN ever convened. Paragraph 118 of that conference's Platform of Action stipulates: "violence against women is a manifestation of the historically unequal power relations between men and women which have led to domination over and discrimination against women by men and to the prevention of women's full advancement" (United Nations General Assembly, February 23, 1994). In the aftermath of these developments, the EP's CWR proposed that the European Commission support efforts to combat various forms of male violence.

The Commission responded swiftly with the 1996 STOP program to counter "the transport of women from third countries into the European Union (including *perhaps* subsequent movements between Member States) for the purpose of sexual exploitation" (COM(96) 567, 4; my emphasis). While the Commission acknowledged its timidity in condemning the trafficking of women *within* Member States in 2000,[1] its initial position was in step with long-standing efforts to liberalize its own market. Recall the Broadcasting Directive of 1989, which had lowered the internal barriers for the distribution of pornography: the graphic depiction of women (and others) in prostitution. Furthermore, the Commission's reluctance to infringe on sex traffickers within the EU is consistent with the Community's conception of itself as free of exploitation and thus in no need of efforts to counter it (Williams 2004).[2]

Over its first five years, STOP received €6.5 million (nearly US$8 million), funding research and information gathering for the development and implementation of training programs for public officials (e.g., law enforcement and migration officers) throughout fifteen Member States. When the Commission renewed the anti-trafficking program in 2001, it encouraged applicant countries to seek funding through 2002. In the aftermath of 9/11 and increased efforts to combat terrorism, this "STOP II" program has since faded. Anti-trafficking efforts continued under the aegis of AGIS, a catch-all criminal justice program, through 2006.[3]

During STOP's tenure, a substantial portion of its funding went to the International Organization for Migration (IOM), an intergovernmental organization established in 1951 to resettle "displaced persons," migrants, and refugees throughout Europe in the aftermath of World War II. The IOM has since expanded to encompass a variety of "migration management activities," including the monitoring of trafficking throughout the world.[4] With STOP funding, this intergovernmental organization became largely responsible for generating the EU's initial research on trafficking. In addition, it was deeply involved with public awareness campaigns and international conferences related to trafficking.

After attempting the first systematic overview of sex trafficking by focusing on women transported from Central and Eastern Europe to the then fifteen Member States, the IOM found a majority of the countries it surveyed had no data on trafficking in women. Nonetheless, the organization concluded in 2000 that it had obtained "valuable information" about why it was "so badly informed about the scale of trafficking" (Salt and Hogarth 2000, 34).[5] It attributed the dearth of data to the covert character of the abuse and emphasized that many countries never bothered to define the problem, much less to maintain comprehensive data on it.

Aware of this problem, and prior to the release of the report, the Council adopted a 1997 Joint Action (OJ L 63, 4.3.97), obliging Member States to review their existing laws with a view to making the trafficking in human beings and the sexual exploitation of children a criminal offense. Other efforts were undertaken as well, such as an EU Ministerial Conference on the traffic in women organized by the Dutch presidency that year. Having excluded those who had campaigned against prostitution, those in attendance echoed the need to increase the awareness and responsiveness of law enforcement, customs, and legal services to only those women *trafficked* throughout the Member States, a position that would be reiterated at later events and through additional legislation.

The Commission established the DAPHNE initiative the same year (1997) to complement STOP's measures. The majority of DAPHNE's funding (of approximately €5 million or US$6 million each year) went to the voluntary (NGO) sector, including the EWL, to support community-wide information and action campaigns. In its first year, DAPHNE funded forty-six NGOs and volunteer programs for projects within the Member States to prevent violence against women and children while supporting survivors. Of these, less than a third (13) related specifically to women.

In its second year, the Commission sponsored forty-nine DAPHNE projects, including a few against trafficking but none that dealt directly with ending prostitution (Marcovich 1999, 199). Antoinette Fouque, former vice chair of the EP's CWR, found that it became almost impossible to confront prostitution in the aftermath of the Beijing and Dutch conferences (Idels, interview, 2005). Not only had the Dutch and their allies convinced numerous MEPs that prostitution existed without coercion and that efforts to end it intruded on women's rights to pursue their own "work" lives, various EU programs began funding operations that actively campaigned to promote its legalization (see European Parliament 2004, 18).

Since then the Commission has twice renewed DAPHNE as a Community Action Program (from 2000 to 2004 and from 2004 to 2008) to support networks and to coordinate programs to protect and assist women and children victimized by male of violence, narrowly defined. If STOP's trajectory provides any clue for DAPHNE's future, one might expect that if the program lasts much longer, it will do so with diminished resources. With this brief introduction to the STOP and DAPHNE programs complete, this chapter discusses these initiatives in further detail and concludes with a consideration of their beneficiaries.

The Commission's support of STOP and DAPHNE initially puzzled those within Parliament whose earlier efforts at reform the Commission had selected to ignore. For example, having entertained several motions against pornography each year since 1990, the Parliament passed a 1993 resolution that recognized pornography as a "systematic practice of exploitation and subordination based on sex that disproportionately harms women and contributes to the inequality between the sexes" (OJ C 20/546). The Parliament further requested that the Commission pursue reform efforts under Article 3 of the European Convention for the Protection of Human Rights and Fundamental Freedoms.

The Parliament's 1993 resolution on pornography acknowledged for the first time, at the European level, what it seems all EU institutions (including perhaps the Parliament) have chosen to overlook ever since—that pornography constitutes sex discrimination and for this reason the women in it are hardly eager and willing participants in its production. Heather Macrae reasons that the Commission's support of STOP and DAPHNE "might be interpreted as a political way of addressing male violence against women without actually taking on the issue of pornography" (2003, 335). In fact, the Commission's sudden willingness to condemn the abuse of children through pornography, a competence it denied it held until the mid-1990s when sexual abuse in Belgium received front page coverage in the European press, suggests a way of addressing pornography without offering any "direct recognition of the role [that it] plays in violence against *women*" (Macrae 2003, 335; my emphasis). The fact that so few regard pornography as evidence of harm testifies to the success that pornographers and others have had in concealing sexual discrimination and assault by photographing it.

Reforming STOP—Regulating Trafficking

2000–Present

Although the Commission has yet to acknowledge its earlier refusal to address the Parliament's call to counter pornography, it did concede that it was mistaken in other ways. In 2000, the Commission recognized that its near exclusive concentration on the movement of third-country nationals for "the purpose of sexual exploitation" contributed to a "paradox," whereby a "European citizen forced into prostitution and trafficked within *its* [*sic*] own country, would be less protected than citizens of third countries" (COM(2000) 854 final, 9; my emphasis).[6] The Commission moreover acknowledged that its 1997 Joint Action had "failed," given "the absence of commonly adopted definitions, incriminations and sanctions in the Member States' penal legislation" (COM(2000) 854 final, 4). Criticism had been mounting for some time, particularly from the CATW, the EWL, and numerous other feminist organizations (Raymond 2001, 3). Even the Organisation for Security and Cooperation in Europe (OSCE) concluded that, in the absence of a European Convention to combat sex trafficking, the problem remained a low law-enforcement priority. The OSCE found that the commitment of Member States was "more verbal than real" (in Salt and Hogarth 2000, 117).

To address these shortcomings, the Commission proposed a 2000 Council Framework Decision on trafficking that broadened the definition to cover EU citizens. The Commission reaffirmed its opposition to sex trafficking by emphasizing that the EU's Charter of Fundamental

Rights also prohibits it, a position since codified by the Community's new constitution despite its 2005 rejection in French and Dutch referenda. Last, the Commission recognized that prohibitions against "sexual exploitation" include prostitution and "the production of pornographic material" (COM(2000) 854 final, 9), but only in cases involving "coercion" and where "there is another form of abuse" (COM(2000) 854 final, 16). In marked contrast to the EP's 1993 resolution on pornography, the Commission maintains that, like pornography, adult prostitution is itself neither a sufficient form of abuse, nor one that is inherently coercive. This position allows it to ignore the practices and industries that sustain and promote trafficking. Yet, through its earlier support of STOP, the Commission is also able to insist that it opposes sexual exploitation.

Soon after the Commission recognized that EU citizens deserved protection against trafficking in 2000, the ECJ affirmed prostitution as work, thus distinguishing it from sexual exploitation. Indeed, in 2001 the Court's support of prostitution in *Aldona Malgorzata Jany and Others v Staatssecretaris van Justitie* (Case C-268/99 [2001] ECR 8615) is unambiguous. The case involved six prostituted women (Ms. Jany and Ms. Szepietowska from Poland and four other women from the Czech Republic), all seeking entry and residence permits in the Netherlands. The Dutch government denied the women their request, insisting that it could not treat prostitution as "self-employment" because it could not determine, to its own satisfaction, that the women voluntarily moved to the Netherlands to perform this activity. The Hague District Court referred the decision to the ECJ. After noting that "prostitution is tolerated, even regulated, by most of [the Member] States," most notably the Netherlands (Case C-268/99 [2001] ECR 8615, paragraph 54), the Court found that prostitution posed no "genuine threat to public order" (paragraph 57). It further ruled, "The activity of prostitution pursued in a self-employed capacity can be regarded as a service provided for remuneration" (Case C-268/99 [2001] ECR 8615, 50).

Moreover, despite its earlier stated promises (in 2000) to combat regional trafficking while providing protection to EU citizens, the EU stayed focused on third-country nationals, a bias especially evident in its 2002 IOM-organized and STOP-subsidized international conference addressing the matter. The European Conference ("Preventing and Combating Trafficking in Human Beings—A Global Challenge for the 21st Century") was a two-day event convened within the Parliament that resulted in the Brussels Declaration.

Requesting the establishment of an "expert" group on trafficking,[7] the conference Declaration proposed legislation extending protection and a *limited period of stay* to third-country nationals who are victims of traffickers, but only if they testify against them (see COM(2002) 71 final). Since their 1997 ministerial conference, the Dutch had been promoting this "particularly cynical policy" to deport the same women who had risked their lives to testify against the men who used them (Louis 1999, 194). Authorities often sent the women back to the same conditions that had exposed them to the traffickers in the first place. In extending Dutch policy to the entire community, the meeting chose to ignore the Parliament's earlier and more generous request of asylum for the victims of gender-related oppression and persecution (e.g., OJ 377/341, 29.12.00). In addition to acknowledging the circumstances of the women, the Parliament's earlier tactic might have encouraged Member States to take action against traffickers for human rights violations.

If the limited period of stay signified a welcome shift from concentrating almost exclusively on traffickers to addressing their victims, others with deeper ties to human rights and feminist organizations emphasized its band-aid character (e.g., Goodey 2004, 30). Whereas some (e.g., within the Commission) emphasized the protection and social benefits available to trafficked women, others (e.g., the CATW, the Association des Femmes de l'Europe Meriondale, and the EWL) noted the temporary quality of the benefit and the risks women faced in cooperating fully with the authorities.

Confronted by mounting criticism from the above-noted women's groups for their insensitivity to trafficking victims, the EU responded in 2002 with the adoption of yet another Framework Decision (2002/629/JHA). It states that protection for and assistance to victims are no longer contingent on the cooperation of these women with authorities.

While this recent change implies a move in the right direction, several problems persist. First, the wisdom of encouraging trafficked women to testify is dubious when no Member State currently offers sufficient witness protection to cover the particular circumstances and needs of trafficking victims (Goodey 2004, 39). Second, the Framework Decision obliged the Member States to inform the Commission and the Council of their enforcement measures by August of 2004 and only four Member States (France, Finland, Cyprus, and Austria) even complied with a general request for information. In a 2006 report concerning the Framework Directive, the Commission notes that while it is without reports from several Member

States (e.g., Portugal, Luxembourg, Ireland, and Lithuania), few others sent relevant information on enforcement (CEC 2006e). Moreover, there is little reason to believe that existing programs will be tailored to the needs of women, not least with the 2006 funding cuts.

That STOP continued for a short time under the AGIS criminal justice program suggests that the issue of sex trafficking has "been subsumed under wider concerns about immigration, crime and security." Jo Goodey concludes that sex trafficking has "become distanced from the underlying global problem of violence against women" (2004, 35). Crucially, her conclusion differs little from an IOM assessment that was written well in advance of the adoption of these recent measures (i.e., the quartet of STOP II, two Council Framework Decisions, and the Brussels Declaration).

There is no evidence to suggest that matters will improve. STOP has been discontinued and the IOM has acknowledged the unwillingness of several governments to appreciate or understand trafficking as a contravention of human rights (Salt and Hogarth 2000, 118). In fact, several Member States have refused to ratify and implement international conventions against trafficking and sexual exploitation. Furthermore, if the many governments that concerned the IOM continue to pursue the women who are bought and sold as criminals, while treating sex trafficking as an immigration issue, traffickers and others will be better able to instill fear in women fearing deportation. This point has been made repeatedly by feminists such as de Dios and Leidholdt, both with the CATW.

Many of the EU's most ardent feminist critics (e.g., CATW) remain on the margins of policy discussions. Their persistent request that the Community concentrate on trafficking and its relationship to other forms of sexual violence (i.e., sex tourism, sexual exploitation on the Internet, mail-order brides, pornography, and organized prostitution) has been ignored, if not dismissed derisively as unrealistic. Instead, like most of its Member States, the EU frames trafficking as separate from prostitution and countless other enterprises that trade in sex through physical abuse, emotional coercion, economic disadvantage, manipulation, and deception (Outshoorn 2004, 12). This frame rests on a separation between the "innocent" victims of traffickers and women who "choose" prostitution, a distinction that discounts the demand that prostitution generates for trafficking while ignoring the women in prostitution who have spoken out against its violence (Farley 2006).[8] Like abused women in general, women in prostitution have rarely been included in policy efforts aimed at countering their own abuse, a condition that prompted the CWR to call for change in 2004.

In conversations with Commission officials, Marianne Eriksson, a rapporteur for the CWR discovered that "no checks were carried out on the organizations" or on alleged experts engaged in policy discussions pertaining to trafficking. She concludes, "In view of the way in which organised crime operates, it is therefore possible that the Commission, the initiator of common legislation, is being advised by representatives of criminal organizations" (European Parliament 2004, 18). This finding led to the request that views of women who have survived the industry be included in deliberations. In addition, the CWR insisted on greater transparency in the awarding of grants to NGOs and experts involved in debates on prostitution (European Parliament 2004, 10). Recall that in DAPHNE's second year (1998–1999) monies went to only those anti-trafficking measures that did not address prostitution. This is like spending money to counter male violence without addressing physical abuse.

With the notable exception of Sweden, which decriminalized prostitution while criminalizing the behaviors of customers, pimps, and traffickers in 1999, recent Community reports on trafficking suggest that matters have become worse.[9] In France, officials estimate that the prostitution trade has increased by 30 percent since 1997, the year after STOP began (U.S. Department of State 2003). The Netherlands concedes that, "Although the government increased anti-trafficking law enforcement personnel, evidence does not indicate that the problem has decreased" (U.S. Department of State 2003).

In retrospect, it would have been naïve to expect otherwise. As Leidholdt notes, "Few countries invest law enforcement resources in the investigation and prosecution of sex industry profiteers and fewer still address the criminal sanctions against their customers, who fuel the demand of the sex industry" (1999, 54). In its remarkably candid "Report on the consequences of the sex industry in the European Union," the CWR estimates that the illegal sex industry generates more in profits annually than the combined military budgets throughout the world (estimated between €5,000 to 7,000 billion) (European Parliament 2004, 8). STOP's initial budget (of €6.5 million) was supposed to cover fifteen countries for five years. This amounts to less than the estimated annual profits from trafficking in any one of several states.[10]

"Europe's Year against Violence" and DAPHNE

1999 and After

When Parliament designated 1999 as the "European Year against Violence," the ideological schism had firmly set between the wealth-generating and sexualized violence of trafficking and commercialized sex, on the one hand, and women battered in their homes, on the other. This understanding is evidenced in campaign literature and the Commission's first and only Eurobarometer survey on violence against women (CEC 1999). The survey asked nearly a thousand people in each of the fifteen Member States a dozen questions relating to male violence. These ranged from what Europeans knew about the problem, what factors they think caused it, and what they believe needs to happen to remedy it. Perhaps more important is not what the survey asked, but what it omitted.

Interestingly, the EU's survey on male violence contained no queries pertaining to sexual abuse and exploitation and made no mention of the shelters that first politicized and continue to provide women refuge from "domestic violence." While it revealed that over two-thirds (67 percent) of the Member State nationals polled believed that the EU should "definitely" be involved in countering violence against women (CEC 1999, 103), the survey excluded shelters from the list of groups and institutions that respondents were encouraged to consider as the most appropriate actors for assisting battered women. After omitting shelters from an array of nine assistance options,[11] the survey misleadingly avers, "Europeans therefore regard all the [before-mentioned] entities as having *a legitimate interest* in the problem of domestic violence" (CEC 1999, 48; my emphasis). More to the point, the survey's authors regard as legitimate only those it listed. (See figure 7.1.)

Moreover, when the instrument asked respondents to select measures that could be taken to mitigate male violence, refuges (a.k.a. battered women's shelters) were again absent from a list that included, among other options, phone lines, contact cards (listing possible services), and sensitivity training for police (see figure 7.2). Whether or not the omission was deliberate matters less than the fact that these findings will be used to determine future measures and appropriations. With shelters excluded from an important policy loop, there is cause for concern.

DAPHNE's public information campaigns comprised a key element of the 1999 year against "domestic" violence. In looking through the materials, one is immediately struck by the ways that Eurocrats had essentially mimicked efforts that feminists had already mounted and had grown weary of at the local level.

Several of the posters from these campaigns entailed direct replicas of those used years earlier within various Member States. One borrowed from Denmark read: "95 per cent of Europeans believe that a man who beats his partner should be sentenced by a criminal court . . . So why is only 1 out of every 20 incidents of domestic violence reported to the

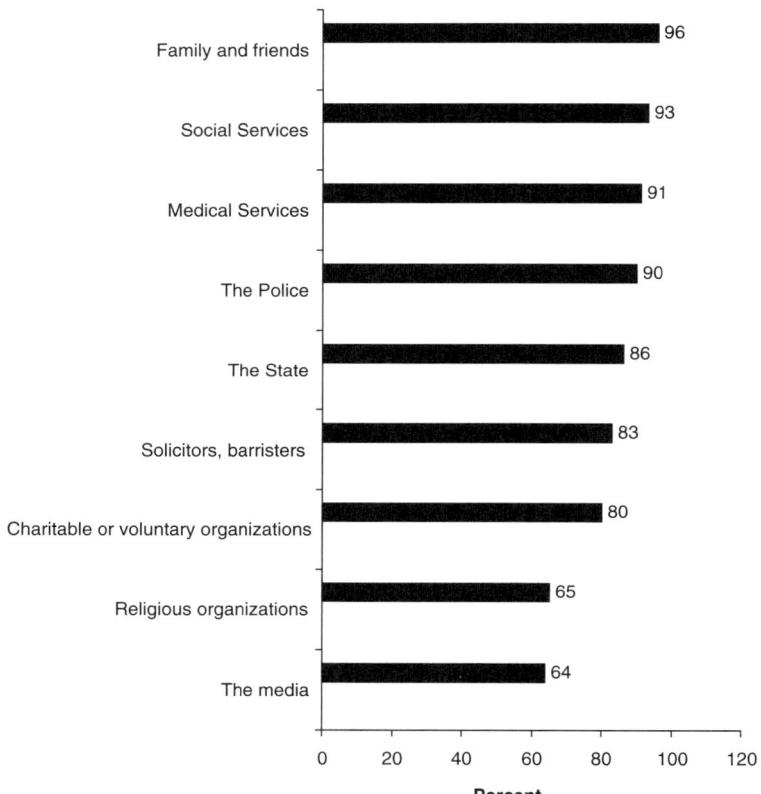

Institutions/groups that should help women who are victims of domestic violence

Figure 7.1 Legitimate assistance for abused women.

Note: The EU provided respondents with this list of nine possibilities.

Source: *Eurobarometer* 51.0, © European Communities, 1999, http://ec.europa.eu/public_opinion/ archives/ ebs/ebs_127_en.pdf.

police?" In the United Kingdom, the publicly financed, feminist inspired "Zero Tolerance" information campaign from 1992 also received renewed attention. In contrast to the Danish campaign, British efforts focused on the perpetrators of violence; they extended public validation to survivors by asserting that responsibility for assault rests squarely in men's hands. Straightforward black posters with white lettering insisted that men have

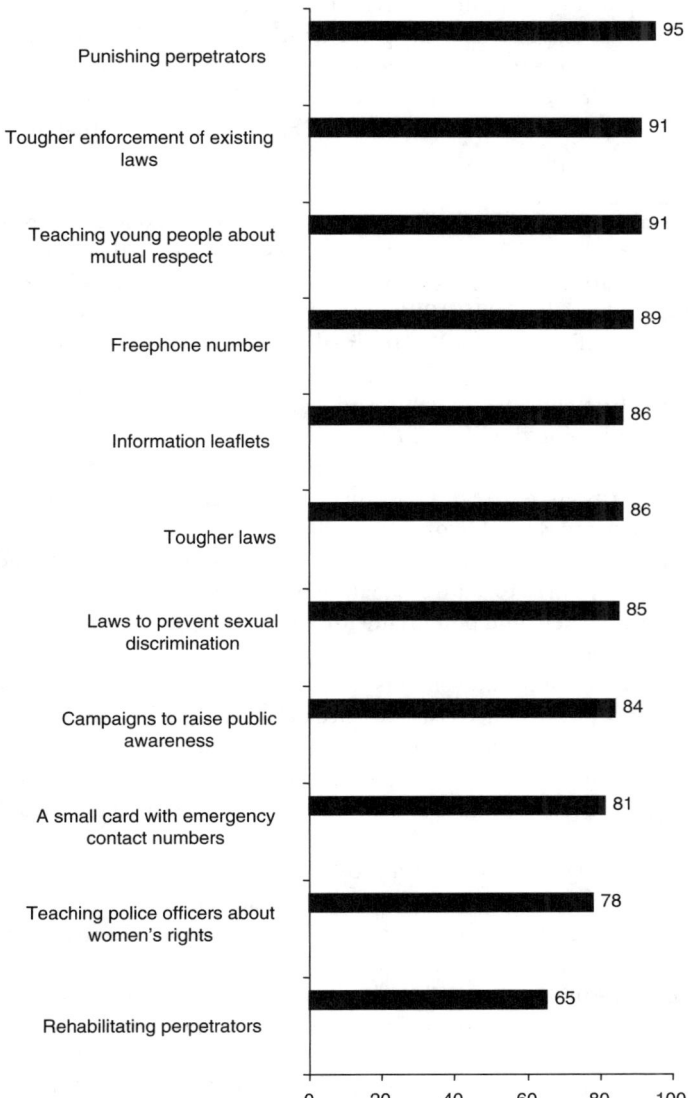

Figure 7.2 Ways of combating domestic violence against women.

Note: The EU provided respondents with this list of eleven possibilities.

Source: *Eurobarometer 51.0*, © European Communities, 1999, http://ec.europa.eu/public_opinion/archives/ebs/ebs_127_en.pdf.

no excuse for abusing women and proclaimed that local administrations (e.g., the police) would not tolerate it. Nonetheless, reality did not conform to rhetoric; years later the percentage of arrests in Britain remained at 12 to 14 percent whereas police records on reported incidents of domestic violence showed increases for nearly a decade (Grace 1995, 139). This fact alone contradicts DAPHNE's insistence that its campaigns to raise public awareness about violence entail and inspire the exchange of "best practices."

Several scholars of male violence have been outspoken critics of these and similar "Zero Tolerance" campaigns, insisting that they have "created an atmosphere in which it appears progress is related to domestic violence" (Kelly 1995/1996, 11). A study in the Spanish region of Cantabria confirms this point. It revealed a decrease in the percentage of women filing official complaints, especially disquieting given that the data were first collected in 1998 and again in 2000, a year prior to and then one following the EU's yearlong campaign to enhance public awareness that the physical assault of women is a crime and that authorities could be trusted to treat it as such (Associacion "Conseulo Berges" Mujeres Separadas y/o Divorciadas 2000).

Whatever criticisms they have of the Commission, the Court, and the Parliament's efforts to address male violence, few women's groups are likely to voice them and potentially forfeit the funding they may have had or hope to receive. In this way, they differ little from their progressive counterparts in other movements. In her candid account of frustrations among anti-poverty activists in Brussels, Sue Cohen observes: "It becomes difficult to challenge the accepted wisdom in these settings, especially if the Commission is your project's funding body" (2000, 18). Funding has been crucial to those with a desire to learn more about the best practices of other states. This is especially the case for activists from less affluent regions that rely more heavily on EU assistance. Still, for women's advocates everywhere, EU recognition may offer respectability and political advantage for activists in their own states (Beausang, interview, 1999; Greboval, interview, 2003; Marcovich, interview, 2003). This can mean, among other things, increased access to desperately needed funding, legislation and those within the criminal justice system willing to implement it.

Moreover, the EU's stated willingness to confront social injustices is itself of such crucial importance to activists that many are able to extend a salutary spin to almost any outcome in order to make it so. This position is reminiscent of international suffragists and inveterate women's rights lobbyists such as the U.S. activist Alice Paul who pretended to have the support of some nation-states to win over others (Rupp 1997, 219). Like Paul and her colleagues, women's rights advocates may exaggerate the support they receive from authorities if only to garner greater backing. Nothing succeeds like the appearance of success. Battered women's shelters may thus assert that police officers and others are reliable allies against male violence, more from a strategic claim for future intervention than from an accurate assessment of current conditions.[12]

The Beneficiaries

After the millions spent on research, select expert groups, and talking shops, and no sign that either "domestic violence" or sex trafficking has diminished or that it is seriously punished, who are the beneficiaries of these efforts to date? By emphasizing its opposition to domestic violence and the trafficking in women and children from outside of the Community, while casting an indifferent or accepting eye toward adult (read: "free") prostitution and pornography within Member States, the EU has been able to appease four groups simultaneously.

First, the EU's anti-trafficking efforts appeal to an increasing number of Europeans opposed to migration by calling for a more stringent policing of their borders. As Goodey explains, "the mainstay of the EU's political and practical response to sex trafficking has been and, arguably, continues to be located within a framework focusing on control of illegal immigration and organized crime." Moreover, "in the aftermath of 9/11, control of unwanted immigration into the EU has been enhanced as it has been wedded to control of terrorism" (2004, 32). What few recognize is that such discursive framing (of illegal immigrants and other "undesirables") often offers an acceptable pretext for racism and xenophobia.

Second, the benefits of this approach to Member State elites cannot be discounted. Recognizing the sovereignty of states to determine migration policies, the EU grants each the ability to determine for itself its policies on prostitution and extends funding to their local authorities in the process.[13] The fact that these authorities "may be complicit with traffickers and may protect them" remains a considerable problem (European Parliament 2000a, 11). For instance, following police raids on brothels in the Czech Republic, court cases against have been "quietly dropped" when senior politicians call in favors (European Parliament 2000a, 65). In Germany, the chief of the Special Commission on Organized Crime in Frankfurt an der Oder, was arrested for working with a German pimp who brought in prostitutes from Eastern Europe

(European Parliament 2000a, 12). Like battered women whose assailant partners work within the criminal justice system, prostituted women are often trapped, particularly in countries with large sex industries. As one survivor explains, "I took the decision to escape but I did not know where to go. I had no confidence in the police because they were clients of the bar. I did not know where to turn" (European Parliament 2000a, 12). Current EU policy offers no meaningful mechanisms to subvert the power of abusive authorities, a position exacerbated by Member States that embrace prostitution as legal.

Third, for women's groups that believe in the erroneous distinction between "free" and "forced" prostitution, there is a measure of relief that action may be taken for those women deemed especially vulnerable. This stance is in keeping with the dominant human rights narrative. It is a discourse that presumes that women within the Community have rights and privileges that make their being in prostitution freely chosen while those (nationals) external to the market lack these resources that render prostitution a "choice." This narrative precludes those with an interest in fundamental rights who "desire to question the Community from within" because the "Community has presented itself externally as a practicing guardian of human rights, a beacon of virtue" (Williams 2004, 200–01).

Most importantly, the "free" versus "forced" dichotomy protects a powerful fourth constituency—Europe's sex industry and its customers. By limiting the numbers of those considered as victims, the EU effectively shields both the industry and its customers from accusations of coercion. As one STOP poster proclaims "forced prostitution = slavery: there is no choice."[14] This approach has helped legitimize the sex trade (i.e., "free prostitution") as a voluntary, rational, economic choice for women. Prostitution becomes an "option" for those who comprise the most impoverished, unemployed, and physically abused segment of the EU market who are nonetheless (unlike third-country nationals) empowered by their Europeanness to embrace "sex work."

The sex industry's triumph rests not only in its increasing profits but also in the growing perception that pornography, trafficking, and organized prostitution are activities entirely separate and distinctive from "violence against women." This perspective causes considerable frustration among feminists. According to Leidholdt, "the victims who are targeted are the same—poor, minority, or so-called Third World women and children, frequently with histories of physical and sexual abuse." The customers are also the same—"men with disposable income who achieve sexual gratification by purchasing" the bodies of women and children. Not least, "whether brothel owners or traffickers employ or threaten violence, debt, imprisonment or brainwashing, the women's experiences of sexually transmitted diseases, substance abuse and physical violence are the same" (Leidholdt 1999, 51–52). Furthermore, the consequences of commercialized sex are often deadly. In 1999 alone, 189 women in prostitution were murdered in Italy (Hawthorne 2004, 252). Ironically, the flurry of anti-violence activity appears to have reached its peak this same year.

Conclusion

If the EU's policies are to be measured by the direct relief that they offer to women who have been abused, it is unlikely they can be regarded as successful. If they are to be measured by either their ability to provoke outrage against male violence or even an attempt to legitimize the movements that politicized it, their success is again doubtful. However, if the reforms that we have considered matter because they embellish the authority of the Union by suggesting its opposition to male violence, the EU has done well by its own measure. This is especially the case because the EU faces few penalties when the expectation for social justice in this arena is disappointed.

At present, well-heeled NGOs (like the IOM) and particular state sectors (e.g., criminal justice and social services) have reaped the fiscal rewards and political prominence from their own rhetoric and related efforts to combat male violence. In contrast, weakened movements have subdued their criticisms of once unresponsive authorities in the hopes of currying favor with them for desperately needed funding—much of it for the provision of direct services to abused women. One reason why women's movements to end violence may be less successful in capturing our attention, to say nothing of state and EU resources, is because they have been replaced by others claiming to do the same (see figures 7.1 and 7.2).

Moreover, while women's movements throughout the EU should be credited with politicizing male violence against women in general, one cannot ignore those other forces that succeeded in focusing more specifically on sexual exploitation. With increased competition from traffickers transporting women from outside the Community, and the ostensible decline in the value of EU nationals in prostitution, a reduction in revenues for Europe's pimps and brothels, whether real or anticipated, brought the issue of sexual exploitation to the fore. While the Commission concedes that accurate figures on trafficking are unavailable, "partly because of the illegal and clandestine activities involved" (CEC 1996d, 4), the CATW estimates the Dutch sex industry alone generates an estimated profit of more than US$500 million per year (Hughes et al. 1999). Such profits help explain the Netherlands' opposition to trafficking and its concomitant promotion of prostitution, a position that is becoming more common throughout Europe.

Over the last two decades, the Netherlands has made tremendous inroads in promoting its policy—both within the EU and well beyond. The Hague played a crucial role in developing the EU's action plan for the Beijing Conference of 1995.[15] There, for the first time, the EU recognized the concept of "forced prostitution" as opposed to the freely chosen kind that the Dutch industry insists it sells. The Dutch achieved similar success when, in 1996, they objected to Belgium's call to criminalize the possession of child pornography. Prior to the Dutch intervention, Belgium's proposal had enjoyed the support of most Member States (Louis 1999, 195).

By 1998, even the EP had begun to capitulate to the Dutch position. Retreating from its more ambitious requests of the past, that body now emphasizes measures "aimed at combating pornography and prostitution *involving children* and trafficking in children" (European Parliament 1998b, 15, paragraph 90). It is more circumspect regarding adult pornography and prostitution (e.g., European Parliament 1998b, 15, paragraph 86). Passing a separate resolution on (adult) prostitution that year, thereafter condemning only "forced" prostitution, the Parliament implied its support for "free" prostitution, a position that it would have been loathe to take years earlier. Leidholdt believes, "To decry the prostitution of a fifteen-year-old girl, but fail to speak out against the prostitution of her seventeen-year-old sister, is to tacitly sanction the sexual exploitation of the older girl" (1999, 52).

Two parliamentary reports, issued four years apart, further epitomize the EU's ambivalent, contradictory response to male violence. The first of these focused exclusively on trafficking in women (European Parliament 2000a), the later one (European Parliament 2004) concerns Europe's sex industry in general, something the first report could not ignore entirely. The earlier report expresses concern for "Western brothel keepers" who "find themselves under increasing pressure from organized gangs based in the CEEC countries to hire eastern European women" (European Parliament 2000a, 11). This worry seems particularly misplaced, not least because the report acknowledges an ever-diminishing distinction between such traffickers and other segments of Europe's sex industry: "analysis shows that they [the traffickers] tend to control the whole sex business" (European Parliament 2000a, 10). In case after case, it has become clear that "organized prostitution is the economic and structural foundation of sex trafficking," all efforts to deny this connection notwithstanding (Leidholdt 1999, 51).

Consider the first report on conditions in Belgium: "the high degree of tolerance attached to the exploitation of prostitution . . . has been fully taken advantage of by eastern European traffickers" (European Parliament 2000a, 39). After offering some terrifying details about the abuse that women endure in prostitution, the report asks whether legalizing it would be a "means of combating the situation of slavery" (European Parliament 2000a, 23). This is especially ironic, given the report's earlier acknowledgment that the main cause of trafficking is the demand for it—one fueled by the sex industry (Raymond 2003).

Whether in this first report or in other EU venues (e.g., the Court's rulings or IOM conferences), one often encounters the suggestion, often within efforts alleged to counter trafficking and other male violence, that Europe legalize (and thus legitimize) the very demand for prostitution that is causing so much harm. This circumstance prompted MEP Marianne Eriksson, a prominent member of the CWR, to call for an investigation in 1999 into "whether lobbying by the sex industry had succeeded in influencing the EU institutions" (Wennberg 2002, 3). Not only was a majority of this committee demure in demonstrating any enthusiasm for her request, Eriksson notes it "repeatedly ensured that any action on it (was) deferred" (Wennberg 2002, 3).[16] A determined Eriksson nonetheless succeeded in producing a final report on Europe's sex industry five years later, though not necessarily on the industry's influence on the EU per se. Issued under the CWR auspices, Eriksson's report insisted that the Commission maintain greater transparency in its deliberations on prostitution (European Parliament 2004).

This second report is remarkable for its clear refusal to regard the EU's legalized sex industry as sympathetic, if not legitimate. It employs candor in claiming that the "sex industry has an adverse impact on equality" and that the women in it "find themselves in situations that might be defined as slavery." Furthermore, it reasons, "Because this industry normalizes sexual violence, it undermines all the efforts which the EU and its Member States have made to give women and men fundamental rights" (European Parliament 2004, 7).

Although the report calls on the Council, Commission, and Member States to adopt it, this is unlikely. Even the committee was divided in its support of this final account (in April 2004), with eleven voting in its favor and nine against (European Parliament 2004, 3). The CWR's reluctance to embrace the report's suggested efforts to censure the sex industry is hardly surprising, in light of its internal divisions (discussed in chapter 5). Indeed, the Committee's ambivalence parallels larger trends.

As this chapter reveals, the EU's greatest denunciations of male violence have been increasingly reserved for those whose behaviors interfere with its labor market (e.g., batterers and traffickers of third-country nationals) and not those who generate profits within it (like European pimps and pornographers).[17] The latter typically enjoy the explicit protection of laws that equate their aggression against women with freedom of expression (European Parliament 2004, 7). It is thus that violence against women remains the most protected bastion of daily terrorism, unrecognized as harm and valued as liberty, a stance that explains how, under the pretense of increasing budgets to combat terrorism and insisting that it will eradicate gender-based violence, the EU cut its program against trafficking in women.

CHAPTER 8

Politicizing Sexuality

Spain is among the few European states that have legalized lesbian and gay marriages. In 1986, a year after that country had entered into the Community, Spanish police officers arrested two lesbians for kissing one another as they strolled in one of Madrid's central squares, the Puerta del Sol. The authorities charged the women with violating Article 431, a law that condemned "public scandals" (Llamas and Vila 1999, 224).

This case ignited public demonstrations within the country, both to counter the social stigma and condemn the violence that police routinely used against lesbians. Lesbians came out and directed their protest to local and national authorities;[1] the transnational level seemed beyond their reach. In 1986, Amnesty International and other human rights organizations did not recognize the routine harassment and incarceration of lesbians (and gay men) as a human rights violation.

Initiating grievances against such discrimination at the European level would have been inconceivable. More recently, activists throughout the Community (and from applicant states) are invoking precisely this transnational tactic against Member States to obtain relief (see Langenkamp 2003, 437). In 2005, the Turkish codirector of the International Lesbian and Gay Association (ILGA), Kursad Kahramanoglu, expressed faith in the EU's accession process, stating: "I would hate to see things happening in Turkey because the EU is forcing its hand, but we have to use this opportunity" ("Turkey's Homosexuals Call for Stronger EU Support" 2005).

By first analyzing the effects of heterosexism on lesbians and exploring the politicization of sexual orientation and lesbian visibility, this chapter outlines the historical foundation from which we can then account for this strategic shift. This chapter credits committed activists with helping to reduce the EU's initial refusal to redress anti-lesbian and gay discrimination so that, by the mid-1990s, the EU began departing from its earlier position of decades past.

Spanish activists may have been distinguished from their European neighbors by the country's recent break with fascism, yet they shared a relatively parochial focus in their efforts to combat heterosexism. Prior to the 1990s, discrimination against lesbians was rarely viewed as connected to Article 119 or the workplace. Like feminist politics in general (and those against male violence more specifically), lesbian politics was largely local and then perhaps national, but not European. This is not because discrimination against lesbians is (and was) confined to Spain and a few other Member States; unlike lesbian activism at the time, anti-lesbian and anti-gay discrimination, prejudice, enforced invisibility, and violence was so pervasive that the Community's borders hardly seemed to matter.

Whether through judicially expressed condemnations, violence, stunned silence, or popular ridicule, lesbians throughout Europe have been denied basic human rights daily, including the right to insist upon their very existence—reform efforts and gay pride parades notwithstanding. When, for example, Austrian activists sought to counter women's social exclusion through a 1988 International Women's Day poster campaign asserting, "Lesbians exist always and everywhere," an advertising firm refused them publication. The firm cited Austria's Article 220 on "public morals," a rarely invoked law that prohibited the production and distribution of material that presents homosexuality in a positive manner (Frölich 1996, 11–12). Although similar legal prohibitions were passed in several other countries around this time, including Italy (in 1984), Belgium (in 1985), the United Kingdom (in 1988),[2] and Ireland (in 1990), Austrian activists prevailed against the firm in 1990 through their courts. However, the Viennese Traffic Management agency then refused to display the slogan on any of its trains. It claimed concern for female passengers whom others might wrongly presume to be lesbians (Frölich 1996, 11–12). That this presumption could prompt anxiety is consistent with and inseparable from the prejudice that these activists were determined to address—as women.

Women's rights and lesbian rights are inextricably linked in substantive ways, not least because "the defense of lesbian rights is integral to the defense of all women's right to *determine* their own sexuality, to work at the jobs they prefer, and to live as they choose with women, men, children, or alone" (Bunch 1996, vi; my emphasis). Thus, lesbian organizations such as France's Radical Lesbian Front declared (in 1981) that heterosexism is "the very cornerstone of society; not challenging it, not endeavoring to destroy it, makes any so-called struggle for Women's Liberation hypocritical and pointless" (Graziella et al. 1988, 474). Put differently, women's rights mean little under conditions whereby "the physical violence, psychological abuse, forced heterosexuality, and compulsory marriages inflicted on women of all ages who love other women" continue unabated (Bunch 1996, vi).

Because it is often easier to equate oppression with blatant discrimination, it is possible to interpret the relative absence of explicit prohibitions against lesbianism as evidence that either heterosexism belongs to a bygone era or that discrimination against lesbians is less severe than for gay men. Rachel Rosenbloom observes, "While legislative silence may lead to a measure of safety" for lesbians, it may also conceal "other, more hidden, human rights violations." In other words, "The rules may be unwritten—or even unspoken—but they are very real, and the official silence surrounding lesbianism does not make the prohibition of it any less powerful; it only makes it harder to document, respond to, or resist the abuses that lesbians experience" (1996b, 8–9). The pervasive power of these rules results, in part, from their ostensible imperceptibility. This renders clearer restrictions less effective and unnecessary.

The distinctiveness of anti-lesbian discrimination stems less from its supposed "infrequent" occurrence than from the recurring inability of the women subjected to it to make such instances public. Many women throughout the EU pretend to ignore the bigotry directed against them and, in order to survive, they conceal their sexual attraction for and/or affectionate attachment to one another. A 1993 survey of 800 lesbians in Britain found 90 percent had to conceal their sexuality at work; nearly half of all respondents had been harassed for it, sometimes violently (cited in Palmer 1996, 26). A German study mapping violence and discrimination against lesbians in 2000 found that almost 98 percent had experienced verbal harassment, 44 percent had been subject to sexual attacks, and 24 percent had been physically assaulted for being lesbians (Ohms 2002, 7). While these studies are unique for their lesbian focus, the condition they describe is hardly unusual.

A Slovak research project from 2002 found that 26 percent of lesbian and gay respondents had been harassed at work because of their sexual preference despite the fact that a large majority (87 percent) of them had hidden this aspect of their identity from at least some of their coworkers (Siposova 2003). A national survey in Germany the same year revealed that nearly one-third of the citizens evidenced negative attitudes toward "homosexuals" (cited in Baer 2004, 206). France's SOS Homophobie, a gay and lesbian rights association, reported that insults and mockery pervade the French labor market (Borrillo 2004). Little of this abuse is reported because the decision to come forward often involves the hazards associated with coming out.

The decision to be "out" (whether at home or at work) is one that few lesbians effectively control; although as the above-noted Slovakian example reveals being "closeted" does not necessarily shield one from harm. Many lesbians are subject to hateful and hurtful comments "*precisely because they pass for heterosexuals* and are therefore assumed to possess a heterosexist perspective" (Petersen 1995, 130). Cynthia Petersen believes that because she is an out law professor, many of her students and coworkers are more likely to correct themselves and less likely to make discriminatory remarks in her presence (1995, 130). Still, being out or staying closeted is itself "continuous and complex, a matter of degree, rather than binary." As Catharine A. MacKinnon notes, "One is never wholly one or the other, as even the most closeted person never knows who guesses their private secret, and even the most open person is not out in every brief encounter" (2001, 1083).

While most lesbians may mask their sexuality to keep their jobs and/or to access safe, affordable housing, many do so also to preserve connections to potentially hostile relatives and/or to retain custody of their children. In 2007, two years after Spain legalized gay and lesbian marriage, a judge in Murcia nonetheless denied a lesbian mother custody of her children. He insisted that she "choose between her daughters and her new partner" because "it's impossible that two homosexual parents can give a child complete education" (ILGA-Europe 2007, 13). Throughout the EU, the status of parenthood is predominantly, if not exclusively, heterosexual.[3] Not only are same-sex couples frequently prohibited from adopting children,[4] "artificial" insemination (by donors) for lesbians has been expressly outlawed in Austria, Denmark, France, Italy, and Sweden.[5] Such circumstances exacerbate the risks of being out.

Current restrictions governing adoption and insemination throughout the EU support the patriarchal "principle of legitimacy" whereby children brought into the world without a man—and one man at that—are regarded as "illegitimate." To date, no EU provision *forcefully* prohibits this or other manifestations of heterosexist discrimination. The serious social consequences of such prejudice are evident early on, particularly for lesbian and gay youth. Comparative rates of suicide indicate that their risk is much higher than for heterosexual youth (Veen and Dercksen 1993, 114, n40). A 2004 survey of lesbian, gay, and bisexual youth in Northern Ireland revealed that nearly one-third had turned to suicide after bullying had become too much for them to withstand ("Northern Ireland: Shocking Statistics on Gay Youth" 2004).[6] While several scholars and social commentators have discussed the willingness of citizens to die for the state (e.g., Walzer 1970), few appear to mourn those whose alienation from it may be manifest in suicide.

Lesbians frequently remain closeted to protect their lives as well as for banal reasons, such as avoiding the ordinary hassles that can attend recognition. Simply being oneself, particularly in public, can be a defiant political act. In *Lesbian Visibility: A Report about Lesbians in the European Community*, a Parisian explains, ". . . being an open lesbian in France means living in a war zone. If you walk hand in hand with your lover, you never know who will react aggressively" (quoted in Nissen and Paulsen 1995, 102). In Sweden, a restaurant owner asked a couple to leave his establishment because they kissed. The case made international headlines, but only after the women won against an earlier judgment that cleared the proprietor of sex discrimination ("Lesbians Win Appeal over Kiss" 2005).

Several analysts emphasize that the EU's Equality Directives offer women general relief from blatant cases of sex discrimination (Hoskyns 2000; Mazey 2002; Walby 2004); yet, lesbians throughout the EU are persons for whom equal rights have been largely a fiction. Furthermore, few regard discrimination against lesbians as sufficiently overt and/or serious to warrant action. Whether in works on "family" and "women's policy" or in discussions of "reproduction" or "homosexuality," the prohibitions on lesbian insemination provoke little or no discussion. For example, while the EWL addressed the issue of maternity rights and related legislation in its campaigns in the early 1990s, it was noticeably silent on matters of lesbian motherhood (Andermahr 1992, 116). In addition, the conspicuous absence of these bans from "standard measures" of gay and lesbian rights (e.g., Waaldijk 2001b, Appendix) has led to an exaggeration of the success in achieving a "clear pattern of steady progress" for "homosexuals" (Waaldijk 2001a, 439). In contrast to the more conventional EU-oriented scholarship on gender equality (e.g., Ellina 2003; Ellis 1991; Hoskyns 1996; Rossilli 2000), family policies (e.g., Guerrina 2002; Hantrais 2000), or sexual orientation (e.g., Bell 2004a; Stychin 1998; Tatchell 1992; Waaldijk and Clapham 1993), this work takes seriously lesbians and the injustices against them.

By placing lesbian struggles for sexual equality at the center of my analysis, this chapter generates insights into the added ambiguities, anomalies, and ironies that are at the very heart of European equality politics. Indeed, an account of the factors that brought lesbians into the

European political arena and beckoned its response illustrates the ways in which EU's equality agenda is both dynamic and diffident.

The Emergence of Community
Action: The 1980s

Those with considerable experience in working for women's rights (for instance, Hedy d'Ancona) were among the first to offer official condemnations of heterosexism at the EU level, usually from within the EP. The heterosexism they experienced first hand may have motivated some of these women; the lesbian-baiting that sexists commonly deploy against feminists may have moved still others. It matters less whether a woman is actually a lesbian than that consequences arise when a woman's "lesbianism" becomes pertinent. As Cynthia Petersen observes, "Women who vocalize their objections to sexist behavior, who actively struggle to improve the material conditions of women's lives, who pursue a feminist agenda for change, or who otherwise challenge their sexual subordination are routinely accused of being lesbian" (1995, 120). Whatever their motivations, those that addressed heterosexism at the EU level constructed their convictions to appeal to progressive political fashions—they were pragmatists.

Citing the Rome Treaty's Preamble and several articles that embrace improved working and living conditions for the people of Europe, women MEPs released the first parliamentary report that was unequivocal in its demand for lesbian and gay equal rights. The Italian Communist MEP, Vera Squarcialupi, sponsored this 1984 report. Entitled *On Sexual Discrimination in the Workplace* (also known as the Squarcialupi Report; European Parliament 1984), it called on the Member States to:

- Abolish laws against homosexuality.
- Ban the maintenance of special records on lesbians and gay men by police and other authorities.
- Reject the classification of homosexuality as a mental illness.
- Outlaw discrimination in the workplace on the grounds of one's sexuality.
- Maintain reports on all aspects of discrimination against lesbians and gay men, including housing and other "social problems."

In addition, the report acknowledged that discrimination excludes lesbians and gay men from certain segments of the wage-labor market.

This parliamentary report suggested that Europe's integration has been accomplished, in part, through the mutual recognition of privileges accorded exclusively to heterosexual EU nationals, their spouses, and families. It further questioned the exclusive character of these rights. The report called on the European Commission to adopt community measures to facilitate increased access to employment, improved working conditions, and freedom of movement for lesbian and gay Community nationals (European Parliament 1984, 46–48).[7] This last right, to freedom of movement, has been especially crucial. Without it and the understanding that it allows family reunion, workers have found the option of movement throughout the common market too onerous.

As the report helped make clear, the Preamble to the 1968 Regulation (1612/68) on freedom of movement is anything but subtle in its preference for the patriarchal family. It states:

> Whereas the right of freedom of movement, in order that it may be exercised, by objective standards, in freedom of dignity, requires that equality of treatment shall be ensured in fact and in law in respect of all matters relating to the actual pursuit of activities as employed persons and to eligibility for housing, and also that obstacles to the mobility of workers shall be eliminated, in particular as regards the worker's rights to be joined by *his* family and the conditions for the integration of that family into the host country. (My emphasis)

Intra-European workers (assumed to be men by this document) can be joined by their dependent relatives, descendants (under twenty-one), and spouses, irrespective of their nationality.

Though the EU has refused to regard cohabitants (including those who are heterosexual) as "spouses" fully deserving of these rights of integration (*Netherlands v Reed*, Case 59/85 [1986] ECR 1283),[8] it has yet to provide an exact definition of additional relations constituting "the family." Tamara Hervey writes, "Rejection of a dynamic interpretation, reflecting social diversity in the member states, has the result of excluding all but those families which conform to the dominant norm" (1995, 105). Nonetheless, settling on a definition would be difficult as the operationalization of the concept varies considerably across the Member States (Hantrais 1999).

Numerous policies, secondary legislation, and ECJ rulings privilege conventional conceptions of family premised on blood and marriage. In cases where the same-sex partners of EU nationals have been denied the right to immigrate and live with their lovers as "family," institutions throughout Europe (including the ECJ and the European Court of Human Rights) have refused them redress—a problem that persists.

Shortly after accepting the Squarcialupi Report and agreeing with its premise that heterosexism is "unacceptable," former Social Affairs commissioner Ivor Richards suggested that the Commission might recommend legislation (i.e., against unfair dismissals). He also noted a need for job protection following the report's discovery of the systematic exclusion of EU lesbians and gays from several occupations (Tatchell 1992, 16–17). For instance, many lesbian and gay teachers find it difficult, if not impossible, to be out at work, given the presumption that they will proselytize. The issue of freedom of movement went ignored.

Women MEPs such as Vera Squarcialupi may have succeeded in capturing the Community's attention by framing heterosexism through the lens of the market and focusing on matters like occupational segregation and not family status, but lesbian activists soon recognized that the Commission's assurances were empty. As the Dutch activist Willemien Ruygrok explains: "On many occasions, we wrote to the European Commission asking them what they were doing to implement the Squarcialupi Report. Most of the times we got no answer. The other times, they were always evasive" (quoted in Tatchell 1992, 17). The Commission's unresponsive behavior did not deter Ruygrok and others.

These activists learned that persistence paid and if success eluded them now, it might come later. Hedy d'Ancona, the Dutch femocrat who helped place male violence on the EU's formal political agenda by recognizing its close connections to economic inequality similarly insisted that the principle of non-discrimination extend to lesbians (and gay men). Her 1986 parliamentary report, "On Violence against Women," called urgently for provisions to "cover both discrimination on the basis of sex or marital status and discrimination on the basis of sexual preference" (European Parliament 1986, 75). Two other reports, issued three years later, reiterated this demand (European Parliament 1989a; European Parliament 1989b).[9] At the decade's close, Britain's newly formed lesbian and gay professional lobbying group, Stonewall, joined the chorus of those calling on the Commission to honor the Social Charter's commitment to combat all forms of discrimination in order to ensure equal treatment.[10]

The Denial of Community Competence: 1990

Under mounting international and inter-institutional pressure, the Commission responded in 1990 to an EP query, denying that it had any competence to adjudicate claims on behalf of lesbians and gays. The Commission asserted, "The Community has no powers to intervene in possible cases of discrimination practiced by Member States against sexual minorities." It observed redress was best offered elsewhere: "The fundamental rights of sexual minorities are protected by other international instruments" (quoted in Clapham and Weiler 1993, 28), a curious claim for a Community that has typically prided itself on its own higher standards of human rights. The Community missed an immense opportunity to demonstrate its affirmation of human rights; though formally it can also be argued that prior to the adoption of the Amsterdam Treaty, it had no strong legal basis.

When the Commission deferred to instruments outside its ambit to protect Europeans against heterosexism, it reasoned: "Since all the Member States are members of the Council of Europe and signatories to the European Convention on Human Rights, the [COE's] Commission and the Court of Human Rights, are best able to guarantee the protection of sexual minorities against discrimination" (in Clapham and Weiler 1993, 28).[11] Without claims of discrimination tethered closely to Article 119, the Community remained aloof.

Still, the legal precedent for the Commission's confidence in these Strasbourg institutions was slim. From the Council of Europe's (COE) founding in 1949 until 1981, it had rejected all complaints of discrimination against gay men and lesbians as unfounded.[12] Then, in 1981, the European Court of Human Rights (ECtHR) changed course. It found the British government in breach of the European Convention on Human Rights (ECHR) when its Royal Ulster Constabulary subjected a gay rights activist (Jeffrey Dudgeon) to over four hours of interrogation about his sexual behavior, following a dubious search of his house and the seizure of his personal papers in Belfast (*Dudgeon v UK* (1981) Series A No 45). Dudgeon persuaded the Court that the legal prohibitions against consensual sex between men in Northern Ireland undermined his right to privacy as guaranteed by the Convention. At the time, it may have seemed an extraordinary victory. However, while many depict this case as the ". . . watershed event in human rights law for lesbian women and gay men" (Sanders 1996, 78; See also Bell 2004a, 90; Tatchell 1992, 26), others are more circumspect about the case and the Council's capacity to combat heterosexist discrimination (Clapham and Weiler 1993; McLoughlin 1996).[13]

However, emphasizing the COE's role as a human rights leader for the Community overlooks more than precedent however. First, because the COE is devoid of supranational governance, the power of its Convention is diluted. Second, the often-uncertain relationship between the COE and the Community has meant that although there is a general respect for established ECtHR jurisprudence, the ECJ is reluctant to admit any obligation to follow it (Toner 2004, 132). Third, in *Dudgeon*, the ECtHR reached no further than the consensus that its constituent states had already achieved. By 1981, most states had decriminalized male homosexuality; others, such as Northern Ireland, rarely enforced their prohibitions. The Court's chief concern hinged on whether criminalizing gay men for their sexual behavior was necessary to preserve the public order. Finding such prohibitions unnecessary, as the Court did, is not the same as finding them inherently violative—which the Court did not. Instead, the ECtHR cautioned the public against construing its ruling to imply its approval of male homosexuality (*Dudgeon v UK* (1981) Series A No 45, 24).

When the ECtHR "succeeded in making gay men equal to lesbians, whose sexual behavior has almost never been criminalized," it failed to find lesbian and gay Europeans equal to their heterosexual counterparts (McLoughlin 1996, paragraph 133), a failing later endorsed by the European Human Rights Commission (ECommHR) in *X and Y v UK* (Application 9369/81 (1983) 32 DR 220). Until 1998, when this Human Rights Commission effectively merged with the ECtHR, it screened all the Court's cases. However, in cases such as *X and Y v UK* (Application 9369/81 (1983) 32 DR 220), the ECommHR reached its own judgment. This 1983 case involved a Malaysian man who relied upon his gay relationship with a British citizen to request a residence permit. The couple petitioned the COE after the British government had refused. They claimed that the decision violated their right to family life.

X and Y v UK marked the first time the ECommHR would determine whether a state's denial of residence rights to same-sex couples violated the Convention's promise that "everyone has the right to respect for his private and family life" (in Article 8). After concluding that same-sex relationships and different-sex relationships are incomparable, the ECommHR declared that states are under no obligation to recognize same-sex couples as "families," deserving the rights and privileges of legal residence. Furthermore, it stated that because it would have reached the same verdict if the couple were lesbian, its position provided no discriminatory interference with its conclusion that the "applicants' relationship is a matter of private life" and not "family life" (Application 9369/81 (1983) 32 DR 221). The ECommHR reinforced this point by declaring to the lesbians that later stood before it that they too had "private" lives that did not conform to "family life."[14]

If the ECtHR was unwilling to recognize lesbian identified couples as families, it was willing to accommodate those in which one partner had altered her "appearance" so drastically that the relationship could conform to the conventional notions of a heterosexual union. Such was the case in *X, Y and Z v UK* (Application 21830/93 (1997) 24 EHRR 143) when the ECtHR accepted a former lesbian couple as "family" once one of the women became a post-operative transsexual and insisted on being recognized as the social father of his partner's child (Toner 2004, 82–83). Years later, in 2002, the ECtHR ruled in favor of transsexuals to enter into (conventional) marriage.[15] In these ways the ECtHR affirmed, rather than undermined, the heterosexual pretensions of "family life." By emphasizing equivalent treatment between gay men and lesbians, the COE denied them both equality with their heterosexual (and transsexual) counterparts. This tactic is one that the ECJ would employ years later. For instance, in *KB v National Health Service Pensions Agency*, the ECJ ruled that Britain's failure to allow KB to marry her transsexual male partner (and thereby allow him the inheritance of a widower's pension) was *in principle* a breach of EU law (Case 117/01 [2004] ECR 541, paragraph 34; my emphasis).

The COE's institutions may have helped obscure the systematic inequality that pervades Europe's public by couching gay and lesbian rights exclusively as a "right to privacy." They appear to have thus legitimized and extended the reach of the closet while depoliticizing the consequences (Sedgwick 1990). Freedom from public intervention may sound appealing, but in the midst of discrimination, privacy offers "an inadequate basis for constructing a broader regime of equality for homosexuals" because it isolates lesbians and gay men from public recourse (Sanders 1996, n 46). Moreover, when one considers the historical reluctance of states and transnational institutions to intervene in matters they have traditionally described as private, such as the physical and sexual abuse of women and girls, it is little wonder that, for many lesbians, "privacy" sounds more like a euphemism for silence than a remedy for injustice.

The Commission's early refusal to redress anti-lesbian and gay discrimination was in keeping with the response of the COE and other international bodies, including NGOs whose main mission is to promote fundamental rights. Amnesty International, a world-renowned human rights organization, underwent nearly two decades of acrimonious debate before it deemed state imprisonment for homosexuality a human rights violation. It took this decision in 1991.[16] Amnesty International was, however, not the only transnational actor to change course.

The Turning Point: 1991

In 1991, the European Commission moved from its earlier refusal to mitigate discrimination concerning sexual preference by issuing a recommended Code of Practice on sexual harassment that recognizes "lesbians and women from racial minorities are disproportionately at risk." The Code declared: "It is undeniable that harassment on the grounds of sexual orientation undermines the dignity at work of those affected and it is impossible to regard such harassment as appropriate workplace behavior" (92/131/EEC, Annex, paragraph 5).

Given its non-binding character, one might conclude that the recommendation's significance was more symbolic than real; however, the historic influence of the Code is impossible to dismiss. By supporting the recommendation, the European Council broached the subject of lesbian and gay rights: ". . . for the first time ever, the EC had explicitly included 'sexual orientation' within its anti-discrimination policies" (Tatchell 1992, 22).

The Code provided a pivotal moment, one that suggested but did not promise that the Commission was becoming attentive to the claims of lesbian and gay constituents whom it insisted it could ignore only a year before. Evelyn Collins attributes the Code's adoption to "timely lobbying during the [Code's] consultative process by Members of the European Parliament and the International Lesbian and Gay Association" (1996, 31). The Commission's preparations for the Maastricht Treaty, with its emphasis on democratization and European citizenship, may also explain its newfound receptivity to such lobbying.

In 1991, at the behest of the EP, the Commission also funded research analyzing the single market's impact on lesbians and gay men, including the now classic legal study, *Homosexuality: A Community Issue* (Waaldijk and Clapham 1993). Groundbreaking in its scholarly analysis of the invidious discrimination against homosexuals under Community law and the Human Rights Convention, the work's gay (male) bias raised objections among prominent lesbian scholars and activists. In one respect, the study's legal emphasis made such bias unavoidable. Most laws specifically pertaining to homosexuality focus almost exclusively on men. However, the conflation of men and homosexuality is not the fault of law alone and one detects a male slant throughout other areas of the text as well. In discussions of an open market, the authors insist on the free movement of "homoerotic goods" and "dating services" while ignoring the connections that these market sectors have to sexual exploitation and abuse (Clapham and Weiler 1993, 19–20).[17] Although women are certainly not of one mind on this issue, the availability of lesbian "dating services" and "cinematographic materials" tend not to be priorities for lesbians striving to achieve sexual equality. Those who have been struggling to organize an autonomous EU-wide network are rather explicit about their opposition to the sex industry (e.g., Coordination Lesbienne 2003). Moreover, mention the single market within lesbian contexts and attention turns instead to poverty, gender segregation, job insecurity, and sexual harassment (see Nissen and Paulsen 1995).

The gay orientation of the 1991 report marginalized lesbians, but it also offered an impetus for research on the special problems confronting lesbians in the market (Nissen and Paulsen 1995, 5). This was hardly the first such project to materialize in response to gay male bias. A decade earlier, Dutch lesbians had established the International Lesbian Information Service (ILIS) to counter male domination within the ILGA. This time, however, lesbian activists turned to the European Commission for support, stressing their project to enhance the visibility of lesbians as a specific group of women coincided with the Commission's newly adopted "Third Medium-Term Community Action Program" (1991–1995), which sought to further "equality between the sexes in favor of underprivileged groups of women" (in Nissen and Paulsen 1995, 7). Furthermore, the new Code of Practice legitimized this request by identifying lesbians as especially vulnerable to sexual harassment in the labor market.

With funding from the Commission's Equal Opportunities Unit and the Danish National Association for Gays and Lesbians, Vibeke Nissen and Inge-Lise Paulsen first released *Lesbian Visibility: A Report about Lesbians in the European Community* in 1993 (2nd ed., 1995). Based on more than one hundred in-depth interviews, this rarely cited pilot study dispels misconceptions (often contained in gay-friendly contexts) that obscure and/or exaggerate lesbian existence. For example, the notion of a gender-neutral "pink economy" in which most "gays" are generally envisaged as affluent professionals suggests that the earning power and consumer behavior of lesbians is comparable to that of (gay) men—a premise that not only conceals gender inequity in general but the poverty that lesbians experience as marginalized women more specifically. Not least, by exaggerating lesbian earning power, heterosexists attempt to disguise their resentment against these women through hallow rationalizations. While the pilot study helped to refute the presumption of political and economic affinity between gay men and lesbians, its subsequent call for more rigorous, gender-specific studies of heterosexism went unheeded amidst the emergence of general calls for GM. The EP soon eclipsed this report on heterosexism with its own.

The EP's Committee on Civil Liberties and Internal Affairs affirmed lesbian and gay rights in its Roth Report (1994),[18] a gender-neutral investigation that resulted in a comprehensive parliamentary resolution the same year. The resolution calls upon Member States to end "the unequal treatment of persons with a homosexual orientation under the legal and administrative provisions of the social security system and where social benefits, adoption, laws on inheritance and housing and criminal law *and all related legal provisions* are concerned" (A3-28/94, Section 7; my emphasis).

The Roth Report urged the Commission to adopt a separate recommendation to end the ban on lesbian and gay marriage and the rights and benefits associated with it. The report seemed to endorse those Member States such as Denmark that had adopted (or were about to pass) registered partnership reforms extending various benefits for same-sex couples. Examples such as this suggest that, compared to some of its Member States, the UN, and other international organizations, the EU's position on lesbian matters, though not stellar, is arguably somewhat more enlightened.

For instance, in 1995, at its Fourth World Conference on Women in Beijing, UN officials persisted in their opposition to lesbian rights and succeeded in omitting any mention of sexual preference from the final conference document on women's rights.[19] The paragraph (96) they succeeded in censoring called upon the world's member states

> to recognize the right to determine one's sexual identity; the right to control one's own body, particularly in establishing intimate relationships; and the right to choose if, when, and with whom to bear and raise children as fundamental components of the human rights of all women regardless of sexual orientation. (in Rosenbloom 1996a, Appendix A)

Granting Rights and Intra-Institutional Conflict: 1997

In January 1997, the EP demonstrated its unwillingness to embrace non-discrimination for itself and other EU institutions after the Committee on Legal Affairs refused to adopt a report guaranteeing equal treatment for lesbian and gay civil servants. This rebuff resulted in the denial of benefits to same-sex couples already enjoyed by married couples if the Commission employs only one partner. Such benefits include but are not restricted to bereavement leave, pensions, and joint health insurance. Exclusion from such benefits can impose financial hardship, particularly for lesbians who, as women workers in Europe, are likely to earn 20 percent lesser than their male counterparts (International Lesbian and Gay Association 1998, 18). This committee's position undermined the Parliament's earlier reforms endorsed in *Roth*.

An EP employee and spokesperson for EGALITE, an advocacy group for lesbian and gay Eurocrats that formed in 1993, Marion Oprel observed:

> The Parliament has repeatedly urged the ending of discrimination against lesbians and gays—but when it has a chance to put its own house in order and set a practical example to other European employers, it has failed. Its credibility as an employer and as a legislator on working conditions has been badly damaged by this.

Oprel then asked, "What does this say about the EU's commitment to equal rights for all Europe's citizens? If it can't even treat its own employees equally, then what hope is there for women, ethnic minorities and lesbians and gays—in Europe as a whole?" (EGALITE 1997, 4). Framing expansive queries in the context of citizenship in post-Maastricht Europe proved astute, especially as the institutions and Member States approached the Amsterdam Treaty.

As gay and lesbian movements mobilized within and across Member States, they precipitated an increased awareness and sensitivity to heterosexism that the institutions of Europe could no longer ignore. Highlighting specific measures to counter discrimination adopted by nearly half of the Member States, EGALITE, ILGA, and others were able to persuade the EP that it could no longer dismiss inequality based on sexual orientation without appearing out of step. Activists engaged at the grassroots level applied similar pressure, citing progressive steps taken from within the EU (such as the Code of Practice or the Roth Report) to convince their states that without reform, they would be out of sync with the rest of Europe (Spindler, interview, 2003).

A month after Ms. Oprel's declaration, the Parliament assumed a more progressive posture; soon it was joined by the Member States, including those previously hesitant to embrace anti-discrimination efforts. Heterosexism was becoming unacceptable, if only in the most public of proclamations. After months of tortuous negotiation over whether and how to prohibit discrimination, including that directed against gay and lesbian EU citizens, the Member States adopted the Amsterdam Treaty. It defines discrimination as bigotry based on race or ethnicity, religion or belief, disability, sex, age, and "sexual orientation." The text, Article 13, reads:

> Without prejudice to the other provisions of this Treaty and within the limits of powers conferred by it upon the Community, the Council, acting unanimously on a proposal from the Commission and after consulting the

> European Parliament may take appropriate action to combat discrimination based on sex, racial or ethnic origin, religion or belief, disability, age or sexual orientation.

The Treaty's requirement that the Council must reach a unanimous vote on a Commission proposal before it "may take appropriate action" tempers the reach of the clause. By declining to assert that the Council "shall" endeavor to take action, Member States did not establish a directly effective provision but, instead, left it to the Community institutions to adopt "appropriate" measures.[20] In order to pursue these measures, however, clarity was a crucial element and the ECJ disappointed many lesbian (and gay) advocates in its rulings to provide it.

The Treaty's distinction between discrimination premised on sex and that based on sexual orientation is noteworthy, insofar as one may read it in two ways. The wording can be construed as an effort to extend official recognition to the distinct injustice(s) of heterosexism, a positive step toward realizing the agenda of gay and lesbian activists. Alternatively, the language of "sex" and "sexual orientation" may be read as redundant or worse—as a means of differentiating discrimination against gays and lesbians from sex discrimination. This latter interpretation is troubling for lesbians who, as women, may not be able to distinguish between the two oppressions because they are often so profoundly interconnected.[21] Moreover, the insistence on such differentiation suggests a lost remedy. As the British legal theorist Virginia Harrison writes: "discrimination against a person for having a partner of the same sex is discrimination on the ground of gender" and thus could be prohibited under existing equality law (e.g., Article 141) (1996, 275). This is precisely the logic that inspired and defeated Lisa Grant's case before the ECJ. Shortly after the ink set on Amsterdam, the ECJ refused to recognize heterosexism as sex discrimination in *Grant v South-West Train* (Case C 249/96 [1998] ECR 621). In this case, a lesbian employee (Lisa Grant) objected to her company's denial of travel benefits to her same-sex partner (Jill Percey), while providing the same concessions for opposite sex partners regardless of marital status.

Invoking EU equality law (Article 119 in *Treaty of Rome* now Article 141 *Treaty of Amsterdam*), Ms. Grant insisted that the company's denial of benefits constituted sex discrimination. The Court had previously recognized concessions as falling within the definition of pay (*Garland v British Rail Engineering*, Case 12/81 [1982] ECR 359) and Grant's male colleague had enjoyed his travel benefit (worth approximately £1,000 per year) for his unmarried woman partner.

Throughout its own calculations of comparison, the Court rebuffed Grant's claim and reasoned: "concessions are refused to a male worker if he is living with a person of the same sex, just as they are refused to a female worker living with a person of the same sex" (Case C 249/96 [1998] ECR 621, paragraph 27). The Court's comparison of a lesbian with a gay man, both of whom are equally ill-treated, concealed the favored treatment extended to heterosexuals. This reasoning is clearly reminiscent of the ECommHR's position years earlier when it held that gay and lesbian relationships are outside the acceptable scope of "family life" because they are incomparable to heterosexual partnerships (e.g., in *X and Y v UK* Application 9369/81 (1983) 32 DR 220).

The ECJ could have rendered a more compelling comparison between Grant and her (heterosexual) male colleague whose unmarried female partner received travel concessions denied Grant's lover. Grant's lawyers argued, "The mere fact that the male worker who previously occupied her post had obtained travel concessions for his female partner, without being married to her, is enough to identify direct discrimination based on sex" (Case C 249/96 [1998] ECR 621, paragraphs 16–17).

The ECJ's imposition of an imaginary gay comparator in *Grant* affirmed its inaction and furthered its position that "stable relationships between two persons of the same sex are not regarded as equivalent to marriages or stable relationships outside marriage between two persons of the opposite sex" (Case C 249/96 [1998] ECR 621, paragraph 35). This aspect of the judgment is especially damaging because it bestowed a doctrinal legacy of flagrant inequality in the aftermath of the Amsterdam Treaty.

The Court's determination that the partners of lesbians (and gays) do not deserve equal treatment is as disappointing as its emphasis on "stability" is bewildering. Scholars have observed that even marriages that are for all practical purposes dead and buried, can still be the basis for a dependent residence right of the spouse of the worker. For the Community, the quality of any relationship has long been unimportant; its legality is what matters (e.g., *Diatta v Land Berlin*,[22] Case 267/83 [1985] ECR 567). For this reason, the ECJ's decision to ignore the increasing trend among a number of its Member States to extend legal recognition to same-sex relationships seemed politically inspired. At the time of *Grant*, nearly half, that is, seven Member States had moved to blunt bigotry against gays and lesbians through policies that extend official recognition of and some privileges to same-sex relationships.

Unsettling as the *Grant* decision is, its reasoning accurately reflects the discriminatory stance of most Member States, including the seven that had already bestowed a measure of recognition to same-sex relationships. In all the states, heterosexual marriage remains a principal means of receiving benefits (e.g., travel concessions) as well as the key to legal entry into the EU for most third-country immigrants.

Without denying the vast differences among states concerning access to citizenship, nationality, residence, and family benefits, most Member States remain strikingly similar in the special provisions they maintain for the foreign spouses of their nationals. Through matrimony, foreign spouses are typically entitled to an array of privileges including, but not limited to rights of residence, the possibility of acquiring their partner's nationality, shared child custody, and the preferential status extended to spouses and/or family for purposes of free movement. Despite these material incentives, marriage rates in all the Member States had declined by nearly one-third between 1960 and 1995 (Eurostat 1996).

Inter-State Conflicts

With EU institutions hesitant to explicitly recognize lesbian and gay relationships as falling within the accepted parameters of legal relationships (i.e., "relative," "family," or "spouse"), same-sex couples from reform-oriented states soon discovered that they resume the status of acquaintances when they travel within an allegedly egalitarian and integrated Europe. Such conditions obviously hamper access to migration and other citizenship rights afforded heterosexual partnerships throughout much of Europe (Stychin 1998; Tanca 1993, 283).

Although lesbian and gay activists have successfully challenged the exclusively heterosexual character of matrimony on a piecemeal basis in states such as the Netherlands and Spain, the overarching principle of marriage as an exclusively heterosexual institution persists throughout the Community. Moreover, as noted earlier, at the European level, "spousal" relationships remain exclusively heterosexual, recognizable only through marriage. Consider *Netherlands v Reed* (Case 59/85 [1986] ECR 1283), a case involving an unmarried heterosexual British couple that moved to the Netherlands where the man had obtained a temporary post and his companion, Ms. Reed, was unable to find employment. When Reed applied for a residence permit to stay with her partner, the Netherlands rejected her application. In an effort to stay, she sought to have her cohabiting relationship of five years recognized as "spousal." The Court responded by refusing to extend the term "spouse" (in Regulation 1612/68/EEC) to unmarried cohabitants.

Endeavors to extend entitlements similar to those of marriage through legal partnerships between homosexuals have sometimes met with renewed affirmations of matrimony's heterosexual character and been punished in the process. For example, France's conservative government (under then president Chirac) suspended the mayor of Bègles, a Bordeaux suburb, for a month after he officiated the country's first gay marriage in 2004. The Court there nullified the marriage, ruling: "A difference of sexes is a condition of marriage under French law" ("France: Court Voids Gay Marriage" 2004). Two years later, the Irish High Court maintained a similar position against two Irish lesbians determined (but now unable) to marry (KAL Advocacy Initiative 2006). Both the French and Irish courts echoed the verdict of Germany's Constitutional Court almost a decade earlier when it had insisted that the right to marry (and accompanying socioeconomic benefits) is, without exception, a heterosexual prerogative (Agence France Presse 1993).

Precluded from lawful matrimony within their Member States, lesbian (and gay) EU nationals face other legal obstacles that undermine their ability to establish intimate, cohabiting relationships (to say nothing of extended families) with third-country nationals. Their heterosexual counterparts do not face these hurdles. To wit, marital privileges (e.g., maintaining legal residency for third-country partners) provide a buffer against pressures from which lesbian and gay EU nationals are unprotected. Thus, lesbians and gay men not only lose the social support offered to their married counterparts, but they also face the destructive pressures from which matrimony can shield heterosexuals. The double standard regarding relationships inherent in state and EU policy renders lesbian and gay EU nationals second-class citizens.

From 1997 until 1999, foreign same-sex partners of British citizens could immigrate; though, for those two years, they faced more stringent standards than did their heterosexual counterparts when it came to demonstrating commitment. That is, whereas policy for cohabiting heterosexuals requires that couples be together for only two years, same-sex couples had to demonstrate that they had been living together for four years.

A subsequent relaxation (in 1999) of the requirement to two years provides the appearance of parity, yet marriage is still an exclusive option for heterosexual cohabitants intent on relatively swift, easy access to migration—in the United Kingdom and throughout the EU. By contrast, lesbians and gay men are burdened with violating residence requirements that typically forbid non-EU nationals from living in Britain for more than several months each year. The procedures that same-sex couples have to endure to authenticate their intimacy with the state's authorities (e.g., the provision of love letters, personal photographs, and detailed testimonials) are often so intrusive that their privacy rights are undermined. This irony results from the reforms efforts undertaken to integrate lesbian and gay citizens and their families.

If the British example falls short in amply demonstrating that a state's recognition of same-sex partnerships affords no ironclad guarantee of equality before the law, the Netherlands offers an additional case in point. Prior to 2001, when the Netherlands became the first Member State to affirm same-sex marriage, Dutch lesbians and gay men could register their relationships with other Dutch nationals, but the state extended neither joint pension benefits nor equal inheritance taxes to these couples. The Netherlands refused same-sex foreign partner's access to immigration until that time. The government attributed its refusal to the fact that same-sex partnerships and marriages lack legal standing within most other Member States. The government's position, though politically objectionable, remains empirically valid and, as chapter 9 suggests, it is unlikely that the tensions within and between these states over this matter will be resolved by the EU's further integration.

Conclusion

Discrimination against lesbians has long pervaded the Member States; however, the expectation that the EU should counteract it is relatively new. The Commission's insistence, in 1990, that it had "no power" to stem the heterosexism of its constituent states may serve as a telling reminder of just how far it has drifted from its more conservative moorings. After all, in 1997, it appeared to have changed course. According to the Amsterdam Treaty that year, the Commission, Council, and EP "may take appropriate action" to combat such discrimination.

This chapter attributes this shift, however slight, to several factors. First, the unprecedented level of success achieved by lesbian and gay movements within several Member States inspired movements in others and accelerated demands for justice at the transnational level. Second, with its rhetoric of democratization, the 1992 Maastricht Treaty offered a powerful discursive weapon of mobilization for equal rights within a European context. Activists pursuing sexual equality had additional leverage as they pursued their claims before varied courts (e.g., ECJ and the ECtHR), NGOs (e.g., Amnesty International), and transnational settings (e.g., UN conferences).

Yet, unlike sex discrimination in general, the often-covert character of lesbianism itself provides a partial explanation for the persistent indifference of most authorities, human rights actors, and academics to heterosexism specific to women, such as the ongoing prohibitions against "artificial" lesbian insemination. It is telling that these restrictions have inspired relatively little outrage and, thus, no transnational reforms. The EU may regard itself as a distinguished proponent of human rights, but it reached no further than the consensus its states and various transnational actors had already achieved in their willingness to combat discrimination against lesbians.

When the EU at last addressed lesbians specifically, it was through a non-binding resolution on sexual harassment (in 1991) that condemned the *indignity* suffered by lesbians *at work*, as opposed to throughout social life. The largely symbolic character of redress for workplace inequality remains, as does the EU's refusal to recognize the legality of same-sex partnerships. As a consequence, numerous workplace benefits (e.g., travel concessions and household allowances) are financial awards extended exclusively to heterosexual partnerships.

The access of lesbians (and gay men) to the labor market and their freedom from harassment within it coincide with the EU's agenda for four reasons. First, access corresponds well with the market's desire for competent workers. Second, harassment poses an obstacle to their productivity. Third, these two issues enable lesbians and gay men the opportunity to unite by offering each temporary relief from the gender-segregation and the relatively sex-specific controversies concerning lesbian insemination, sodomy laws, and concern over HIV-AIDS. Last, access to work (as opposed to the added benefits that derive from it) resonate with other market-oriented demands in ways that are removed from more radical requests concerning the redistribution of workplace benefits.

In sum, while the EU regards itself as a distinguished proponent of human rights, it reached no further than the consensus its states and various transnational actors had already achieved in their willingness to combat discrimination against lesbians. Thus, while several of the EU's own institutions adopted progressive public proclamations concerning gay and lesbian equality, they were unwilling to insist that the material benefits extended to heterosexual partners (married or not) be extended to all couples regardless of sexual orientation—a point that is clarified in the EU's legal wrangling over same-sex marriage and household benefits.

CHAPTER 9

Wedding Rights to Marriage

At the dawn of this century, the ECJ emphasized the power of the Member States to define marriage, and the Council underscored their obligation to combat sexual orientation discrimination through the adoption of a new directive and a five-year Community Action Program to Combat Discrimination (2001–2006). In proposing this plan, the Commission claimed that the "Community is already active in the fight against discrimination," and then insisted that the "responsibility for implementing the fight against discrimination rests principally with the Member States" (COM(99) 567 final, paragraphs 5–6).

The ramifications of this position and the political prominence extended to intimate partnerships form the subject of this chapter. I argue that an erratic effect of European integration on sexual equality is especially apparent as each level of "integrated Europe" off-loads responsibility onto another for the promise of fulfilling it. Watch closely as the language and politics of integration can increase expectations through discussions of equity and equality, while the responsibility for inequality and the implementation of measures to end it are scattered. Reforms thus become so elusive that equality's promise is deferred.

To comply with the 2000 Framework Directive (2000/78/EC), Member States must prohibit discrimination in employment on the grounds of religion or belief, disability, age, and sexual orientation; yet, unlike the separate Racial Equality Directive (2000/43/EC) passed the same year, the Framework Directive's reach does not extend to discrimination in the domains of education, housing, and healthcare. The Framework Directive does not apply to state social security or social protection schemes (as called for in *Roth* years ago), nor does it require (as does the Racial Equality Directive) that states establish bodies for the promotion of equal treatment. Furthermore, the Framework Directive promises no interference with those state measures deemed "necessary for public security, for maintenance of public order and the prevention of criminal offences, for health protection and for the protection of rights and freedoms of others" (2000/78/EC, Article 2(5)). Mark Bell posits that the ambition of this provision is to reassure the public that "a ban on sexual orientation discrimination cannot be interpreted as according protection to paedophiles or other persons engaging in unlawful sexual behavior" (2004a, 115–16). Still, he notes that the Member States could use the provision's ambiguity to defend restrictions against lesbians and gay men in, for example, the military.[1]

While it is too early for a thorough assessment of the Framework Directive's impact, one group of researchers released a tentative analysis in 2004, just a year after the Member States were required to adopt the laws, regulations, and administrative procedures necessary to comply with the legislation (Waaldijk and Bonini-Baraldi 2004). The Commission funded this research with monies from the Community Action Program. Of the fifteen countries that comprised the EU up until May 1, 2004, the study found that only twelve had "more or less fully implemented the Directive" by adopting the new anti-discrimination measures, half of these had done so after the implementation deadline had expired (Waaldijk 2004).[2] The same four states that had earlier refused to implement the Race Equality Directive (i.e., Austria, Finland, Germany, and Luxembourg) proved similarly reluctant to implement the Framework Directive. Again, these states were called before the ECJ (European Union Monitoring Centre on Racism and Xenophobia 2004).

If, as this background suggests, the compliance of older members has been sluggish and inconsistent, the ten newest Member States seemed to offer a welcome contrast. Within a year of their admission, the Commission's 2005 annual report on equality and non-discrimination found that only Latvia had not fully transposed the ban on sexual orientation discrimination in employment—a position that directly contradicts that state's obligation under EU law (CEC 2005d, 15). However, by the end of 2005, Latvia had gained company.

As the case of Poland demonstrates, one administration's compliance does not guard against another's transgression. Poland's new rightist government came to power in October 2005, months after its leader Mr. Kaczynski, the former mayor of Warsaw, banned that city's lesbian and gay pride rally. The European Commission reminded the new president of Poland's duty to abide by European laws on discrimination the morning after his election, to little effect. Kaczynski swiftly abolished the ministry for women and, weeks later, banned the (gay and lesbian) March for Equality and Tolerance in Poznan, a city in western Poland.

Still, focusing entirely on the formal (national) legislation of Member States can prove misleading; general remedies are often ineffectively applied. As the only European country to have explicitly banned sexual-orientation discrimination in its constitution, Portugal may epitomize the gap between official policy and common practice—its best intentions notwithstanding.[3] Judge Miguel Freitas describes several conditions in Portugal that hamper the constitution's promise and, thus, the Directive's enforcement (2004). First, he describes the low level of awareness regarding sexual orientation issues among those charged with the law's enforcement, a shortcoming that has also plagued the implementation of the earlier adopted sex-equality provisions described in chapter 2 in this book. Second, he notes unwillingness among victims to litigate, though he does not openly attribute their reluctance to the questionable competence of those in whose hands their fate would rest. Third, he questions whether Portugal's penalty structure (e.g., modest fines) conforms to the Framework Directive's expectation that sanctions be "effective, proportionate and dissuasive" (2000/78/EC, Article 17). Such shortcomings are not unique to Portugal.

Mark Bell concludes his investigation of Ireland noting, "The principal challenge in Ireland is not formal compliance with the provisions of [the] Framework Directive. Rather, it is ensuring that individuals vulnerable to sexual orientation discrimination feel sufficiently confident to make use of the legislation" (2004b, 275–76). Yet in taking the constraints of the Directive seriously, along with the inexperience of most authorities to implement it, lesbians and gay men have scarce reason to place much confidence in either Member State or EU authorities.

Few doubt that the Framework Directive offers improved protection in many Member States, but the fact that it lacks the more comprehensive character of the Racial Equality Directive might encourage a difference in treatment and/or add logistical hurdles for those suffering from multiple discriminations. This is a troubling prospect for equality advocates (CEC 2005d, 6).[4] For example, on what directive should an Asian lesbian suffering from harassment depend? As Bell notes, for many women, distinguishing between the harassment based on sex, race, or religion may prove impossible given the inextricability of these elements. Yet, the EU's legislative framework "contains only a right to assistance in respect to those aspects of harassment based on racial or ethnic origin" (2004a, 114–15).

If the EU is able to evade action against sexual (orientation) inequality while appearing to provide redress through its current legal framework, Member States can take a similar position of circumvention by emphasizing their formal policies as well as the EU's power to intervene through its varied institutions. After all, the Commission is expected to ensure the proper and effective implementation of EU directives. The ILGA's guide for NGOs on implementing the Framework Directive informs readers: "If your government is failing to implement the Directive properly, it may be possible to persuade the Commission to take this up with your government. Consult ILGA-Europe about this" (ILGA-Europe 2001, 11).

Perhaps no case better illustrates how Member States *and* EU institutions can appear honorable while dodging responsibility for sexual-orientation discrimination than *D v Council* (Case T-264/97 [1999], Reports of European Community Staff Cases II-1) and the appeal that followed from it. After the Council chose to ignore its own 1998 staffing regulations prohibiting sexual-orientation discrimination by denying a household allowance to a Swedish Union official whose same-sex "marriage" it refused to recognize, the official (Sven Englund) sought legal redress from the EU's Court of First Instance (CFI). This Court endorsed the Council's defiance.

In *D v Council*, the CFI reasoned that the EU's staffing regulations refer exclusively to civil marriage in the conventional sense of the term. According to this Court, the Council is not obliged to extend a household allowance to the same-sex Swedish couple, an exclusive privilege for heterosexual spouses. Given the Council's potential prominence in alleviating discrimination as defined in the Amsterdam Treaty, its position is cause for concern.

When the Swedish government objected to the Community's treatment of Sven Englund and appealed to the ECJ on his behalf in 1999, it was joined by Denmark and the Netherlands. All three Member States insisted that their national law, and not Community law, stipulates the notion of marriage that recognizes Mr. Englund's relationship.

The ECJ responded in 2001 by affirming *both* the sovereignty of these Member States *and* the finding of its lower Court. In *D and Sweden v Council*, the ECJ took a position reminiscent of the CFI and reasoned that the regulations governing EU civil servants refer exclusively to marriage in the conventional sense of the term because "apart from their great diversity," domestic partnerships are themselves recognized by Member States as legally distinct from marriage (Cases C-122/99P and C-125/99P [2001] ECR 4319, paragraph 36). This is especially true in Sweden where the law recognizes same-sex couples, both as domestic partners (cohabitants) and registered partners, but not as married. Registered partnerships, like the one entered into by Englund with his partner, have been available since 1995. They are restricted to gay and lesbian couples though the government insists that they involve most of the rules that apply to marriage. This separate but nearly equal status nonetheless contradicts Sweden's insistence on equal treatment, though few noted this double standard until after the ECJ's ruling.

In assessing the merits of Mr. Englund's case, the ECJ invoked precedent from *Grant* to insist that the Council had *not* violated the principle of equal treatment. "It should be observed first of all that it is irrelevant for the purposes of granting the household allowance whether the official is a man or a woman." Second, "it is clear that it is not the sex of the *partner* which determines whether the *household allowance is granted but the legal nature of the ties between the official and the partner*." Again, "the principle of equal treatment can apply only to persons in comparable situations, and so it is necessary to consider whether the situation of an official who has registered a partnership between persons of the same sex, such as the partnership entered into by *D* under Swedish law, is comparable to a married official" (paragraphs 46–48; emphasis in the original). As in *Grant* and the Member States at the time, the ECJ concluded that same-sex and opposite-sex relationships are not comparable, a position even the ECHR abandoned in 2003 (in *Karner v Austria* Application 40016/98 [2003] ECHR 395).[5]

The Court's denial of Mr. Englund's claim by affirming the sovereignty of those states that insisted on supporting him provides the most remarkable aspect of *D and Sweden v Council*. After all, when the three states insisted upon stipulating their own notion of marriage, the Court agreed and then exposed their hypocrisy in defining marriage as exclusively heterosexual. At the time of the Court's decision, Sweden, Denmark, and the Netherlands had codified their recognition of same-sex partnerships, albeit as relationships distinct from "real" marriage. In short, the Court emphasized what many, until then, may have wished to keep implicit. To be either a domestic or a registered partner in Sweden (and throughout the EU) is not to be a married one (see table 9.1).

Shortly after the Court's 2001 *D and Sweden v Council* verdict, the Dutch made marriage available to lesbian and gay couples. The Commission's Directorate General of Personnel and Administration dispatched a memo to the Netherlands clarifying that the EU's staffing regulations would extend to the same-sex couples of that state (cited in Bonini-Baraldi 2004, 16). In this manner, the Commission embraced Dutch sovereignty while ignoring the Court's contention that same-sex relationships are not equivalent to heterosexual ones. Dutch newlyweds were thus entitled to a household allowance, pension and sickness insurance, access to EU cafeterias, and language courses—all of which

Table 9.1 Legal recognition for same-sex partnerships[*]

No recognition	Unregistered cohabitation	Registered partnerships/ cohabitation	Same-sex marriage
Bulgaria	Austria 2003	Czech Republic 2006	Belgium 2003
Cyprus	Hungary 1996	Denmark 1989	(registered partnerships 2000)
Estonia	Portugal 2001	Finland 2001	Netherlands 2001
Greece		France 1999	(unregistered cohabitation
Ireland		Germany 2000	1979; registered partnerships
			1998)
Italy		Luxembourg 2004	Spain 2005
Latvia		Slovenia 2005	
Lithuania		Sweden 1994	
Malta		(unregistered	
		cohabitation 1988)	
Poland		United Kingdom 2005	
Romania			
Slovak Republic			

[*] All dates in the table refer to the year the legislation was adopted.

Notes: For unregistered cohabiting partners, legal recognition, rights, and responsibilities automatically accrue after a specified period of cohabitation. The details of these laws vary between states. The rights and responsibilities granted to registered partners vary between Member States and are distinct from heterosexual marriage in a number of important ways. These include, but are not limited to, pension and inheritance rights, rights for foreign partners, shared custody, and child adoption. Only Spain extended identical rights for heterosexual and same-sex married couples. The Netherlands prohibits same-sex married partners from adopting children from abroad, a position currently under reconsideration. Belgium similarly denied adoption rights for same-sex married partners until 2006. Thereafter, same-sex married partners have had equal rights to heterosexual spouses. Sweden has called for the repeal of its 1994 Registered Partnership Act to be replaced with same-sex marriage in 2008.

Source: ILGA-Europe site for same-sex marriage and partnership: country by country.

the Court had just denied to Mr. Englund, whose Swedish sanctioned relationship did not constitute marriage.

With various benefits typically limited to married couples, and many same-sex partners registered but prohibited from matrimony, indirect discrimination on the ground of sexual orientation has remained the rule rather than the exception. If neither the Amsterdam Treaty nor the Framework Directive empowered the Commission to intrude into the distribution of partner benefits within Member States, it could still put its own house in order by amending its own staffing regulations. In 2004, the Commission reformed its personnel statutes to treat non-marital registered partnerships like matrimonial ones. In addition, the new policy provided "reduced social packages" for those unmarried officials living in *de facto* (i.e., unregistered) relationships, provided they supply proof with legal documents (Bonini-Baraldi 2004, 16). Non-EU employees, by contrast, continue to labor throughout the Community under significantly less generous policies and court rulings that privilege the sovereignty of states in matters of relationship discrimination.

As an increasing number of registered partners throughout the Community confront the limitations of their legal status, many have come to regard such partnerships as "an important step forward for same-sex couples, but . . . not enough" ("Lesbian Couple's High Court Test" 2005). In 2006, Britain's highest court denied two lesbian nationals (Celia Kitzinger and Sue Wilkinson) full legal recognition for a marriage they entered into while residing in Canada ("UK: Same Sex Couple Lose Marriage Laws Challenge" 2006). It is likely that the women will appeal. Meanwhile, Sweden is considering the legalization of same-sex marriage for 2008.

More legal challenges are sure to follow, insofar as Belgium (in 2003) and Spain (in 2005) joined the Netherlands in sanctioning same-sex marriages. Others, like Austria and a majority of the CEEC countries, have declared their refusal to recognize them. A case decided by Austria's Federal Constitutional Court in 2004 involved a U.S. citizen who had married his German partner in the Netherlands. When the German national secured employment with an international organization in Vienna, Austria refused to recognize his marriage and, thus, declined to issue residence and work permits to his third-country spouse. By denying the U.S. citizen his right to free movement as a "spouse," Austria prevented the German national from assuming his new post. When the couple appealed to that state's Federal Constitutional Court, the Court observed that Austrian law limits the definition of marriage to opposite-sex couples (HOSI Wein 2004, 6), a decision that trumps the matrimonial recognition the Netherlands extends to lesbians and gays.

Those activists expecting the EU to resolve such conflicts should examine the revised 2004 Directive on freedom of movement: despite its egalitarian inclinations, the rights of EU lesbians and gay men have been sacrificed on the altar of subsidiarity. First, Member States that do not permit same-sex marriages or registered partnerships for their own nationals are not obliged to recognize the rights of EU nationals from others that grant this status. Thus, lesbian and gay couples moving from Member States recognizing their relationships to those that do not lack an *automatic* right to free movement that EU citizenship implies, and that married heterosexuals can take for granted. Second, the Directive limits a guarantee of free movement *primarily* to "spouses" and the children related to them (2004/38/EC). It is doubtful whether the Directive provides for the recognition of same-sex marriages as constituting "spousal" relationships.

According to the Directive, lesbian and gay EU citizens are entitled to have their partners join them in other parts of Europe only "*if* the legislation of the host Member State treats registered partnership as *equivalent* to marriage" (2004/38/EC, 79; my emphasis). The ECJ's precedents in *Grant* and *D and Sweden v Council* afford little optimism that such partnerships will meet the EU's demand of "equivalence." In fact, because the Court has been adamant in its refusal to regard same-sex relationships as comparable to intimate heterosexual relationships (Wintemute 1995, Chapter 5), its decisions threaten to undermine the EU's legislative efforts to prohibit sexual-orientation discrimination (Carolan 2005).

With public discourse focusing predominantly on the socioeconomic benefits of marriage, one tends to ignore the reluctance of many Europeans to embrace and enter into an institution that has long been difficult to escape. Although divorce has been legally available in most Member States from the 1970s and even in Ireland since 1995, fewer Europeans are getting married than they were decades ago. This comes as no surprise with the demise of prohibitions against cohabitation and nuptials that frequently involve cumbersome contractual arrangements sanctioned by states.

Malta, a new Member State, distinguishes itself as one of only two countries in the world that reject divorce, a position that did not threaten its EU membership. In Sweden, where divorce is usually granted upon request, the law requires parents of offspring younger than sixteen to endure a six-month waiting period for the sake of the children. The Czech Republic takes a similar stance and does not grant a divorce before the subsequent care of the children has been settled; in Italy, the Parliament rejected a 2003 bill that would have reduced the time it takes to get a final divorce decree from three years to one. Equality advocates in these countries and others have objected strongly to such legal limitations, especially for mothers married to and seeking divorce from physically and/or psychologically abusive husbands (Elman 2001; Eriksson and Hester 2001; Hester and Radford 1996). Their objections, among others, serve as a caution against viewing modern marriage as a panacea, regardless of sexual orientation.

Proposing Justice

If lesbians insist on the right to same-sex marriage, it may be less because they esteem matrimony as an institution than because they wish to end the societal discrimination that reinforces their exclusion from it. Feminists have long decried heterosexual wedlock as a major site of women's oppression (Hodgkinson 1988),[6] explaining the long and contentious debates between lesbian feminists and gay men over the wisdom of pursuing marriage rights. Writing from Germany, Judith Rauhofer analyzes this definitive split over state-registered partnerships. While many gay male organizations in that country favor the codification of same-sex relationships, Rauhofer insists that lesbian activists have been so "closely entwined with the feminist movement, [they are] too critical of the institution of 'marriage' to actually claim it for themselves" (1998, 73–74, 79). Statistics from several states that have legalized registered partnerships appear to substantiate her claim. In all such states, far more men than women have registered their relationships (Waaldijk 2001a, Appendix VI, 463),[7] a point rarely discussed. Given the economic foundation of marriage as an institution that protects private property and men's greater earning power, it makes sense that more men in partnerships with each other enter into registered relationships; as women, lesbians receive incommensurate benefits.

The state's recognition of sexual relationships clearly entails regulation, to say nothing of the worrying potential of its agencies in later discriminating against the very couples that trusted authorities enough to register their partnerships in the first instance. Legal theorist Ruthann Robson warns that the promotion of domestic partnerships "tacitly promises lesbians protection if we conform our relations to traditional family values and threatens persecution if we do not" (1994, 989). A noted lesbian legal practitioner explains that official recognition has enabled greater "state surveillance and regulation of lesbians, in return for the 'right' of lesbians to fight each over in court over property." She despairs that "this is an intolerable prospect for lesbians who wish to keep their power to define their own lesbian relationships" (Ocean quoted in Rankine 1996/1997, 10). Moreover, the heterosexist history and destructive capacity of states should not be ignored. If Member States were nearly as benevolent as the trust that many activists who seek its recognition imply, registered recognition would be unnecessary.

Considering the small inroads lesbians (and gay men) have made through the legal recognition of their "intimate" relationships, one wonders whether the commitment such legal strategies require inhibits the search for superior solutions to the concrete problems their recognition was designed to eliminate. Rather than seeking the extension of health care and housing allowances to the sexual partners of (and/or those "related" to) insured employees, the ethically ambitious project would entail mass mobilization for guaranteed access to quality health care and decent living conditions for all, regardless of their cohabiting status (Rieder 1992, 107-10). Instead of insisting that "lovers" have unconditional access to their hospitalized partners, perhaps it would better to inquire about the conditions that led to hospitalization. The fact that male violence is the main cause of death and disability for women throughout Europe should give pause to the assumption that "intimate" partners are necessarily kind and always deserving of unrestricted visitation rights. Intimate violence is no stranger to lesbian and gay communities (see Renzetti and Miley 1996); it is dangerous to overlook the lessons learned from feminists while accepting clichés that abound about familial relationships offering haven in a heartless world.

Preventing heterosexism by ending the particularized privileges of (heterosexual) couples is not only principled, but it may also be more effective than embracing the illusion of stable domesticity in an effort to secure equivalent advantages. Lisa Grant's objection was not that benefits constituted (additional) pay extended to the spouses and lovers of her heterosexual coworkers. Rather, Grant requested that she and her lesbian partner receive the same privileges, a demand that went unfulfilled.

Conclusion

In a Europe where more women than ever are neither living with a spouse nor a partner,[8] the emphasis on partnership benefits undermines the long-standing demand for equal pay for equal work by expecting employers to calculate remuneration based on one's dependency/marital status and not one's job performance. The assumption that such policies are fair because nearly everyone has (or wants) a "stable relationship" can be insulting, not least to Europe's sizable single population.

It is one of the great ironies of social movements and EU policy that, on the one hand, demands for sexual equality have long hinged on an individualization of benefits and, more recently, the same goal may ostensibly be achieved through the extension of household benefits to same-sex couples. Helen Toner reveals this paradox well: "The ECJ has often been criticised for its traditional attitude to the family and one may be skeptical as to whether a choice to remain unmarried is something that it would be quick to protect" (2004, 171). Moreover, it is time that we ask whether the choice to remain "single" is one that feminist, lesbian, and gay movements will continue to defend. Recent efforts to end discrimination have almost exclusively called for the "recognition of lesbian and gay *relationships* and families as *equally valid to heterosexual relationships and families* within laws and social policies pertaining to the family, parenting, the care of children, adoption and fostering, and immigration" (International Lesbian and Gay Association 1998, 26).

The continuing exclusion of gays and lesbians from the rubric of "family" may best be countered not by begging for inclusion but, instead, by resorting to truly equal treatment. That is, movements could insist that "equal treatment" means that there shall be no discrimination (directly or indirectly) whatsoever on the grounds of marital or family status. In pursuing this more radical "equal treatment" position, lesbians and gay men could free themselves from the burden of demonstrating the equivalence and/or merit of their intimate relationships. In seeking justice, Sven Englund and his Swedish legal counsel could have pursued an innovative challenge to the Council's heterosexism by insisting that marital benefits (and by extension, marital comparators) are inherently prejudicial. This argument would actually have been in keeping with Swedish rhetoric that the state's model of "gender-neutral citizenship" is one in which entitlements do not extend to anyone primarily due to their spousal status (Sommestad 2002).[9]

Concomitantly, those interested in social change must not relinquish the demand to know the basis by which couples (or any groupings) constitute a preferential class, deserving of socioeconomic benefits and rights denied to others. As the political theorist Jacqueline Stevens notes, the most fundamental structures of the modern state rest on the rules regulating marriage and immigration; these "make possible the power relations associated with nationality, race, and family roles." She concludes that until this is understood, "it is clear that piecemeal approaches to eradicating certain inequalities will not work" (1999, xv).

For most European social movements, the successful assertion of claims at the EU level can obviate the need for local campaigns within all twenty-seven Member States, just as losing may obliterate any local victories that movements may have already chalked up. However, the special difficulty for lesbian and gay movements is that their claims for justice often challenge policy areas where states maintain sovereignty and the EU refuses to intervene (e.g., migration and marital policies).

As Virginia Harrison has pointed out, "Community case law indicates that the Court will avoid making far-reaching decisions which challenge important institutions such as marriage and the family" (1996, 280, n58). Lesbian and gay activists are forced repeatedly to assert claims within all Member States while knowing that progressive policy gains within any one state rarely transfer to other national contexts, a condition amply demonstrated by the legal cases discussed in this chapter.

CHAPTER 10

Self-Negating Policies and Polities

The core question of this book was straightforward. What role, if any, does the EU have for Member States in defining, maintaining, constructing, or remedying sex discrimination? In exploring the EU's policies pertaining to equal pay and equal treatment, GM and decision-making, sexual violence and same-sex marriage, the answers were anything but simple. They can be summarized briefly: in general, the EU has played a role, albeit limited, in defining and even maintaining sex discrimination. It has accomplished this through decades of sometimes-contradictory legislative and funding initiatives, court rulings, and other institutional studies and statements—a majority of which emphasize that remedies for discrimination must begin at places of work, with Member States expected to assume responsibility for their implementation. The qualifiers in the previous sentences such as "limited" and "sometimes" recognize that there are marked differences between the Member States. Further, not all anti-discrimination policies are the same, and opportunities for positive social change are difficult to discern because principled consistency has not been a hallmark of the EU, much less of the Member States.

Given the historical origins of Europe's first equality law (i.e., Article 119) and the Court's reasoning in the cases related directly to it (e.g., *Defrenne*), one cannot be sanguine about equating efforts alleged to end sex discrimination with support for women. First, in the aftermath of World War II, gendered pay disparities became a problem, worthy of political solution, only after equal-pay provisions served as a means of offsetting male wage stagnation and economic competition among the Member States. Second, more recent efforts to cultivate labor have less to do with liberating women per se than with balancing women's contribution to economic development with their fertility, an ongoing concern given the graying of Europe and the growing need to "reconcile" home and work life to resolve this demographic shift. Last, when the ECJ first insisted that equal pay only covered wages and not social security schemes, it bolstered its authority as the final arbiter of European law in general and gender policies more specifically. In *Defrenne II*, the Court insisted that the principal aim of equal-pay legislation was to promote the market's efficiency within the Member States, while countering sex discrimination to ensure social progress (i.e., women's rights) came second. This background helps to explain the Court's later position in *Barber* when, in 1990, it broadened the principle of equal pay to include occupational pensions, but insisted that its judgment did not apply retroactively. Fearing the potentially disastrous consequences that sexual-equality claims would have on national budgets, Member States joined with the Court and confirmed this limitation. They annexed a Protocol to Article 119 of the Maastricht Treaty that read: "Benefits under occupational social security schemes shall not be considered remuneration if and in so far as they are attributable to periods of employment prior to 17 May 1990," the date of the *Barber* decision.

These equal-pay cases illustrate how the Community and its Member States rebuffed efforts to redress sex discrimination while claiming to decry it, a position that holds for other matters as well. Consider, for instance, the Community's mixed messages on parental leave. Soon after the Court suggested (in *Hofmann*) that it would not interfere in "private" family matters such as the division of labor within the home, the Commission unveiled its Second Action Program in 1986. The program explicitly recognized that equality between women and men is unattainable without reconciling work life and family caretaking. When, a decade later, the Commission composed a directive extending parental leaves to fathers, a majority of the fifteen Member States already had leave arrangements similar to what the Commission proposed. However, thereafter, as before, few men elected to take them if only because to do so may not have been in their family's best financial interest. Even with the Council's 2006 request that Member States promote policies that "better balance professional and private life in order to meet the challenges of demographic change" (CEC 2007b, 3), circumstances are unlikely to change with men continuing to earn significantly more than women earn and no sign of the wage gap decreasing. The Council's emphasis is less on promoting women's rights than on using measures that promote gender equality as "essential instruments for economic growth, prosperity and competitiveness" (CEC 2007b, 6).

The Community's reluctance to combat sex discrimination on principle rather than merely because it is economically and/or politically expedient parallels its ambivalence about affirmative action, an indecisiveness mirrored by the very term used to depict it—"positive discrimination." That the EU officially characterizes measures intended to prevent, offset, or eliminate disadvantages to women as "discrimination," albeit of a "positive" sort, is telling (MacKinnon 2006). After denouncing an affirmative action program for advancing "impermissible discrimination" in *Kalanke* in 1995, the Court was persuaded to rethink its position in *Marschall* in 1997 and recognize that seemingly gender-neutral promotion criteria such as seniority could place women at disadvantage in practice. This progressive shift in consciousness appears to have been short-lived. The controversy surrounding *Kalanke* may have informed the Court's reversal and contributed to the Commission's willingness to adopt a proviso in the 1997 Treaty of Amsterdam that expressly permits positive measures for the underrepresented sex, but the debate over "positive discrimination" is far from resolved.

If from *Marschall* we learn that the persistence of equality advocates pays off, the Court's position in *Cadman* in 2006 reminds us that struggles won can later be lost. First, the *Cadman* ruling undermines the Burden of Proof Directive's promise that the onus to prove discrimination does not rest with employees. In addition, the Court's heavy reliance in *Cadman* on seniority for financial reward contradicts its chief insight in *Marschall* that such measures are insufficient guarantors of just outcomes at best and, at worst, may perpetuate indirect discrimination. After all, determining wage structures by simply equating additional work experience with better job performance disadvantages women who, on average, have shorter periods of service due to their greater share of unpaid caretaking.

The EU's fickle approach to sexual equality suggests that, in the absence of a foundational commitment to this principle, victories remain hollow, subject to rapid reversal and/or authorities indifferent (or even hostile) to their implementation. As one of the EU's most ambitious and least understood policies, GM seems to exemplify this problem. In theory, GM promises a systematic examination of policies to determine their gendered consequences. This proves easier to execute than a thorough analysis of the structural underpinnings of women's subordination. The goal of GM is to neutralize myriad disadvantages for any one gender that result from seemingly unbiased practices. In practice, therefore, it was used to undermine positive action by calling for an end to the policies and programs that privileged women's concerns.

Although the advocates of GM succeeded in stemming this tide, another predicament has emerged whereby some of the most outspoken opponents of gender-equality policies work within the same institutions that promoted policies they previously decried. Consider, for example, the Vatican and its membership with the EWL[1] or the Parliament's Women's Rights Committee, led by Anna Zaborska, a woman vociferously opposed to both abortion rights and lesbian and gay rights. Indeed, following a loud scuffle involving Polish MEPs over abortion that necessitated the intervention of Parliamentary guards, a well-known British MEP commented: "On women's rights and gay equality, we are fighting battles that we thought we had won years ago" (Bowley 2005).[2] It is small wonder that there has been a "reduced visibility and a loss of momentum" when it comes to "gender issues" (CEC 2006b, 6), a point perhaps lost in the Commission's 2007 efforts to promote "equal opportunities for all," as opposed to promoting prospects for those women who have been specifically denied them.

Consider the Community's circuitous approach to sexual harassment in the workplace. After both the Council and the Commission condemned this abuse through a resolution in the early 1990s, they took little additional action to stem it, insisting instead that the 1976 ETD provided relief to the victims of it. When a decade of data mounted that suggested otherwise, at substantial cost to EU business, the Commission passed a Directive in 2002 to prohibit sexual harassment at work. Whether the newer legislation proves any better in practice, it is too soon to tell as Member States had until 2005 to comply with it.

Despite the clearly cautious and incremental character of the EU's response to sexual harassment, proponents of reform in some states (e.g., the Netherlands, France, and Sweden) insist that the EU has provided an additional and important venue to promote measures that their governments have been otherwise reluctant to adopt. Battered women's activists as well as advocates for lesbian rights, particularly in the newer Member States, have sometimes reached similar conclusions. Unlike equal pay and sexual harassment, woman battery and lesbian rights are relatively novel matters for the public sphere, concerns that women's movements politicized. The fact that activists are convinced that the EU, and not their national governments, has offered some amelioration in these areas raises interesting questions about public perception, expectations, and the relative efficacy of each level.

Might this then suggest that activists regard the EU as a leader—at least for some states, promoting positive social change in what for them may be the newly politicized arenas of sexual life and inequality?

Perhaps, but again, the EU's restrained approach to sexualized discrimination provides insight. Whereas the 2000 Framework Directive affords lesbians and others some redress for employment discrimination, it is notably silent on discrimination against them in education, housing, and healthcare. This partial, piecemeal approach suggests that activists (national and otherwise) cannot rely on supranational institutions such as the EU to provide a solid foundation for their claims.

Recall, as well, that the EU recognizes sexual harassment as sex discrimination when it transpires in the wage-labor market, but does not regard it as injurious when it happens elsewhere or is inherent to an industry—as in prostitution and the production of pornography. Paradoxically, this explains, in part, why the Directive on Burden of Proof (whatever its limitations after *Cadman*) could not extend to women exploited in the EU's growing sex industry, even though they risk losing their lives if they testify against the men who profit from exploiting them. The now common distinction between trafficking (sexual coercion) and "free" (occupational) prostitution serves that industry well by legitimizing sexual exploitation and thus lowering public outrage against it. Germany provides a case in point. After legalizing pimping in 2002, Germany hosted the 2006 World Cup Games and its sex industry "imported" an additional 40,000 women from Central and Eastern Europe to "sexually service" the nearly 3 million (mostly male) football fans (Coalition Against Trafficking in Women 2006). In a nod to the sovereignty of Member States and the protection of their markets, the Court had earlier ruled that it too regards prostitution as "work" (e.g., *Aldona Malgorzata Jany and Others v Staatssecretaris van Justitie*). Moreover, the Commission funded efforts (e.g., STOP) to counter the traffic of third-country nationals coming into its Member States through 2006, suggesting that third-country nationals offered unwelcome competition to the local sex industry. Together, these examples of sexual harassment, prostitution, and pornography suggest that the EU takes action against sex discrimination only when it fundamentally hampers production and diminishes profits within its own market (Baer 1996).

A historical analysis of the EU and its response to sexual inequality have revealed that because its agenda is primarily economic and because it lacks any specific and detailed legislation concerning human rights, the EU can contend that such issues as violence against women and sexual self-determination are extraneous to its political mission, beyond its purview, or even substantively inconsequential. The EU's general reluctance to regard the sexual subordination of women as political in nature, economic in consequence, and worthy of EU action in general has meant that, relative to many of its numerous constituent states (though certainly not all), it is a laggard.

Not only did the EU address discrimination against lesbians and male violence against women years after many of its Member States had already done so, but those Eurocrats with an avid interest in these issues often labored in relative obscurity within the Community's least powerful institutions, such as the Parliament. We witnessed how, for nearly a decade, the Commission ignored the Parliament's requests to confront male violence, including its 1986 comprehensive resolution on male violence. Soon after, a similar dynamic emerged when, in 1990, the Parliament broached the subject of equal rights for lesbians and gays. This time, however, the Commission's rebuff was explicit. It insisted that it had no power to combat discrimination against "sexual minorities," a position it reconsidered in adopting the 1997 Treaty of Amsterdam.

In its efforts against heterosexism, the EU's economic emphasis has led to a partial embrace of equality, one resembling its general approach to equal pay. That is, through its denunciations of inequality, the EU affirms sexual equality in the abstract, a stance exemplified by its Treaty that empowers, but does not oblige, the Community to combat sexual-orientation discrimination. In the absence of a concrete obligation to act, the Council had adopted for itself a policy of non-discrimination for its gay and lesbian staffers that it later chose to ignore. The Council's noncompliance and the Court's support of its defiance (in *D v Council*) is attributable, in part, to the EU's fundamentally flawed and incomplete conception of discrimination.

EU equality law conceals harm by obstructing moves against it. According to Union law, discrimination entails a difference in treatment for similarly situated persons under conditions where differentiation is unjustifiable. Discrimination, thus, means treating likes unequally. Historically, in the EU and throughout the world, this approach has rationalized the denial of fundamental rights (such as suffrage) to women, Jewish men, and men from other minorities, whose imagined difference from the rights-bearing standard (of propertied men from the racially privileged group, e.g.) disqualified them from the likeness required by this Aristotelian notion of equality. While to be sure, the EU has repudiated such discrimination, the Court has sustained the logic that promotes it. Thus, in *Grant*, the Court established that because lesbians and gays can be equally ill-treated, their subordination does not trigger a judgment of "discrimination" based on sex.[3] Furthermore, the Court privileged the favored treatment extended to heterosexuals by refusing to recognize the second-class status of lesbian partnerships as unlawful discrimination because, it insisted, lesbian and heterosexual relationships are incomparable even though both involve women ("like" parties eligible for equality by virtue of their similarity).

Today's advocates for social justice must mobilize throughout a fragmented European polity within which several ostensibly progressive constituent states maintain marriage as exclusive to heterosexuals by extending official, though not full, legal recognition to lesbian (and gay) partnerships. As the case of *D v Council* amply demonstrates, a Member State's recognition of same same-sex partnerships guarantees neither equality within that state nor beyond it, throughout the EU and within EU institutions. In addition, the same states that afford lesbians (and gay men) the right to register their relationships with other nationals typically fail to extend joint pensions, adoption rights, or equal inheritance taxes to these couples. Last, states such as the Netherlands, Spain, and Belgium expressly permit marriage for all their citizens, but are fully aware that the same-sex marriages they recognize lack standing within most other Member States, a condition the EU is poorly positioned to change and unlikely to challenge.

The divergent approaches to lesbian rights among the Member States and the EU's reluctance to counter heterosexism forcefully are of obvious concern to Europe's lesbian and feminist communities. They know, as do most other European social movements, that a victory at the EU level can render the need for local campaigns within all twenty-seven Member States obsolete, while losing may also obliterate the local victories that they may have already accrued. In consequence, advocates of sexual equality must often assert claims at the EU level *and* within every state, knowing that progressive policy gains within any one Member State rarely transfer to other national contexts. This circumstance is clearly demonstrated by migrating same-sex partners as well as Swedish feminists who succeeded in having their state recognize prostitution as a violation of women's equality.[4]

Activists throughout Europe must determine the emphasis they should extend to each level of governance so that they may effectively meet their goals. This is an arduous determination, especially considering the history and current character of the EU, its twenty-seven Member States and, not least, the Court's appropriation of sexual equality to justify discrimination where claimants (lesbian, gay, or other) are equally ill-treated. The conservative legal norms that are foundational to the Court, the Community's economic emphasis, and the sometimes-conflicting positions of the Member States simultaneously reinforce and conceal the EU's refusal of equality through the politics of integration.

Within this context of Europe's growing integration, women's rights are frequently lost in the shell game of accountability that is subsidiarity. Each level of governance that one might expect to offer redress can defer to another until no remedy materializes. While this is especially clear in the case of same-sex partnerships, the struggle over abortion rights offers another example. Although the ECJ ruled that abortion is a service to which all European citizens are entitled and unification involves a harmonization of laws that would seem to support this, the politics of integration permitted Ireland the autonomy to deny women this right of European citizenship when it had a Protocol inserted in the Maastricht Treaty. Ailbhe Smyth reveals the impossible situation faced by the women of Ireland in the Maastricht referendum: "in voting against the Treaty, Irish women would be voting against their own best interests, although in point of fact, voting in favor of the Treaty ensured that repressive Irish law overrode the EU in the matter of abortion" (Smyth 1996, 118).

Like the other EU constituents, Ireland's power points to a crucial paradox for modern states where "power and privilege operate increasingly through disavowal of potency, repudiation of responsibility, and diffusion of sites and operations of control" (Brown 1995, 194). This insight extends beyond the power of modern states to include transnational institutions. Thus, just as the EU offers a central site for its Member States to locate power as they deny their own, the Member States serve a similar function for the EU. That is, in deference to state sovereignty, the EU is able to insist that its Members are the primary unit for dispensing and protecting rights and privileges that it continually credits itself with having initiated but that the Member States endlessly defer. For instance, in proposing its Community Action Program to Combat Discrimination (2001–2006), the Commission insisted that it was already engaged in efforts to end discrimination and that the responsibility for implementing measures now rested with the Member States. In 2006, the Commission reiterated this position in its "Roadmap for equality between men and women" (2006–2010), stating "the centre of gravity for action lies at the Member State level" (CEC 2006c, paragraph 1).[5] The Member States have responded in kind through a dramatic increase in the number of referrals that their courts send up to the ECJ. If to former ECJ judge Federico Mancini this reference procedure is an exercise in "child's play," it is important to recognize that many women's lives hang in the balance (in Ward 2003, 82, n2).

The interplay between the EU, its Member States, and women's advocates is complicated and there are, to be sure, challenges for those seeking meaningful rights within the rhetoric of universal human rights, free markets, and fragmented polities. First, women throughout the EU are similar to women elsewhere in the world in that they do not have access to full human status in social reality. Women are recognizably not "like" men (the androcentric standard for right-bearing beings); the "treat likes alike" model of equality thus fails women (MacKinnon 2005). For this reason, much of the abuse that is largely specific to women (e.g., "women's work," sexual harassment, prostitution, and domestic violence) falls outside the EU's rubric of human rights violations. Characterized as a "violation of dignity" and/or "contrary to the principle of equality" and separate from the sex of those involved, sex discrimination so defined risks becoming abstract and often unrecognizable to the women who experience it. Employing the rhetoric of commerce to gain social justice is no less a Faustian bargain than this feeble model of redress for sexual inequality, especially within fragmented structures of governance and authoritative avoidance.

The good news is that once movements focused on the heavy costs of sex discrimination, gender equality achieved the rhetorical status of a good business practice, opening jobs and other possibilities to women. Indeed, the Commission reasons: "In order *to fully exploit the potential of European workplace productivity*, it is essential to promote women's long-term participation in the labour market and to eliminate the disparities between men and women across the board" (CEC 2007b, 6; my emphasis). Women have undoubtedly been good for commerce. However, can the reverse be true: that is, has commerce been good for women? First, the increase in women in the wage-labor market has afforded business a highly profitable and flexible, if not expendable, labor source. Nevertheless, what is profitable for commerce rests on the exploitability of labor and while exploitation is no less odious for being called "equality," the EU is no less elitist and inaccessible for being called transparent and "democratic."

My analysis of the EU's numerous efforts to combat inequality and the language used to describe them observes a Community that ensures a modicum of protection for those who suffer from sex discrimination as the EU defines it. However, for the vast majority of women, including those suffering from the worst injuries of inequality—such as sex-based poverty, physical and sexual abuse—the Community's emphasis on market liberalization substitutes rhetoric for relief. In the absence of clear success or new ideas for effective measures, one finds an affirmation of past policies slightly modified in ways that do not impinge on the presumed efficiency of the market, the sovereignty of the state, or masculine privilege.

Notes

Chapter 1   Rhetoric and Reality

1. According to the Commission, "measures targeted at a particular group and intended to eliminate and prevent discrimination or to offset disadvantages arising from existing attitudes, behaviors and structures" are sometimes referred to as "positive discrimination" (CEC 1998a, 45).

2. One must not confuse this Charter with the 1989 "Community Charter of the Fundamental Social Rights of Workers." Commonly referred to as the "Social Charter" and signed by all member countries of that time save Britain, the earlier agreement is a register of certain rights and principles that extend almost entirely to working conditions (e.g., social security and occupational health and safety). Of the twenty acts that implement the Social Charter, half cover occupational health and safety, three concern improvements in living and working conditions, and three others concern equal treatment for women and men, disabled persons, and child welfare (Majone 1993, 155).

3. Theo van Gogh's first film, in 1981, was a misogynistic farce about the kidnapping of a wheelchair-bound woman. It depicts a man firing a gun into her vagina. Women were not, however, the only ones to experience his contempt. Theo van Gogh was also notorious for his anti-Semitic and anti-Muslim tirades against other men. For example, he ridiculed Muslim men as "goat fuckers" and suggested that the respected Jewish Dutch filmmaker Leon De Winter bind his penis with barbed wire while yelling "Auschwitz." Ian Buruma suggests that van Gogh's interest in directing "Submission" with Hirsi Ali was in keeping with his insatiable hunger for publicity (Buruma 2006).

4. "The American law of equality has," by contrast, "been forged in the crucible of racial inequality, in particular through resistance by people of color to white racism" (MacKinnon 2001, 51).

5. Throughout this work, unless otherwise noted, Germany refers to West Germany since 1940 and, from 1990 onward, the unified Germany.

6. For a detailed history concerning the adoption of Article 119, see Hoskyns (1996b, chapter 3); for a legal appraisal, see Ellis (1991, chapter 2).

Chapter 2   Sexual Equality Conceived

1. It was only after the Treaty on European Union (i.e., the "Maastricht Treaty") had come into force, in 1993, that the European Community became more commonly known as the "European Union." The former is often invoked with reference to the central activities of the EC prior to this treaty. I often use the terms interchangeably, though am inclined to use the term "Community" when referring to matters prior to 1993.
2. By contrast, according to the same survey, nearly one in five Europeans had also never heard of the European Commission or European Court of Justice, institutions discussed later in this chapter (CEC 2004c).
3. As well, one must not confuse the European Council with the Council of Europe. The Council of Europe is Europe's oldest pan-European institution and its institutions are located in Strasbourg. Founded in 1949, it comprises over forty nation states. Unlike the EU, its principal aim is the promotion of parliamentary democracy and human rights throughout Europe as affirmed in its European Convention on Human Rights (ECHR). The case law generated by the Council's Court of Human Rights (also ECtHR) is, however, influential for the EU's Court of Justice.
4. The allocation of seats to each Member State is based on the principle of digressive proportionality. This means that while the size of the population of each country is taken into account, smaller states elect more MEPs than would be strictly justified by their populations alone. Whereas treaty negotiations determine the number of MEPs granted to each country, there is no precise formula for the apportionment of seats among Member States. Moreover, no change can occur without the unanimous consent of all governments.
5. Three years prior, in 1963, the ECJ established that the Community "constitutes a new legal order of international law" and encouraged litigants to employ Community law before domestic courts. *Van Gend en Loos v Nederlandse Administratratie der Belastingen*, Case 26/62 [1963] ECR 1.
6. This was no easy feat. For a candid overview of the sexism that then permeated the UN, see Hedervary (1984).
7. Indeed, according to Lisa Baldez, governments continued to prepare "showpiece" policies for international conferences throughout the 1980s and 1990s, including the most recent UN Women's Conference in Beijing in 1995 (in Ellina 2003, 39). We will examine several of these policies later in this book.

Chapter 3   Fashioning Interventions

1. The details of this new Directive are covered in greater detail in chapter 4.
2. From 1960 until 1995, the divorce rate doubled (except in Ireland where divorce was illegal) despite marriage rates declining by nearly one-third (CEC 1997a, 20).

3. In their in-depth study of women MEPs, Vallance and Davies found that "Although some of the women consider their male colleagues as allies, many of them claim to have noticed some hostility among the men to working with women politicians, particularly if they believe the women to be feminists" (1986, 62).

4. Since 2004, the assembly also elects an administrative board and executive committee of five every two years, charged with overseeing policy development and organizational management.

5. Their article offers an excellent examination of the Court's "mixed messages" regarding sex-equality laws through the lens of caretaking.

6. In 1992, the Commission adopted the Pregnancy Directive (1992/85/EEC). It prohibited the dismissal of pregnant employees throughout the Community and established minimum requirements for maternity leave. Promoted primarily as a health and safety measure, few regarded this legislation as an "Equality Directive" because "pregnancy and maternity were not treated under the rubric of gender equality but as matters concerning working conditions, under the label of 'sickness'" (Ostner and Lewis 1995, 166).

7. Only after a decade's worth of empirical evidence began to suggest sexual harassment increased turnover at substantial cost to European business did the Commission revisit this position. However, as recently as 1998, then Commissioner Pádraig Flynn insisted that most Member States opposed creating an instrument to counter sexual harassment at work (Zippel 2006, 116).

8. In this respect, the Recommendation made the same distinction between a "hostile work environment" and "quid pro quo" harassment established in the U.S. courts, similarly providing women with remedy for both sorts of harm. *Meritor Savings Bank v Vinson*, 106S. Ct. 2399 (1986).

9. Although Baer's comment may hold for the Commission, it is less true of the European Parliament, which has opposed pornography, prostitution, and trafficking since the 1980s; note chapters 6 and 7.

10. My emphasis.

11. Mentioned briefly in the introduction, co-decision is a procedure that bestowed the EP with a limited form of joint legislative power with the Council of Ministers in some areas such as the internal market, public health, education, culture, and the free movement of persons.

12. This view is anchored in, among other instruments, a 1984 Council Recommendation on the Promotion of Positive Action for Women. It advised Member States to adopt policies "designed to eliminate existing inequalities affecting women in working life and to promote a better balance between the sexes in employment" (84/635 EEC. OJ L 331/34, paragraph 1).

Chapter 4   Assessing Material Reforms

1. For earlier years, comparable Eurostat data are missing, inconsistent, and incomplete. Only Italy, Luxembourg, the Netherlands, the United Kingdom,

and West Germany provided data since the 1970s. However, even cross-national comparisons among these countries pose problems because the surveys often used different definitions and methodologies.

2. More recently, the Commission acknowledged that more women than men participate in adult education or training in twenty-one Member States, with an average participation rate of 11.7% among women and 10% among men (CEC 2006b, 12).

3. The OECD provides the governments of thirty market democracies a forum to address the economic, social, and governance challenges of globalization. The OECD is renowned for its published reports, containing detailed statistics on economic and social conditions.

4. The Commission observed that 23.3% of women with children worked part-time as opposed to 15.9% of women without them (CEC 2006b). In 2003, the employment rate for women aged 20–49 without children under twelve in the EU-25 was 75% compared to 60% for those with children under twelve. For men in the same age group, the opposite effect was observed: their employment rate increased from 86% for those without children to 91% for those with them (Eurostat 2005).

5. Business may be every bit a "man's game," but so too is academics. Although women outnumber men as graduates, within education and research "their presence decreases consistently as they progress on the career ladder, from 43 per cent of PhDs down to only 15 per cent of full professors" (CEC 2006b, 6).

6. On average, 15% of women are employed in temporary jobs in the EU-25, compared to 14% for men (Eurostat 2006).

7. This incongruity is discussed in the book's conclusion.

8. See note 1 in this chapter. For a comprehensive analysis of many of the methodological problems involved when comparing different (EU) labor markets see Rubery et al. (1999).

9. Indeed, because so many Swedes regard their country as one where equality has already been achieved, they view themselves as uniquely innovative. This perspective is sometimes born of ignorance. Unaware of progressive policies adopted elsewhere, Swedes will suggest that "women friendly" policies originated with them. The authors of a 2002 study concerning GM note, for example, that Swedish officials credit themselves with the invention of mainstreaming (OPTEM 2002, 13).

10. Alter and Vargas demonstrate that European litigation favored Britain's Equal Opportunities Commission at the height of Conservative Party power.

11. The data must, however, be viewed with some caution as no data were compiled for 1996.

12. Jennifer Corcoran proves a notable exception (1988).

13. The reasons for this ignorance have not been comprehensively studied and represent a great opportunity for future research.

14. Remember, in *Kalanke* the Court held that favoring a female candidate when choosing between equally qualified applicants for public service was

contrary to the ETD. Two years later, in *Marschall*, the Court reversed itself and acknowledged that equally qualified candidates still stand different chances based on gender. On both these cases, see chapter 3 in this book. After discussing the Court's contradictory positions on pregnancy, one critic writes: "There are occasions when judicial stupidity, and tastelessness, almost beggars belief" (Ward 2003, 183).

15. In the press, see "A Retrograde Decision" (2006). I discuss this editorial in more detail later. Note, as well, that Socialist MEPs followed the decision with a letter to Social Affairs Commissioner Vladimir Spidla, requesting the reexamination of Union legislation on equal pay (GMB 2006).

16. The legislation will be discussed in detail in chapter 9. However, knowledge is limited concerning the effects of this measure because some aspects of this legislation have been in effect only since 2006. Moreover, Member States remain empowered to decide for themselves what mechanisms should be in force to resolve claims.

17. Parental leave conditions were more limited in Greece, Ireland, Luxembourg, and the United Kingdom (Lohkamp-Himmighofen and Dienel 2000, 56).

18. The network was discontinued in 1996, after ten years.

19. Domestic work refers to work done for one's own household. According to Eurostat: "The most important categories are food management, care for textiles, cleaning and household upkeep, gardening, repairs, shopping and childcare" (2004, 44–45).

20. Reader take note, these times are all self-reported.

Chapter 5   Assessing Political Equality and Mainstreaming

1. Although the practice of citizenship remained largely invisible before Maastricht, the roots of citizenship policy and its actual practice can be traced to the early 1970s. See (Durand (1979), Evans (1984), and Wiener (1997). As Carole Lyons explains, "The term 'Citizens' Europe' had been in circulation on an irregular basis since 1974, and rights conferred mainly under the EEC Treaty (1957), together with jurisprudence, had created some elements of citizenship" (Lyons 1996, 98).

2. Consider the former Social Democratic German chancellor, Gerhard Schroeder. After announcing that he would further trim Germany's "nanny state," tens of thousands of teachers, police officers, and other public sector employees closed down the center of Berlin in October of 1999. The same month, Ireland witnessed the largest work stoppage in the nation's history as 27,500 nurses went on strike for nine days over paltry wages.

3. Lackluster leadership may offer one explanation. Consider Commissioner Charlie McCreevy's remarks following the French and Dutch constitutional referenda. Pondering how the EU's elites might best reconnect with their "ordinary" constituents, he explains the need to reach "the great majority of

people for whom transatlantic dialogues, inter-institutional committees, gender institutes and the like hold little interest. They are people who just want to earn a decent living, be able to afford a few pints, go to a game of football and have a bit of sex" ("Different Voices" 2005).

4. Many MEPs often sign in Friday morning for a full day's work at a per diem stipend of €262 (ca. $320) and depart for a flight home for which they are reimbursed at the highest available economy fare, regardless of the actual cost. A scandal over these perks erupted shortly before the 2004 elections when a former reporter for Germany's *Der Spiegel*, Hans-Peter Martin, then serving as an elected MEP, surreptitiously filmed his colleagues boasting about this practice. Subsequent criticisms have prompted reforms to both cleanse the Parliament's reputation and enhance its power. With regard to the former, stipends and reimbursement practices are now on the table.

5. According to Annette Borchorst, a prominent Danish political scholar, "In Denmark, statistical data reveals [*sic*] that the corporate channel has been the most male-dominated area of the political system" (in Lovenduski and Stephenson 1999, 36). Borchorst's colleague, Drude Dahlerup, furthermore advises that we recognize that "even if the relative number of women in the Danish parliament increased gradually over time, there were more feminist women in parliament in the 1980s than in the 1990s." She continues, "Now, experienced feminists have begun to keep a low profile in parliament, and young women politicians have been eager to stress that they were not feminists" (Dahlerup 2006, 520, n5).

6. This strategy first emerged at the UN's Third World Conference on Women in Nairobi in 1985, a decade before the Commission pledged to adopt this tactic for itself. The plan emerged from efforts to ensure the integration of "women's values" in development programs.

7. Although it is true that the Court issued this judgment in 1984, it is worth noting that the Court has not yet distanced itself from this position.

8. More recently, on the matter of sex trafficking in women, expertise was again at issue. See chapter 4 and the request made by the Committee on Women's Rights that there should be greater transparency in the determination of "experts" and their contracts. Still, it is worth noting that the Commission refers repeatedly to those whose positions it actively solicits as "experts." In this manner, the body reinforces itself and the legitimacy of those selected for their "expertise."

9. Of the main organizations working to militate against discrimination in the EU, only ILGA is clear in its vehement opposition to having the Vatican at various related round-tables. In 2003, ILGA stated: "Not only do we think it is inappropriate because the Vatican has no democratically elected parliament or government, we consider its recent attacks on lesbians and gays as incitement to hatred, and call upon law makers and politicians to oppose legislation in favor of same-sex couples as an assault on human rights, disqualifying the Holy See to be a serious part of such organizations" (Hardt 2003).

Chapter 6   Politicizing Male Violence

1. While Member States hold exclusive competence for their criminal and thus antiterrorist measures, the Commission calls for a stronger antiterrorism policy and stepped up *cooperation* between law enforcement and judicial authorities throughout the Community, especially following 9/11 in the United States, the Madrid bombings of 2004, and the London bombings of 2005. By July of 2005, all Member States had implemented a European-wide arrest warrant to replace old extradition procedures and by the year's end they also adopted a European-wide evidence warrant. The later provides law enforcement authorities with the ability to obtain objects, documents, and data in cross-border cases without court approval.

2. For example, in Britain, approximately 50% of all homicides involve men who murder the women in their lives (Kotatakos 1999, 8). In Sweden, by contrast, authorities estimate that percentage at sixty (Elman 1996a, 34).

3. Consider AFEM, a federation of Mediterranean women's organizations. Established in the mid-1990s, AFEM represents the interests of southern Europe at the European level. More recently, one finds networks seeking to bridge the gap between activists in older and newer Member States. Consider the Network of East West Women—Polska (NEWW/P) and the KARAT Coalition, an association of twenty Central and Eastern European feminist organizations. As well, there is ASTRA, the Central and Eastern European Women's Network for Sexual and Reproductive Heath Rights. It has organized informational tours of the EP for its members. Cécile Greboval, policy coordinator for the EWL, emphasized these networks in my interview with her (2003).

4. Writing from Spain, Juanjo Medina-Ariza and Rosemary Barberet insist that many simply find the issue of male violence "too threatening" to address (2003, 303).

5. In 2001, the Court explicitly recognized prostitution as work in *Aldona Malgorzata Jany and Others v Staatssecretaris van Justitie* (Case C-268/99 [2001] ECR 8615). I discuss this case in chapter 7.

6. The Green group within Parliament welcomed the second conference of "international sex workers" in Brussels in 1985. As chapter 7 reveals, it took them another decade to succeed in their efforts to have prostitution increasingly described as "sex work."

7. The principle of subsidiarity was articulated in Article 3b of Maastricht: "In areas which do not fall within its exclusive competence, the Community shall take action, in accordance with the principle of subsidiarity, only if and in so far as the objectives of the proposed action cannot be sufficiently achieved by the Member States and can therefore, by reason of scale or effects of the proposed action, be better achieved by the Community." Interestingly, subsidiarity cannot be extended to matters where the Community holds "exclusive competence." Moreover, there are no certainties about whether an action is best achieved by the Member States or the larger Community. Such

uncertainties are a central dimension of European integration. See the Commission's reasoning in its communication regarding the DAPHNE Programme, COM (1998) 335 final, 7.

8. See note 22 in chapter 8 for the details of this case.

9. It is interesting to note that of the eighty-four battered women I surveyed in 1999, only one specifically requested protection under the Violence Against Women Act.

10. This term of art describes the very *indirect* and, at times, *insignificant* influence of EU citizens on most decisions made within EU institutions. Further, several EU bodies make key decisions in meetings that are closed to the press and public.

11. It was not until 2000 that the EU adopted a Charter on Fundamental Rights.

12. Remember that the Danish first rejected Maastricht in a referendum and the French gave it less than an enthusiastic response in their referendum, approving the Treaty by a tiny margin. The Germans sent Maastricht to their constitutional court, which in the end voted for it. The United Kingdom pushed it through Parliament under unprecedented pressure. When the Maastricht finally came into force in November 1993, it was hardly to great fanfare.

13. A series of interviews that I conducted in Brussels with numerous EU officials (e.g., Duffin, interview, 1999; Gradin, interview, 1999; Simpson, interview, 1999) confirmed Pollack's point. That is, the EP and Commission responded, in part, to a Belgian public that was horrified and agitated by these crimes that received extensive coverage in the European press. Remember too, from chapter 2, that the fight to end wage discrimination against women began in Belgium.

14. It must be said that, when compared to their European counterparts, Swedish women appear to enjoy greater political strength and economic influence. However, impressive portraits of Sweden's exceptionalism notwithstanding, in the area of sexual politics, this Member State is second-rate (Elman 1996a). Indeed, a comparative exploration of sexual harassment policy at the state and EU levels suggests that Sweden was advantaged by the Europeanization of its domestic policy on sexual harassment (Elman 2000b). Also note Zippel (2004, 74–75).

15. Carl Stychin reaches a similar conclusion in his pointed exploration of European gay rights movements: "the economic teleology of rights in the EU can 'sanitise' the claim, making it more likely that a court will conclude that it can legitimately find in the claimant's favour" (2000, 290). I explore this point further in chapter 7.

16. In 2005 alone, the World Health Organization estimated that a record 4.9 million people were newly infected with HIV. As well, the organization emphasized that infection rates in Asia and Eastern Europe are rising at an alarming rate, stating a twenty-fold increase in the number of people living with HIV just over the last decade (Jack and Johnson 2005).

Chapter 7 The Programs—Stop and Daphne

1. The conditions that motivated this acknowledgment are soon considered. For now, see Communication from the Commission to the Council and the European Parliament, Proposal for a Council Framework Decision on Combating Trafficking in Human Beings and Combating the Sexual Exploitation of Children and Child Pornography, COM (2000) 854 final, 7–9.

2. Andrew Williams characterizes the EU's human rights agenda as bifurcated and marred by an underlying assumption that human rights possess a distinctive European heritage that is largely absent outside the Member States. He warns that this perspective is not only rife with hypocrisy and hubris, but that it also has the potential to undermine the EU's human rights objectives. His candor is refreshing.

3. Two years prior, the Commission warned in a Communication (COM(2004) 101 final) of the need to "revisit" such expenditures so that it could focus further on *internal* security and by December of 2006 it discontinued AGIS.

4. For more information on the IOM, see International Organization for Migration (2005).

5. Researchers from the IOM distributed 345 questionnaires to different government bodies, NGOs, and various academics throughout all fifteen Member States, as well as Switzerland, Norway, and Central and Eastern Europe. Its conclusions were based on 188 completed questionnaires from twenty-five countries (Salt and Hogarth 2000, 34–35).

6. This language is telling in that it underscores the objectification of those in prostitution by denying them even personal pronouns.

7. In 2003, the Commission established the "Experts Group on Trafficking in Human Beings." Commission Decision (2003/209/EC).

8. Farley's article (2006) offers the most comprehensive, empirically based analysis to date.

9. For information on Sweden, see Swedish Government (2004). Impressed with Sweden's success, Denmark's Socialist Party has called for the country to establish a law that is similar to that of Sweden (Kolthoff, interview, 2005).

10. In 1978, e.g., France's Ministry of Interior estimated that pimping and procuring accounted for France's third-largest business, with an annual estimated profit of US$7 billion. Due to the illicit nature of the sex industry, precise profits are impossible to calculate. However, several Member States, such as France, have attempted to track them nonetheless (Barry 1995, 237).

11. Options included, but were not limited to, religious organizations, social services, police, medical personnel, and charitable groups.

12. Ironically, scholars may interpret such spin as a movement's satisfaction with or endorsement of authorities. Yet, this understanding, however mistaken, is also not without benefit as even the most symbolic interventions (and interpretations) have the potential to evoke something substantive.

13. Ironically, the Broadcasting Directive undermines the emphasis on sovereignty insofar as states cannot exercise any meaningful control over pornography—because the community remains an open frontier. In consequence, national politicians can effectively evade responsibility for pornography within their states.

14. One can find this poster (and photos of those like it) at the official STOP Conference website http://www.belgium.iom.int/STOPConference/photos .shtm (accessed November 15, 2004).

15. That this declaration appears to have little, if any, effect in the actual reduction of violence for women in their daily lives is evident in the telling fact that those dignitaries employed within the UN are immune from prosecution for the crimes they perpetrate, including acts of violence against women.

16. Eriksson's suspicions about the sex industry's influence were well founded. Five years later, the Commission was forced to open disciplinary proceedings against two of its staff members after the Belgian newspaper, *De Morgen*, revealed that they were owners of Studio Europe, an alleged Brussels brothel. Under Article 12 of the staff regulations, "an official shall refrain from any action or behaviour which might reflect adversely upon his position" (King 2005).

17. See, for instance, Council Resolution of October 20, 2003, on initiatives to combat trafficking in human beings, in particular women (OJ C 260/4, 29.10.3).

Chapter 8   Politicizing Sexuality

1. Two years later, Spain repealed Article 431.

2. Most notably, Britain's Section 28 of the Local Government Act prevents the "promotion" of homosexuality by local authorities. Section 28 followed on the heels of the lesbian feminist movement's long-standing promotion of lesbianism as a "positive choice for women." This assertion countered biological determinism and infuriated Tories to the point that it led to the law's passage (Harne 1996, 21–24).

3. In *Kerhoven and Hinke v The Netherlands* (Case 15606/89), a lesbian couple claimed they and their child had been discriminated against because of his "birth and status in comparison with legitimate children." The ECommHR responded, "as regards parental authority over a child, a homosexual couple cannot be equated to a man and a woman living together," unpublished case cited in Robert Wintemute (1995, 193). See below for further discussion of the Council of Europe, its various institutions, and their response to heterosexism.

4. With the limited and qualified exceptions of Denmark, Belgium, Spain, Sweden, and the Netherlands, all Member States currently refuse adoption to same-sex couples. In England, such couples are challenging policy that permits them to adopt children, but not *qua* couple, while in Germany the

Social Democrats passed a bill permitting lesbians and gay men to co-adopt the children of their partners. Green MEP Volker Beck, the German bill's cosponsor explains, "It must be stressed that this is not a blank cheque for gays to adopt children. It does however permit children who are the off-spring of one partner to be co-adopted by the other gay partner in the relationship. The best interests of the child are always the priority" (DPA 2004).

5. In light of the HIV epidemic and the need for rigorous and reliable testing of sperm for disease, this last restriction poses especially serious health risks for those women resorting to private donors. In 2005, the Swedish government reversed its discriminatory prohibition against lesbian insemination, acknowledging, "Lesbian couples will be on an equal footing with heterosexual couples when it comes to assisted fertilization" ("Sweden to Allow IVF for Lesbians" 2005). The year before, Italy reaffirmed its restrictions through the adoption of a new law that restricts assisted fertilization to "stable" heterosexual couples—not single (heterosexual) mothers or lesbians.

6. In addition, almost as many of those surveyed acknowledged they regularly harmed themselves ("Northern Ireland: Shocking Statistics on Gay Youth" 2004).

7. As it is, the Commission estimates that a miniscule 1.5% of 370 million nationals availed themselves of this right in the mid-1990s (High Level Panel 1997, 6).

8. The details of this particular case are discussed later in this chapter, on page 134.

9. One of these requested an action program dedicated to the equal protection of rights for all workers, not least lesbians and gays. The other concerned HIV/AIDS and restated this basic proposition of non-discrimination.

10. Stonewall was established in 1989, in response to Britain's Section 28. See note 2 above.

11. It is also worth noting that membership in the Council of Europe is a pre-requisite for any application to join the EU.

12. The COE's historic hostility to homosexual rights is clear. When, for example, a German citizen insisted that his conviction for being gay under paragraph 175 of the German Penal Code violated the Convention, the Council's Commission found paragraph 175 accorded with the legal codes for health and morals (McLoughlin 1996, paragraph 25). Between 1933 and 1945, the Nazis sentenced approximately 15,000 men under paragraph 175, deporting some 5,000 of them to concentration camps. This keystone of anti-gay discrimination remained in effect in Germany until 1994 (Grau 1995, 6).

13. While McLoughlin recognizes *Dudgeon* as civil rights "milestone," he views it less as a tool for social change than a document of "incremental change in societal attitudes toward lesbian and gay Europeans, especially gay men" (1996, paragraph 85). More critically, Andrew Clapham and J.H.H. Weiler suggest that the conservative approach of the European Commission and Court of Human Rights might inhibit the progressive development of EC law (1993, 65).

14. In a case of the same name (*X and Y v UK*), an Austrian woman relied upon her lesbian relationship with a British citizen to apply for a residence permit for herself and her daughter. After the British government denied her request, she and her British partner petitioned the Council. Its Commission responded, "that a lesbian partnership involves private life within the meaning of Article 8 of the Convention" but insisted that lawful deportation could not be regarded as interference with this provision as states possess the right to impose control and limits on immigration (*X and Y v UK* Application 14753/89; see also *Simpson v UK* Application 11717/85 (1986) 47 DR 274, *C and LM v UK* Application 14753/89). In both *Simpson* and *C and LM*, the Commission reasserted its position about same-sex couples and dismissed their complaints as "manifestly ill-founded" and "inadmissible."

15. Two years later, the ECJ did the same.

16. Three years later, Human Rights Watch issued a statement opposing state-sponsored violence, detention, and prosecution of lesbians and gays. The UN, by contrast, remained obstinate and, as late as 1995, censored a call from feminists that requested women's right to determine their own sexuality (see this chapter's conclusion).

17. For a critical view of the market in sex, see chapter 7 in this book.

18. Named after its chief author, Green MEP Claudia Roth, the report's formal title is "Report for the Committee on Internal Affairs and Citizens Rights on Equal Rights for Homosexuals and Lesbians in the European Community."

19. Despite the defeat, commentators such as Rachel Rosenbloom emphasize the historic dimension of the debate, noting it marked the first substantive discussion of lesbian rights in any UN forum (1996b, x–xi). Charlotte Bunch, by contrast, demonstrates rare candor in criticizing the UN for its antifeminism in general and its long-held contempt for lesbians in particular (1996). By contrast, conventional criticisms of the women's world conferences concentrate most on the "cultural" clashes between "First" and "Third" World women, often in ways that fail to address the bigotry against lesbians everywhere (e.g., Rosen 2001, 340–43). Carl F. Stychin offers an astute analysis of the seemingly progressive uses of anti-Western discourse used to justify heterosexism. He notes such rhetoric "relies upon the right to defend the oppressed, geographically based community from powerful interests seeking to sweep away ways of life and belief systems shared by a people that simply wants to be left alone, with lives uncomplicated by gay rights" (2004, 964).

20. Elspeth Guild thus concludes that the Council has little incentive to change matters given that the Treaty itself lacks sufficient clarity, precision, and strength to have effect (2001, 687).

21. When, for instance, the Parliament's Equality Division chief Elvy Svennerstål insists that sex discrimination is "totally different" and must be "treated separately" from heterosexism, it suggests that lesbians have had

little influence on the discussion. However, it is impossible to know if this assertion results from sensitivity to the gender-specificity of discrimination or from a desire to avoid confronting heterosexism. Regardless, lesbians are nonetheless vulnerable (Svennerstål, interview, 1999).

22. *Diatta* involved a Senegalese woman separated, though not formally divorced, from her French husband. The Court ruled that the woman was, despite the collapse of the relationship, still entitled to the protections of Community law *until* the marriage was formally annulled. The ruling indirectly grants the EU national husband control over expulsion of his third-country wife because, once divorced, she ceases to be a member of the family for purposes of Community law (Hervey 1995, 106). Commenting on the decision, Joseph H.H. Weiler argues that the Court essentially stripped the woman of her "humanness" (1992, 90). Over a decade later, the High Level Panel addressed this issue in its report to the Commission. It suggested that Community provisions "should be amended so as to recognize a right of residence for the divorced spouse who is a third-country national" (High Level Panel 1997, 60–61). The revised directive (2004/38/EC) concerning freedom of movement extends rights of residence to third-country national divorcees and former cohabitants whose past partnerships endured for at least three years. As well, it provides refuge to survivors of violence who suffered abuse from their former spouse or partner (OJ L 158/77, 30.4.2004, 102). Chapter 9 offers further details on this legislation as it relates to same-sex partnerships.

Chapter 9 Wedding Rights to Marriage

1. For instance, the Greek army has banned gay men from military service since 2002 and the state's committee on human rights has, to date, been unsuccessful in demanding an end to this practice (Political Gateway 2006).

2. Germany and Greece failed to publish their final proposals for implementation and Luxembourg did not even bother to adopt a proposal for legislation on the matter of sexual orientation.

3. In July 2004, Portugal became the fourth country in the world to offer such a constitutional guarantee of equality. It follows Ecuador, Fiji, and South Africa.

4. In a small survey of equality authorities and related NGOs throughout the Community, the Directorate-General for Employment, Social Affairs and Equality found 82% of 150 respondents "agreed there should be greater links between efforts to combat discrimination on different grounds, including sex" (CEC 2005d, 6). The desire for this connection was also apparent from various interviews I conducted with activists from the European Network against Racism (e.g., De Jonckheere, interview, 2003) and ILGA-Europe (e.g., Spindler, interview, 2003).

5. The case entailed a comparison between same-sex and different-sex unmarried partners and the ECtHR ruled, "Differences based on sexual orientation require particularly serious reasons by way of justification" (*Karner v*

Austria Application 40016/98 [2003] ECHR 395, paragraph 37). It remains to be seen what reasons the ECtHR will find sufficiently serious to warrant a difference in treatment.

6. Through the codification of matrimony, women lost their rights to property ownership and individual legal status. Indeed, they lost their rights to their own identity. For example, until the 1990s, several member states (e.g., Austria and Germany) prohibited women from retaining their "maiden" name after marriage. In spite of feminist attempts in the twentieth century to redress these problems through reforms, Liz Hodgkinson reveals that marriage still renders women second-class citizens (1988). More recently, Laura Kipnis offers a persuasive polemic that reveals that despite the demise of "arranged marriages" throughout the world, contemporary partnerships in industrialized societies are less about "falling in love" than calculating the assets of an "appropriate mate" (2003).

7. These gendered comparisons are not without methodological problems. Namely, evidence suggests that there are more gay men than lesbians, at least, in terms of those willing to self-identify in survey populations about sex and relationships. Thus, whether "unequal" registration is nevertheless "proportionate" is impossible to know.

8. In 2005, one of every eight persons is a single adult living alone in the EU-25. Germany and Finland had the highest percentage of singles (17%) and Malta (where divorce is illegal) had the lowest (4%) (Eurostat 2007, 19). According to Eurostat, there are fewer and later marriages, and more divorce. In 2001, for example, there were only five marriages per 1,000 inhabitants in the EU-15 compared with almost eight in 1970. Moreover, for marriages entered into in 1960, the divorce rate was 15%. By 1980, this figure nearly doubled to 28%. Analysts conclude, "The trend towards smaller households, with more people living alone at all ages, is continuing" (Eurostat 2003, 12).

9. Ms. Sommestad, a former Social Democratic cabinet minister, insists that in Sweden "No entitlements are targeted at women in their capacity as wives" (2002). It is thus somewhat ironic that this Member State demands that the Council extend housing allowances to Swedish spouses and partners.

Chapter 10   Self-Negating Policies and Polities

1. See note 9 in chapter 5.

2. In 2005, a handful of MEPs (i.e., seventeen representing twelve Member States) organized a meeting entitled "Abortion—Making it a right for all women in the European Union," with the goal of returning legal abortion to the EU agenda as a human rights, gender equality, and public health issue. Because the EU considers abortion only as a health issue, and health matters are left to the decisions of each member state, several Member States (e.g., Poland, Portugal, Malta, Lithuania, Ireland, and the Slovak Republic) have succeeded in prohibiting abortions. As a consequence, women from states that ban them

have had to either travel to other states to obtain abortions or receive them in clandestine clinics where they risk unsanitary conditions and even death. The meeting closed with a declaration (written by the Hungarian MEP Katalin Levai) that calls upon Member States to ensure safe and legal access to abortion for all women.

3. The ECJ's position on same-sex partnerships is reminiscent of the logic employed by myriad U.S. states in their efforts to maintain miscegenation laws. Virginia was unable to convince the Supreme Court in 1967 (in *Virginia v Loving*) that its ban on interracial marriage was not racist because it equally forbade both races from entering into it, but miscegenation laws remained (unenforced) in several states until 2000 when Alabama became the last state to remove its law against mixed-race marriage. This example demonstrates, in part, the persistence of bigotry despite its formal repudiation.

4. The case of Sweden also offers a cautionary tale to those interested in comparative assessments of Member States and/or social policies. Sweden may favorably distinguish itself on the matter of prostitution, but on the matter of sexual harassment—it was a laggard that was very much helped by the EU in drafting policies more beneficial to women.

5. This "roadmap" is similar to other action programs and includes six priorities.
   - Achieving equal economic independence for women and men.
   - Enhancing reconciliation of work, private, and family life.
   - Promoting equal participation of men and women in decision-making.
   - Eradicating gender-based violence and trafficking.
   - Eliminating gender stereotypes in society.
   - Promoting gender equality outside the EU.

References

Advisory Committee on Equal Opportunities between Women and Men. *Opinion on Men in Gender*. Brussels: European Commission, 2006.

Agence France Presse. "Gay Couples Can't Marry in Germany, Court Rules." October 19, 1993. Accessed http://lexis-nexis.com/universe.

Alter, Karen and Jeannette Vargas. "Explaining Variation in the Use of Litigation Strategies: European Community Law and British Gender Equality Policy." *Comparative Political Studies* 33, no. 4 (2000): 452–82.

Amara, Fadela and Sylvia Zappi. *Breaking the Silence: French Women's Voices from the Ghetto*. Berkeley: University of California Press, 2006.

Andermahr, Sonya. "Subjects or Citizens? Lesbians in the New Europe." In *Women and Citizenship in Europe*, ed. Anna Ward, Jeanne Gregory, and Nira Yuval-Davis, 111–22. Exeter: Trentham Books and EFSF, 1992.

Ashworth, Georgina. *Changing the Discourse: A Guide to Women & Human Rights*. London: The Book Factory, 1993.

Associacion "Conseulo Berges" Mujeres Separadas y/o Divorciadas. *Estudio Sociologico Mujeres Asesoradas, Mujeres Victimas De Malos Tratos, Actualizacion, 16 November 1998–31 Diciembre 2000*, 2000.

Baer, Susanne. "Pornography and Sexual Harassment in the EU." In *Sexual Politics and the European Union: The New Feminist Challenge*, ed. R. Amy Elman, 51–65. Oxford: Berghahn Books, 1996.

———. "Germany." In *Combating Sexual Orientation Discrimination in Employment: Legislation in Fifteen EU Member States*, ed. Kees Waaldijk and Matteo Bonini-Baraldi, 209–28. Accessed August 10, 2005. Commission of the European Communities, 2004.

Banaszak, Lee Ann, Karen Beckwith, and Dieter Rucht. "When Power Relocates: Interactive Changes in Women's Movements and States." In *Women's Movements Facing the Reconfigured State*, ed. Lee Ann Banaszak, Karen Beckwith, and Dieter Rucht, 1–29. New York: Cambridge University Press, 2003.

———. *Women's Movements Facing the Reconfigured State*. New York: Cambridge University Press, 2003.

Barry, Kathleen. *The Prostitution of Sexuality: The Global Exploitation of Women*. New York: New York University Press, 1995.

Bell, Mark. *Anti-Discrimination Law and the European Union.* Oxford: Oxford University Press, 2004a.

———. "Ireland." In *Combating Sexual Orientation Discrimination in Employment: Legislation in Fifteen EU Member States*, ed. Kees Waaldijk and Matteo Bonini-Baraldi, 247–76. Accessed August 10, 2005. Commission of the European Communities, 2004b.

Bergqvist, Christina and Ann-Cathrine Jungar. "Adaptation or Diffusion of the Swedish Gender Model?" In *Gendered Policies in Europe: Reconciling Employment and Family Life*, ed. Linda Hantrais, 160–79. New York: St. Martin's Press, 2000.

Bergqvist, Christina and Nordiska ministerrådet. *Equal Democracies?: Gender and Politics in the Nordic Countries.* Oslo: Scandinavian University Press in cooperation with the Nordic Council of Ministers, 1999.

Berkovitch, Nitza. *From Motherhood to Citizenship: Women's Rights and International Organizations.* Baltimore: Johns Hopkins University Press, 1999.

Beveridge, Fiona, Sue Nott, and Kylie Stephen. "Mainstreaming and the Engendering of Policy: A Means to an End?" *Journal of European Public Policy* 7, no. 3 (2000): 385–405.

Bonini-Baraldi, Matteo. "European Law." In *Combating Sexual Orientation Discrimination in Employment: Legislation in Fifteen EU Member States*, ed. Kees Waaldijk and Matteo Bonini-Baraldi, 7–48. Accessed August 10, 2005. Commission of the European Communities, 2004.

Booth, Christine, and Cinnamon Bennett. "Gender Mainstreaming in the European Union: Towards a New Conception and Practice of Equal Opportunities?" *European Journal of Women's Studies* 9, no. 4 (2002): 430–46.

Borrillo, Daniel. "Summary of Chapter 7 on France." In *Combating Sexual Orientation Discrimination in Employment: Legislation in Fifteen EU Member States*, ed. Kees Waaldijk and Matteo Bonini-Baraldi, 37–42. Accessed August 10, 2005. Commission of the European Communities, 2004.

Bowley, Graham. "Conservative Poland Roils European Union." *The New York Times*, December 4, 2005, 18.

Broughton, Andrea. "European Foundation Survey Reveals that Working Conditions in Europe Are Deteriorating." January 28, 2001. Accessed http://www.eiro.eurofound.eu.int/about/2001/01/feature/eu0101292f.html.

Brown, Wendy. *States of Injury: Power and Freedom in Late Modernity.* Princeton, NJ: Princeton University Press, 1995.

Brückner, Margrit. "Reflections on the Reproduction and Transformation of Gender Differences among Women in the Shelter Movement in Germany." *Violence Against Women* 7, no. 7 (2001): 760–78.

Brush, Lisa D. "Understanding the Welfare Wars: Privatization in Britain under Thatcher." *Berkeley Journal Of Sociology* 32 (1987): 261–79.

———. "Changing the Subject: Gender and Welfare Regime Studies." *Social Politics: International Studies in Gender, State & Society* 9 (Summer 2002): 161–86.

———. *Gender and Governance.* New York: Alta Mira Press, 2003.

Buckley, Mary and Malcolm Anderson, eds. *Women, Equality and Europe.* London: Macmillan, 1988.

Bunch, Charlotte. "Foreword." In *Unspoken Rules: Sexual Orientation and Women's Human Rights*, ed. Rachel Rosenbloom, iii–viii. London: Cassell, 1996.

———. "The Intolerable Status Quo: Violence against Women and Girls." December 4, 2003. Accessed http://www.unicef.org/pon97/women1.htm.

Buruma, Ian. *Murder in Amsterdam: The Death of Theo Van Gogh and the Limits of Tolerance.* New York: Penguin Press, 2006.

Cameron, David. "The 1992 Initiative: Causes and Consequences." In *Euro-Politics: Institutions and Policymaking in the "New" Europe*, ed. Alberta Sbragia, 23–74. Washington, DC: The Brookings Institute, 1992.

Carolan, Bruce. "The Legislative Backlash to Advances in Rights for Same-Sex Couples: Judicial Impediments to Legislating Equality for Same-Sex Couples in the European Union." *Tulsa Law Review* 40 (2005): 527–60.

Carter, Victoria. "Working on Dignity: EC Initiatives on Sexual Harassment in the Work Place." *Northwestern Journal of International Law and Business* 12 (1992): 431–60.

CEC. *Equal Opportunities for Women in the Community.* Luxembourg: Office for Official Publications of the European Communities, 1993.

———. *Intergovernmental Conference 1996: Commission Report for the Reflection Group.* Luxembourg: Office for Official Publications of the European Communities, 1995a.

———. *The European Community Facing the Challenges of the Fourth World Conference on Women*, 1995b.

———. *Communication from the Commission to the European Parliament and the Council on the Interpretation of the Judgments of the Court of Justice on 17 October 1995 in Case C-450/93, Kalanke v Freie Hansestadt Bremen.* COM (96) 88 final, 27.03.96, 1996a.

———. *Eurobarometer 44.3: Employment, Unemployment and Gender Equality.* Brussels: European Commission, 1996b.

———. *For a Europe of Civic and Social Rights—Report by the Comité Des Sages*, Luxembourg: Office for Official Publications of the European Communities, 1996c.

———. *Communication from the Commission to the Council and the European Parliament on Trafficking in Women for the Purpose of Sexual Exploitation.* COM (96) 567 final, 20.11.96, 1996d.

———. *Communication on Incorporating Equal Opportunities for Women and Men into All Community Policies and Activities.* COM (96) 67 final, 21.02.96, 1996e.

———. *The State of Women's Health in the European Community: Report from the Commission to the Council, the European Parliament, the Economic and Social Committee and the Committee of the Regions, Employment & Social Affairs.* Luxembourg: Office for Official Publications of the European Communities, 1997a.

CEC. *Annual Report from the Commission: Equal Opportunities for Women and Men in the European Union.* COM (96) 650 final, 12.2.97, 1997b.

———. *One Hundred Words of Equality.* Luxembourg: Office for Official Publications of the European Communities, 1998a.

———. *Special Report No 22/98 Concerning the Management by the Commission of the Implementation of Measures to Promote Equal Opportunities for Women and Men Accompanied by the Replies of the Commission.* OJ C 393, 16.12.98, 1998b.

———. *Sexual Harassment in the Workplace in the European Union.* Brussels: European Commission, 1998c.

———. *Communication from the Commission on Violence against Children, Young Persons and Women and a Proposal for a Council Decision on a Medium Term Community Action Programme on Measures Providing a Community-Wide Support to Member States Action Relating to Violence against Young Persons and Women (the Daphne Programme).* COM (98) 335 final of 20.5.98, 1998d.

———. *Progress Report from the Commission on the Follow-up of the Communication: Incorporating Equal Opportunities for Women and Men into All Community Policies and Activities.* COM (98) 122 final, 1998e.

———. *Eurobarometer 51: Europeans and Their Views on Domestic Violence against Women.* Brussels: European Commission, 1999.

———. "European Campaign against Domestic Violence: Rationale." July 29 2000. Accessed http://europa.eu.int/comm/dg10/women/violence/index3_en.html.

———. *Asylum: Commission Proposes a Common Definition of Refugee and a Common Standard of Refugee Rights.* IP/01/1262, 12.9.01, 2001a.

———. *Communication from the Commission to the Council and the European Parliament Programme of Action for Mainstreaming of Gender Equality in Community Development and Co-Operation.* COM (2001) 295 final, 21.6.01, 2001b.

———. *Employment in Europe 2002: Recent Trends and Prospects.* Luxembourg: Office for Official Publications of the European Communities, 2002a.

———. *Eurobarometer 57.* Brussels: European Commission, 2002b.

———. *Eurobarometer 57: Executive Summary—Discrimination in Europe.* Brussels: European Commission, 2003.

———. *Handbook on Concepts and Methods for Mainstreaming Gender Equality.* Brussels: European Commission, 2004a.

———. *Glossary of Gender and Development Terms.* Brussels: European Commission, 2004b.

———. *Eurobarometer 61.* Brussels: European Commission, 2004c.

———. *Communication on Strengthening the Implementation of the European Employment Strategy—Proposal for a Council Decision on Guidelines for the Employment Policies of the Member States—Recommendation for a Council Recommendation on the Implementation of Member States' Employment Policies.* COM (2004) 239 final, 7.4.04, 2004d.

————. *EQUAL Guide on Gender Mainstreaming.* Luxembourg: Office for Official Publications of the European Communities, 2005a.

————. *Employment in Europe 2005: Recent Trends and Prospects.* Luxembourg: Office for Official Publications of the European Communities, 2005b.

————. *Commission Activities in the Fight against Terrorism— Memo 05/332,* 21.9.05, 2005c.

————. *Equality and Non-Discrimination: Annual Report 2005.* Luxembourg: Office for Official Publications of the European Communities, 2005d.

————. *Women and Men in Decision-Making—A Question of Balance.* Brussels: European Commission, 2006a.

————. *Report from the Commission to the Council, the European Parliament, the European Economic and Social Committee and the Committee of the Regions on Equality between Women and Men,* COM (2006) 71 final, 22.2.06, 2006b.

————. *Communication from the Commission to the Council, the European Parliament, the European Economic and Social Committee and the Committee of the Regions—A Roadmap for Equality between Women and Men 2006–2010.* SEC(2006)275, COM (2006) 92 final, 1.3.06, 2006c.

————. *Communication from the Commission to the European Council: A Citizens' Agenda.* COM (2006) 211 final, 10.5.06, 2006d.

————. *Report from the Commission to the Council and the European Parliament Based on Article 10 of the Council Framework Decision of 19 July 2002 on Combating Trafficking in Human Beings.* COM (2006) 187 final, 2.5.06, 2006e.

————. *Special Eurobarometer 263/Wave 65.4: Discrimination in the European Union Summary.* Brussels: European Commission, 2007a.

————. *Report from the Commission to the Council, the European Parliament, the European Economic and Social Committee and the Committee of the Regions on Equality between Women and Men.* COM (2007) 49 final, 7.2.07, 2007b.

Charlemagne. "A Crucible—or a Zoo?: Odd Behaviour Is the Only Thing that Stirs Interest in the European Parliament." *The Economist,* July 24, 2004a, 51.

————. "A Rigged Dialogue with Society." *The Economist,* October 21, 2004b, 54.

Clapham, Andrew and Joseph H.H. Weiler. "Lesbians and Gay Men in the European Community Legal Order." In *Homosexuality: A European Community Issue— Essays on Lesbian and Gay Rights in European Law and Policy,* ed. Kees Waaldijk and Andrew Clapham, 7–72. London: Martinus Nijhoff Publishers, 1993.

Coalition Against Trafficking in Women. *"Buying Sex Is Not a Sport"—CATW Launches Campaign against Promotion of Prostitution During the World Cup Games in Germany.* North Amherst, MA: Coalition Against Trafficking in Women (CATW), 2006.

Cohen, Sue. "Social Solidarity in the Delors Period: Barriers to Participation." In *Democratizing the European Union: Issues for the Twenty-First Century,* ed. Catherine Hoskyns and Michael Newman, 12–38. Manchester: Manchester University Press, 2000.

Coleman, Isobel. "The Payoff from Women's Rights." *Foreign Affairs* 83, no. 3 (2004): 80–95.

Collins, Evelyn. "European Union Sexual Harassment Policy." In *Sexual Politics and the European Union: The New Feminist Challenge*, ed. R. Amy Elman, 23–33. Oxford: Berghahn Books, 1996.

"Controversial MEP Elected to Chair Womens' Committee." *European Voice.com*, July 29, 2004.

Coordination Lesbienne. *Motion on Prostitution Voted by the Voted by the French Lesbian Coordination, 8 February* CATW, 2003 [cited February 13, 2007]. Available from http://action.web.ca/home/catw/readingroom.shtml? x=32981 &AA_EX_Session=4a9a1b9a608786d7cd7e79cf1d292378.

Corcoran, Jennifer. "Enforcement Procedures for Individual Complaints: Equal Pay and Equal Treatment." In *Women, Equality and Europe*, ed. Mary Buckley and Malcolm Anderson, 56–70. London: Macmillan Press, 1988.

Council of Europe. *Violence against Women in Europe*, Strasbourg: Council of Europe, 2000.

Dahlerup, Drude. "The Story of the Theory of Critical Mass." *Politics & Gender* 2, no. 4 (2006): 511–22.

Dassu, Marta and Daniel Franklin. "Corporate Europe Ignores Diversity at Its Peril." *Financial Times*, November 29, 2005.

Delphy, Christine. "The European Union and the Future of Feminism." In *Sexual Politics and the European Union*, ed. R. Amy Elman. Providence, RI: Berghahn Books, 1996.

"Different Voices." *European Voice.com*, June 16, 2005.

Dobash, R. Emerson and Russell Dobash. *Women, Violence, and Social Change*. London; New York: Routledge, 1992.

DPA. "Germany Proposes Adoption Rights." *ILGA Euro-Letter*, September 2004, 3.

Duchen, Claire. "Understanding the European Community." *Women's Studies International Forum* 15, no. 1 (1992).

Durand, A. "European Citizenship." *European Law Review* 4 (1979): 3–14.

EGALITE. "MEPs withhold Equal Treatment for Gays and Lesbians." *ILGA Euro-Letter*, February 1997, 3–4.

Ellina, Chrystalla A. *Promoting Women's Rights: The Politics of Gender in the European Union*. New York: Routledge, 2003.

Ellis, Evelyn. *European Community Sex Equality Law*. Oxford: Oxford University Press, 1991.

Elman, R. Amy. *Sexual Subordination and State Intervention: Comparing Sweden and the United States*. Oxford: Berghahn Books, 1996a.

———. "The EU and Women: Virtual Equality." In *The State of the European Union: Deepening and Widening*, ed. Pierre-Henri Laurent and Marc Maresceau, 225–39. Boulder: Lynne Rienner Publishers, Inc., 1998.

———. "Sexual Harassment Policy: Sweden in European Context." Paper presented at the Twelfth International Conference of Europeanists, Chicago, March 30–April 1, 2000b.

————. "Unprotected by the Swedish Welfare State Revisited: Assessing a Decade of Reforms for Battered Women." *Women's Studies International Forum* 24, no. 1 (2001).

————, ed. *Sexual Politics and the European Union: The New Feminist Challenge*. Providence, RI: Berghahn Books, 1996b.

Equal Pay Task Force. *Just Pay*, Manchester: Equal Opportunities Commission, 2001.

Eriksson, Maria and Marianne Hester. "Violent Men as Good-Enough Fathers? A Look at England and Sweden." *Violence Against Women* 7, no. 7 (2001): 779–98.

European Forum of Left Feminists. *Confronting the Fortress: Black and Migrant Women in the European Community*. Brussels: The European Women's Lobby, 1993.

European Monitoring Centre on Change (EMCC). "The Childcare Services Sector—Visions of the Future." [September 18, 2006]. Accessed http://www.eurofound.europa.eu/emcc/content/source/eu06016a.html?p1=ef_publication&p2=null.

European Monitoring Centre on Racism and Xenophobia. *Manifestations of Anti-Semitism in the European Union*. Vienna: EUMC, 2003.

European Parliament. *Report on Sexual Discrimination in the Workplace (Squarcialupi Report)*, OJ C 104/16, 16.4.84, 1984.

————. *Report Drawn up on Behalf of the Committee on Women's Rights on Violence against Women (D'ancona Report)*, A-2 44/86, OJ C 176/85, 14.7.86, 1986.

————. *Report on the Fight against Aids*, OJ C 158/477, 26.6.89, 1989a.

————. *Report on the Community Charter of the Fundamental Social Rights of Workers*, OJ C 323/44, 27.12.89, 1989b.

————. *Report of the Committee of Inquiry on Racism and Xenophobia*. Luxembourg: European Parliament, 1991.

————. *Working Document on Gender Mainstreaming and the Targeting of Women in the Budget*, PE 227.895, 29.7.98, 1998a.

————. *Annual Report on Respect for Human Rights in the European Union*, A4-0034/98, 28.1.98, 1998b.

————. *Trafficking in Women*. Brussels: Division for Social, Legal and Cultural Affairs. Working Paper by Carmen Galiana, 2000a.

————. *Report on Countering Racism and Xenophobia in the European Union*. Luxembourg: European Parliament, Final A5-0049/2000, 2000b.

————. *Report on the Consequences of the Sex Industry in the European Union*. Brussels; Strasbourg: Committee on Women's Rights and Equal Opportunities, Final A5-274/2004, 2004.

European Union Monitoring Centre on Racism and Xenophobia. *Racism and Xenophobia in the EU Member States—Trends, Developments and Good Practice. EUMC Annual Report 2003/2004 Part 2*. Vienna: EUMC, 2004.

European Women's Lobby. "Newsflash #9." Brussels: European Women's Lobby, 1995.

Eurostat. *Social Portrait of Europe*. Luxembourg: Office for the Official Publications of the European Communities, 1996.

———. *The Social Situation in the European Union: In Brief*. Eurostat home page, 2003 [cited October 12, 2006]. Available from http://ec.europa.eu/employment_social/social_situation/docs/SSR2003_brief_en.pdf.

———. *How Europeans Spend Their Time: Everyday Life of Women and Men— Data 1998–2002*. Brussels: Eurostat, 2004.

———. *Reconciling Work and Family Life in the EU25 in 2003: Employment Rates Lower and Part-Time Rates Higher for Women with Children*. Brussels: Eurostat, 2005.

———. *Labor Force Survey 2005: Employment Rate in the EU25 Was 63.8% in 2005*. Brussels: Eurostat, 2006.

———. *Living Conditions in Europe: Data 2002–2005*. Luxembourg: Office for Official Publications of the European Communities, 2007.

Evans, A.C. "European Citizenship: A Novel Concept in EEC Law." *American Journal of Comparative Law* 32 (1984): 679–715.

Falkner, Gerda, Oliver Treib, Miriam Hartlapp, and Simone Leiber. *Complying with Europe: EU Harmonisation and Soft Law in the Member States*, *Themes in European Governance*. Cambridge; New York: Cambridge University Press, 2005.

Farley, Melissa. "Prostitution, Trafficking, and Cultural Amnesa: What We Must Not Know in Order to Keep the Business of Sexual Exploitation Running Smoothly." *Yale Journal of Law and Feminism* 18 (2006): 109–44.

Ferree, Myra Marx. "Making Equality: The Women's Affairs Offices in the Federal Republic of Germany." In *Comparative State Feminism*, ed. Dorothy M. Stetson and Amy G. Mazur, 95–113. London: Sage, 1995.

"Forced Fatherhood." *The Economist*, January 10, 2004, 46.

Fouque, Antoinette. *Women in Movements: Yesterday, Today, Tomorrow*. Trans. Anne Berger, Arthur Denner, and Nina McPherson. Paris: Des Femmes, 1992.

"France: Court Voids Gay Marriage." *New York Times*, July 28, 2004. Accessed on-line.

Freitas, P. Miguel. "Portugal." In *Combating Sexual Orientation Discrimination in Employment: Legislation in Fifteen EU Member States*, ed. Kees Waaldijk and Matteo Bonini-Baraldi, 377–406. Commission of the European Communities, 2004. Accessed August 10, 2005.

Frölich, Barbara. "Austria." In *Unspoken Rules: Sexual Orientation and Women's Human Rights*, ed. Rachel Rosenbloom, 9–13. London: Cassell, 1996.

GMB, Britain's General Trade Union. "Cadman Equal Pay Case." *European News Bulletin*, November/December 2006, 3–4.

Goodey, Jo. "Sex Trafficking in Women from Central and East European Countries: Promoting a 'Victim-Centered' and 'Woman-Centered' Approach to Criminal Justice." *Feminist Review* 76 (2004): 26–45.

Goodwin, Jan. "These Women Are Prisoners." *Marie-Claire*, November 2005.

Gould, Arthur. *Developments in Swedish Social Policy: Resisting Dionysus*. New York: Palgrave, 2001.

Grace, Sharon. *Policing Domestic Violence in the 1990s*. London: Home Office Research Study, 1995.

Gradin, Anita. "Speech by Commissioner Anita Gradin." Paper presented at the EU Conference on Violence Against Women, Cologne, March 30, 1999a.

Grau, Günter. "Persecution, 'Re-Education' or 'Eradication' of Male Homosexuals between 1933 and 1945." In *Hidden Holocaust?*, ed. Günter Grau, 1–7. London: Cassell, 1995.

Graziella, Irene, Martine, and Françoise. "Feminism and Radical Lesbianism." In *For Lesbians Only: A Separatist Anthology*, ed. Sarah Lucia Hoagland and Julia Penelope, 472–84. London: Onlywomen Press, 1988.

Griffin, Gabriele. *Feminist Activism in the 1990s*. London: Taylor & Francis, 1995.

Grunell, Marianne. "A Good Practice: The Role of Women's Studies in the Coalition of Feminists and the State against Physical and Sexual Violence." *The European Journal of Women's Studies* 6 (1999): 341–58.

Guerrina, Roberta. "Mothering in Europe: Feminist Critique of European Policies on Motherhood and Employment." *The European Journal of Women's Studies* 9, no. 1 (2002): 49–68.

Guild, Elspeth. "Free Movement and Same-Sex Relationships: Existing EC Law and Article 13 EC." In *Legal Recognition of Same Sex Partnerships: A Study of National European and International Law*, ed. Robert Wintemute and Mads Andeneaes, 677–89. Oxford: Hart Publishing, 2001.

Hagemann-White, Carl. "European Research on the Prevalence of Violence against Women." *Violence Against Women* 7, no. 7 (2001): 732–59.

Hantrais, Linda. "What Is a Family or Family Life in the European Union?" In *The Legal Framework and Social Consequences of Free Movement of Persons in the European Union*, ed. Elspeth Guild, 19–30. The Hague: Kluwer Law International, 1999.

———. *Gendered Policies in Europe: Reconciling Employment and Family Life*. New York: St. Martin's Press, 2000.

Hardt, Birgit. "ILGA-Europe Questions the Role of the Vatican in International Organization." [October 3, 2003]. Accessed http://www.thevillage.org.uk/displaystory.php?recordID = 94.

Harne, Lynne. "Dangerous Liaisons: Reasserting Male Power through Gay Movements." In *All the Rage: Reasserting Radical Lesbian Feminism*, ed. Lynne Harne and Elaine Miller, 10–30. London: The Women's Press, 1996.

Harrison, Virginia. "Using EC Law to Challenge Sexual Orientation Discrimination at Work." In *Sex Equality Law in the European Union*, ed. Tamara Hervey and David O'Keeffe, 267–81. New York: John Wiley & Sons, 1996.

Harvey, Brian. "The Problem of Homelessness: A European Perspective." In *Homelessness: Public Policies and Private Troubles*, ed. Susan Hutson and David Clapham, 58–73. London: Cassell, 1999.

Hawthorne, Susan. "Wild Politics: Beyond Globalization." *Women's Studies International Forum* 27 (2004): 243–59.

Hedervary, Claire de. "The United Nations: 'Good Grief, There Are Women Here!'" In *Sisterhood Is Global: The International Women's Movement Anthology*, ed. Robin Morgan, 692–95. Garden City, NY: Anchor Press/Doubleday, 1984.

Helfferich, Barbara and Felix Kolb. "Multilevel Action Coordination in European Contentious Politics: The Case of the European Women's Lobby." In *European: Protest and Politics in an Emerging Polity*, ed. Doug Imig and Sidney Tarrow, 143–59. Oxford: Rowman & Littlefield Publishers, Inc., 2001.

Hernes, Helga Maria and Eva Hanninen-Salmelin. "Women in the Corporate System." In *Unfinished Democracy: Women in Nordic Politics*, ed. Elina Haavio-Mannila, 106–33. New York: Pergamon Press, 1985.

Hervey, Tamara. "Migrant Workers and Their Families in the European Union: The Pervasive Market Ideology of Community Law." In *New Legal Dynamics of European Union*, ed. Jo Shaw and Gillian More, 91–110. Oxford: Oxford University Press, 1995.

Hervey, Tamara and Jo Shaw. "Women, Work and Care: Women's Dual Role and Double Burden in EC Sex Equality Law." *Journal of European Social Policy* 8, no. 1 (1998): 43–63.

Hester, Marianne and Lorraine Radford. *Domestic Violence and Child Contact Arrangements in England and Denmark*. Bristol: Polity Press, 1996.

High Level Panel. *Report of High Panel on Free Movement of Persons*. 1997.

Hodgkinson, Liz. *Unholy Matrimony: The Case for Abolishing Marriage*. London: Columbus Books, 1988.

HOSI Wein. "Austria's Constitutional Court Dismisses Same-Sex Freedom of Movement Case." *ILGA Euro-Letter*, December 2004, 6.

Hoskyns, Catherine. "The European Union and the Women Within: An Overview of Women's Rights Policy." In *Sexual Politics and the European Union: The New Feminist Challenge*, ed. R. Amy Elman, 13–22. Oxford: Berghahn Books, 1996a.

———. *Integrating Gender: Women, Law and Politics in the European Union*. London: Verso, 1996b.

———. "A Study of Four Action Programmes on Equal Opportunities." In *Gender Policies in the European Union*, ed. Mariagrazia Rossilli, 43–59. New York: Peter Lang, 2000.

Hubert, Agnès. *L'Europe & Les Femmes: Identités En Mouvement, Collection Politique Européenne*. Rennes: Apogée, 1998.

———. "Moving Beyond Quotas in the EU: An Emerging Stage of Democracy." In *The Implementation of Quotas: European Experiences*. Budapest, Hungary: International Institute for Democracy and Electoral Assistance (IDEA)/CEE Network for Gender Issues Conference, 2004.

Hugendubel, Katrin. *Gender Budgeting*, Brussels: European Women's Lobby, 2004.

Hughes, Donna M., Laura Joy Sporcic, Nadine Z. Mendelsohn, and Vanessa Chirgwin. *The Factbook on Global Sexual Exploitation*. Coalition Against

Trafficking in Women, 1999 [cited February 3, 2007]. Available from http://www.catwinternational.org/factbook/index.php.

Hull, Gloria, Patricia Bell Scott, and Barbara Smith, eds. *All the Women Are White, All the Blacks Are Men, but Some of Us Are Brave: Black Women's Studies.* Old Westbury, NY: The Feminist Press, 1982.

ILGA-Europe. "Implementing the Framework Directive: A Guide for LBGT Organizations in the EU Member States and the Accession Countries." *Euro-Letter,* October 2001.

———. "Spain: Murcia judge removes custody from mother because she is a lesbian." *Euro-Letter,* June 2007.

International Lesbian and Gay Association. *Equality for Lesbians and Gay Men: A Relevant Issue in the Civil and Social Dialogue,* Brussels: ILGA-Europe, 1998.

International Organization for Migration. *Managing Migration for the Benefit of All,* IOM, 2005 [cited December 8, 2005]. Available from http://www.iom.int/.

Irish Government. *Report on Sexual Harassment in the Workplace in EU Member States,* The Irish Presidency of the European Union in association with Farrell Grant Sparks Consulting and Professor Aileen McGolgan, 2004 [cited December 23, 2006]. Available from http://www.justice.ie/80256E010039C5AF/vWeb/pcJUSQ63QLTX-en.

———. *Promoting Gender Equality.* Dublin: NDP/CSF Information Office, 2006.

Jack, Andrew and Jo Johnson. "WHO Concedes Battle with AIDS Still Being Lost." *Financial Times* 2005, 3.

Kagan, Robert. *Of Paradise and Power: America and Europe in the New World Order.* New York: Alfred A. Knopf, 2003.

KAL Advocacy Initiative. "Ireland: High Court Does Not Recognize Same-Sex Marriage." *ILGA Euro-Letter,* December 2006, 14.

Katzenstein, Mary Fainsod and Carol Mueller. *The Women's Movements of the United States and Western Europe: Consciousness, Political Opportunity, and Public Policy, Women in the Political Economy.* Philadelphia: Temple University Press, 1987.

Kelly, Liz. "Zero Commitment." *Trouble and Strife* 32 (1995/1996): 9–16.

King, Tim. "Commission Launches Brothel Probe." *EuropeanVoice.com,* July 7, 2005.

Kipnis, Laura. *Against Love.* New York: Vintage Books, 2003.

Kotatakos, Christine. *Europeans and Their Opinion about Domestic Violence against Women.* Brussels: European Commission Women's Information Sector, 1999.

Kramer, Jane. "Refugee: An Afghan Woman Who Fled Tyranny on Her Own." *The New Yorker,* January 20, 2003, 64–73.

———. "Taking the Veil: How France's Public Schools Became the Battleground in a Culture War." *The New Yorker,* November 22, 2004, 59–71.

Lahav, Gallya. *Immigration and Politics in the New Europe: Reinventing Borders.* Cambridge: Cambridge University Press, 2004.

Langenkamp, Travis J. "Finding Fundamental Fairness: Protecting the Rights of Homosexuals under European Accession Law." *San Diego International Law Journal* 4 (2003): 437–66.

Lanquetin, Marie-Thérèse, Jacqueline Laufer, and Marie-Thérèse Leablier. "From Equality to Reconciliation in France?" In *Gendered Policies in Europe: Reconciling Employment and Family Life*, ed. Linda Hantrais, 68–88. New York: St. Martin's Press, 2000.

Leghorn, Lisa and Katherine Parker. *Woman's Worth: Sexual Economics and the World of Women*. Boston: Routledge and Kegan Paul, 1981.

Leidholdt, Dorchen. "Sexual Trafficking of Women in Europe." In *Sexual Politics and the European Union: The New Feminist Challenge*, ed. R. Amy Elman, 83–95. Oxford: Berghahn Books, 1996.

———. "Prostitution: A Form of Modern Slavery." In *Making the Harm Visible: Global Sexual Exploitation of Women and Girls*, ed. Donna Hughes, 49–55. Kingston, Rhodes Island: Coalition Against Trafficking in Women, 1999.

"Lesbian Couple's High Court Test." August 12, 2005. Accessed http://news.bbc.co.uk.

"Lesbians Win Appeal over Kiss." *The Independent*, April 26, 2005, 26.

Llamas, Ricardo and Fefa Vila. "Passion for Life: A History of the Lesbian and Gay Movement in Spain." In *The Global Emergence of Gay and Lesbian Politics: National Imprints of a Worldwide Movement*, ed. Barry D. Adam, Jan Willem Duyvendak, and André Krowel, 214–41. Philadelphia: Temple University Press, 1999.

Lohkamp-Himmighofen, Marlene and Christiane Dienel. "Reconciliation Policies from a Comparative Perspective." In *Gendered Policies in Europe: Reconciling Employment and Family Life*, ed. Linda Hantrais, 49–67. New York: St. Martin's Press, 2000.

Lombardo, Emanuela. "EU Gender Policy: Trapped in the 'Wollstonecraft Dilemma'?" *The European Journal of Women's Studies* 10, no. 2 (2003): 159–80.

Longo, Patrizia. "Revisiting the Equality/Difference Debate: Redefining Citizenship for the New Millennium." *Citizenship Studies* 5, no. 3 (2001): 269–84.

Louis, Marie-Victoire. "Legalizing Pimping, Dutch Style." In *Making the Harm Visible: Global Sexual Exploitation of Women and Girls*. ed. Donna Hughes, 192–96. Kingston, Rhode Island: Coalition Against Trafficking in Women, 1999.

"Love Bridge to Sweden." *Economist*, July 10, 2004, 46.

Lovenduski, Joni and Susan Stephenson. *Women in Decision-Making: Report on Existing Research in the European Union*, Luxembourg: Office for the Official Publications of the European Communities, 1999.

Lubin, Carol Riegelman and Anne Winslow. *Social Justice for Women: The International Labor Organization and Women*. Durham: Duke University Press, 1990.

Lundgren, Eva, Gun Heimer, Jenny Westerstrand, and Anne-Marie Kalliokoskim. *Captured Queen: Men's Violence against Women in "Equal" Sweden–A Prevalence Study*. Stockholm: Fritzes Offentliga Publikationer, 2001.

Lyons, Carole. "Citizenship in the Constitution of the European Union: Rhetoric or Reality." In *Constitutionalism, Democracy and Sovereignty: American and European Perspectives*, ed. Richard Bellamy, 96–110. Aldershot, UK: Avebury, 1996.

MacKinnon, Catharine A. "Feminism, Marxism, Method and the State: Toward Feminist Jurisprudence." *Signs* 8 (1983).

———. *Sex Equality, University Casebook Series*. New York: Foundation Press, 2001.

———. *Women's Lives—Men's Laws*. Cambridge, MA: Belknap Press of Harvard University Press, 2005.

———. *Are Women Human?: And Other International Dialogues*. Cambridge, MA: Belknap Press of Harvard University Press, 2006.

Macrae, Heather. "Morality, Censorship, and Discrimination: Reframing the Pornography Debate in Germany and Europe." *Social Politics: International Studies in Gender, State & Society* 10, no. 3 (2003): 314–44.

Majone, Giandomenico. "The European Community between Social Policy and Social Regulation." *Journal of Common Market Studies* 31, no. 2 (1993): 153–70.

Malos, Ellen and Gill Hague. "Women, Housing, Homelessness and Domestic Violence." *Women's Studies International Forum* 20, no. 3 (1997): 397–409.

Marcovich, Malka. "Human Rights: A European Challenge." In *Making the Harm Visible: Global Sexual Exploitation of Women and Girls*, ed. Donna Hughes, 197–202. Kingston, Rhodes Island: Coalition Against Trafficking in Women, 1999.

Marshall, T.H. *Social Policy*. London: Hutchinson, 1975.

Mazey, Sonia P. "European Community Action on Behalf of Women: The Limits of Legislation." *Journal of Common Market Studies* 27, no. 1 (1988): 63–84.

———. "Introduction: Integrating Gender—Intellectual and 'Real World' Mainstreaming." *Journal of European Public Policy* 7, no. 3 (2000): 333–45.

———. "The Development of EU Gender Policies: Towards the Recognition of Difference." *EUSA Review* 15, no. 3 (2002): 1–3.

Mazur, Amy G. "The Interplay: The Formation of Sexual Harassment Legislation in France and EU Policy Initiatives." In *Sexual Politics and the European Union: The New Feminist Challenge*, ed. R. Amy Elman, 35–49. Oxford: Berghahn Books, 1996.

McGee, Hannah, Rebecca Garavan, Mairead deBarra, Joanne Byrne, and Ronan Conray. *The SAVI Report: Sexual Abuse and Violence in Ireland; A National Study of Irish Experiences, Beliefs and Attitudes Concerning Sexual Violence*. Dublin: Dublin Rape Crisis Centre; Liffey Press, 2002.

McGlynn, Clare. "A Family Law for the European Union." In *Social Law and Policy in an Evolving European Union*, ed. Jo Shaw, 223–41. Oxford: Hart, 2000.

McLoughlin, Micheal T. "Crystal or Glass?: A Review of Dudgeon v United Kingdom on the Fifteenth Anniversary of the Decision." *Murdoch University Electronic Journal of Law* 3, no. 4 (1996).

Medina-Ariza, Juanjo and Rosemary Barberet. "Intimate Partner Violence in Spain." *Violence Against Women* 9, no. 3 (2003): 302–22.

Mirlees-Black, Catriona. *Domestic Violence: Findings from the British Crime Survey Self Completion Questionnaire Research Study.* London: Home Office, Volume 191, 1999.

Mushaben, Joyce Marie. "The Other 'Democratic Deficit': Women in the European Community before and after Maastricht." In *Europe after Maastricht*, ed. Paul Michael Lützeler, 251–75. Providence: Berghahn Books, 1994.

Nelsen, Brent F. and James L. Guth. "Exploring the Gender Gap: Women, Men and Public Attitudes toward European Integration." *European Union Politics* 1, no. 3 (2000): 267–91.

"New Steps Proposed in Equality Dance." *European Voice*, January 9, 1997.

Nissen, Vibeke and Inge-Lise Paulsen. *Lesbian Visibility: A Report about Lesbians in the European Community.* Århus: Commission of the European Communities' Equal Opportunity Unit and LBL (the National Danish Association of Gays and Lesbians) and ILGA (the International Lesbian and Gay Association), 1995.

Nordic Council of Ministers. *Shelters for Battered Women and the Needs of Immigrant Women.* Copenhagen: Nordic Council of Ministers, 1998.

"Northern Ireland: Shocking Statistics on Gay Youth." *ILGA-Europe Newsletter*, March 2004, 19.

Ohms, Constance. "'I Don't Mind, but . . .' Violence against Lesbians." *ILGA Europe Newsletter*, February 2002, 7–9.

Okin, Susan Moller, ed. *Is Multiculturalism Bad for Women?* New Jersey: Princeton University Press, 1999.

OPTEM. "Study on Integrating Gender Mainstreaming into Employment Policies: Covering Public-Authority Officials Responsible for Employment Policies and Social Partners in the 15 Member States of the European Union." [December 12, 2002]. Accessed http://europa.eu.int/comm/public_ opinion/quali/ql_gender2002_en.pdf.

Organization for the Economic Co-operation and Development. "Focus on Part-Time Work." In *Employment Outlook.* Paris: OECD, 1999.

Orwell, George. *Why I Write.* New York: Penguin Books, 2005.

Ostner, Ilona. "From Equal Pay to Equal Employability: Four Decades of European Gender Policies." In *Gender Policies in the European Union*, ed. Mariagrazia Rossilli, 25–42. New York: Peter Lang, 2000.

Ostner, Ilona and Jane Lewis. "Gender and the Evolution of European Social Policies." In *European Social Policy: Between Fragmentation and Integration*, ed. Stephan Leibfried and Paul Pierson, 159–93. Washington, DC: The Brookings Institution, 1995.

Outshoorn, Joyce. "Introduction: Prostitution, Women's Movements and Democratic Politics." In *The Politics of Prostitution: Women's Movements,*

Democratic States, and the Globalisation of Sex Commerce, ed. Joyce Outshoorn, 1–20. Cambridge, UK; New York: Cambridge University Press, 2004.

Palmer, Anya. "Britain." In *Unspoken Rules: Sexual Orientation and Women's Human Rights*, ed. Rachel Rosenbloom, 25–33. London: Cassell, 1996.

Penn, Michael L. and Rachel Nardos. *Overcoming Violence against Women and Girls: The International Campaign to Eradicate a Worldwide Problem*. Oxford: Rowman & Littlefield, 2003.

Petersen, Cynthia. "Envisioning a Lesbian Equality Jurisprudence." In *Legal Inversions: Lesbians, Gay Men, and the Politics of Law*, ed. Didi Herman and Carl Stychin, 118–37. Philadelphia: Temple University Press, 1995.

Phillips, Andrew. "Porn from the Skies." *Maclean's* 1993, 48.

Political Gateway. "Greece Does Not Want Gays in Its Armed Forces." *ILGA Euro-Letter*, April 2006, 8.

Pollack, Mark A. "EU Equal Opportunity Policy: Towards a Broader Agenda?" Paper presented at the Conference of the European Community Studies Association, Pittsburgh, June 3–6, 1999.

Pollack, Mark A. and Emilie M. Hafner-Burton. "Mainstreaming Gender in the European Union." *Journal of European Public Policy* 7, no. 3 (2000): 432–56.

———. "No Revolution: The Disappointing Implementation of Gender Mainstreaming in the European Union." *European Politics & Society: Newsletter of the European Politics & Society Section of the American Political Science Association* 6, no. 1 (2007): 11–13.

Randall, Vicky. "Childcare Policy in the European States, Limits to Convergence." *Journal of European Public Policy* 7, no. 3 (2000): 346–68.

Rankine, Jenny. "For Better or for Worse." *Trouble and Strife*, Winter 1996/1997, 5–11.

Rauhofer, Judith. "The Possibility of a Registered Partnership under German Law." In *Legal Queeries: Lesbian, Gay and Transgender Legal Studies*, ed. Leslie J. Moran, Daniel Monk, and Sarah Beresford, 68–80. New York: Cassell, 1998.

Raymond, Janice G. *Guide to the New UN Trafficking Protocol*, North Hampton, MA: Coalition Against Trafficking in Women, 2001.

———. "Ten Reasons for Not Legalizing Prostitution and a Legal Response to the Demand for Prostitution." *Journal of Trauma Practice* 2 (2003): 315–32.

Rees, Teresa L. *Mainstreaming Equality in the European Union: Education, Training and Labour Market Policies*. London; New York: Routledge, 1998.

Reid, T.R. *The United States of Europe: The New Superpower and the End of American Supremacy*. New York: Penguin Books, 2004.

Renzetti, Claire M. and Charles Harvey Miley, eds. *Violence in Gay and Lesbian Partnerships*. Binghamton, NY: Harrington Park Press, 1996.

"A Retrograde Decision." *The Irish Times*, October 9, 2006, 15.

Rieder, Ines. "Lesbianism in the House of Europe." In *Women and Citizenship in Europe*, ed. Anna Ward, Jeanne Gregory, and Nira Yuval-Davis, 107–10. Exeter: Trentham Books and EFSF, 1992.

Rifkin, Jeremy. *The European Dream: How Europe's Vision of the Future Is Quietly Eclipsing the American Dream*. New York: Tarcher/Penguin, 2004.

Robson, Ruthann. "Resisting the Family: Repositioning Lesbians in Legal Theory." *Signs: Journal of Women in Culture and Society* 19, no. 4 (1994): 975–96.

Römkens, Renée. "Prevalence of Wife Abuse in the Netherlands: Combining Quantitative and Qualitative Methods in Survey Research." *Journal of Interpersonal Violence* 12 (1997): 99–125.

Rosen, Ruth. *The World Split Open: How the Modern Women's Movement Changed America*. New York: Penguin Books, 2001.

Rosenbloom, Rachel. "Introduction." In *Unspoken Rules: Sexual Orientation and Women's Human Rights*, ed. Rachel Rosenbloom, ix–xxxi. London: Cassell, 1996b.

———, ed. *Unspoken Rules: Sexual Orientation and Women's Human Rights*. London: Cassell, 1996a.

Rossilli, Mariagrazia. *Gender Policies in the European Union*. New York: Peter Lang, 2000.

Roth, Claudia. *Report for the Committee on Internal Affairs and Citizens Rights on Equal Rights for Homosexuals and Lesbians in the European Community*. Strasbourg: European Parliament, 1994.

Rubenstein, Michael. *The Dignity of Women at Work: A Report on the Problem of Sexual Harassment in the Member States of the European Communities*. Brussels: Office for Official Publications of the European Communities, 1988.

Rubery, Jill, Mark Smith, and Colette Fagan. *Women's Employment in Europe: Trends and Prospects*. London; New York: Routledge, 1999.

Rucht, Dieter. "Interactions between Social Movements and States in Comparative Perspective." In *Women's Movements Facing the Reconfigured State*, ed. Lee Ann Banaszak, Karen Beckwith, and Dieter Rucht, 242–74. New York: Cambridge University Press, 2003.

Rupp, Leila J. *Worlds of Women: The Making of an International Women's Movement*. Princeton, NJ: Princeton University Press, 1997.

Salt, John and Jennifer Hogarth. "Migrant Trafficking and Human Smuggling in Europe: A Review of the Evidence." In *Migrant Trafficking and Human Smuggling in Europe: A Review of Evidence with Case Studies from Hungary, Poland and Ukraine*, ed. Frank Laczko and David Thompson, 11–163. Geneva: International Organization for Migration, 2000.

Sanders, Douglas. "Getting Lesbian and Gay Issues on the International Human Rights Agenda." *Human Rights Quarterly* 18, no. 1 (1996): 67–106.

Schneider, Peter. "The New Berlin Wall." *The New York Times*, December 4, 2005.

Sedgwick, Eve Kosofsky. *Epistemology of the Closet*. Berkeley: University of California Press, 1990.

Shaw, Jo. "Gender Mainstreaming and the EU Constitution." *EUSA Review* 15, no. 3 (2002): 4–5.

Simon, Robert. "NGO's Mobilisation against Homophobic Crime in France." *ILGA Euro-Letter*, May 2004, 5.

Simons, Marlise. "A Graphic Film of Protest, and Cries of Blasphemy." *The New York Times*, September 27, 2004, A4.

Siposova, Marianna. *Slovakia—Sexual Orientation Discrimination: The Employment Framework Directive and Beyond.* Accessed on-line. European Parliament Hearing, 2003.

Smyth, Ailbhe. "The Contemporary Women's Movement in the Republic of Ireland 1970–1990." In *Irish Women's Studies Reader*, ed. Ailbhe Smyth, 245–69. Dublin: Attic Press, 1993.

———. "'and Nobody Was Any the Wiser': Irish Abortion Rights and the European Union." In *Sexual Politics and the European Union: The New Feminist Challenge*, ed. R. Amy Elman, 109–30. Oxford: Berghahn Books, 1996.

Sommestad, Lena. *Gender Equality—A Key to Our Future.* The Swedish Government, 2002 [cited February 14, 2007]. Available from www.sweden.gov.se.

Stevens, Jacqueline. *Reproducing the State.* Princeton, NJ: Princeton University Press, 1999.

Stratigaki, Maria. "The EU and the Equal Opportunities Process." In *Gendered Policies in Europe: Reconciling Employment and Family Life*, ed. Linda Hantrais, 27–48. London: Macmillan Press, 2000.

———. "Gender Mainstreaming vs Positive Action: An Ongoing Conflict in EU Gender Equality Policy." *European Journal of Women's Studies* 12, no. 2 (2005): 165–86.

Stychin, Carl F. *A Nation by Rights: National Cultures, Sexual Identity Politics, and the Discourse of Rights, Queer Politics, Queer Theories.* Philadelphia: Temple University Press, 1998.

———. "Grant-Ing Rights: The Politics of Rights, Sexuality and European Union." *Northern Ireland Legal Quarterly* 51, no. 2 (2000): 281–302.

———. "Same-Sex Sexualities and the Globalization of Human Rights Discourse." *McGill Law Journal* 49 (2004): 951–68.

Sullerot, Evelyn. "Equality of Remuneration for Men and Women in the Member States of the EEC." *International Labour Review* 112, no. 2–3 (1975): 87–108.

"Sweden to Allow IVF for Lesbians." [March 3, 2005]. Accessed http://news.bbc.co.uk/go/pr/fr/-/2/hi/europe/4315145.stm.

Swedish Government. "Prostitution and Trafficking in Women." [March 20, 2004]. Accessed http://www.sweden.gov.se/content/1/c6/01/87/74/ 6bc6c972.pdf.

Tanca, Antonio. "European Citizenship and the Rights of Lesbians and Gay Men." In *Homosexuality: A European Community Issue*, ed. Kees Waaldijk and Andrew Clapham, 267–88. London: Martinus Nijhoff Publishers, 1993.

Tatchell, Peter. *Europe in the Pink: Lesbian & Gay Equality in the New Europe.* London: GMP, 1992.

Toner, Helen. *Partnership Rights, Free Movement and EU Law.* Oxford and Portland: Hart Publishing, 2004.

"Turkey's Homosexuals Call for Stronger EU Support." *Agence France Presse—English*, February 15, 2005. Accessed http://lexis.nexis.com/universe.

U.S. Department of State. *Country Reports on Human Rights Practices.* Bureau of Democracy, Human Rights, and Labor: 2003.

"UK: Same Sex Couple Lose Marriage Laws Challenge." *ILGA Euro-Letter*, August 2006, 9.

United Nations. "Geneva Convention Relating to the Status of Refugees. Adopted on 28 July 1951 by the United Nations Conference of Plenipotentiaries on the Status of Refugees and Stateless Persons Convened under General Assembly Resolution 429 (V) of 14 December 1950." 1951.

United Nations General Assembly. "Declaration on the Elimination of Violence against Women." General Assembly resolution 48/104 of December 20, 1993, February 23, 1994.

Valiente, Celia. "Reconciliation Policies in Spain." In *Gendered Policies in Europe: Reconciling Employment and Family Life*, ed. Linda Hantrais, 143–59. New York: St. Martin's Press, 2000.

Vallance, Elizabeth and Elizabeth V. Davies. *Women of Europe: Women MEPs and Equality Policy.* New York: Cambridge University Press, 1986.

van Ham, Peter. "The Rise of the Brand State: The Postmodern Politics of Image and Reputation." *Foreign Affairs* 80, no. 5 (2001): 2–6.

Veen, Evert van der and Adrianne Dercksen. "The Social Situation in Member States." In *Homosexuality: A European Community Issue*, ed. Kees Waaldijk and Andrew Clapham, 131–62. London: Martinus Nijhoff Publishers, 1993.

Verloo, Mieke. "Multiple Inequalities, Intersectionality and the European Union." *European Journal of Women's Studies* 13, no. 3 (2006): 211–28.

Vogel-Polsky, Eliane. "L'article 119 Du Traité De Rome—Peut-Il Être Considéré Comme Self-Executing?" *Journal des Tribunaux* (1967).

———. "Parity Democracy—Law and Europe." In *Gender Policies in the European Union*, ed. Mariagrazia Rossilli, 61–85. New York: Peter Lang, 2000.

Waaldijk, Kees. "Small Change: How the Road to Same-Sex Marriage Got Paved in the Netherlands." In *Legal Recognition of Same Sex Partnerships: A Study of National European and International Law*, ed. Robert Wintemute and Mads Andeneaes, 437–64. Oxford: Hart Publishing, 2001a.

———. "Toward the Recognition of Same-Sex Partners in European Union Law: Expectations Based on Trends in National Law." In *Legal Recognition of Same Sex Partnerships: A Study of National European and International Law*, ed. Robert Wintemute and Mads Andeneaes, 635–51. Oxford: Hart Publishing, 2001b.

———. "Comparative Analysis." In *Combating Sexual Orientation Discrimination in Employment: Legislation in Fifteen EU Member States*, ed. Kees Waaldijk and Matteo Bonini-Baraldi, 533–97. Accessed online August 10, 2005. Commission of the European Communities, 2004.

Waaldijk, Kees and Matteo Bonini-Baraldi, eds. *Combating Sexual Orientation Discrimination in Employment: Legislation in Fifteen EU Member States.* Accessed online August 10, 2005. Commission of the European Communities, 2004.

Waaldijk, Kees and Andrew Clapham, eds. *Homosexuality: A European Community Issue— Essays on Lesbian and Gay Rights in European Law and Policy.* London: Martinus Nijhoff, 1993.

Walby, Sylvia. "The European Union and Gender Equality: Emergent Varieties of Gender Regime." *Social Politics: International Studies in Gender, State & Society* 11, no. 1 (2004): 4–29.

Walby, Sylvia and Andrew Myhill. "New Survey Methodologies in Researching Violence against Women." *British Journal of Criminology* 41 (2001): 502–22.

Walzer, Michael. *Obligations; Essays on Disobedience, War, and Citizenship.* Cambridge: Harvard University Press, 1970.

Ward, Ian. *A Critical Introduction to European Law.* 2nd ed. London: Lexis Nexis, 2003.

Weatherill, Stephen and Paul Beaumont. *EC Law.* 2nd ed. London: Penguin Books, 1995.

Weiler, Joseph H.H. "The Transformation of Europe." *Yale Law Journal* 100 (1991): 2403–83.

———. "'Thou Shalt Not Oppress a Stranger': On the Judicial Protection of Human Rights of Non-EC Nationals." *European Journal of International Law* 3 (1992): 65–91.

Wennberg, Jenny. *EU Financial Support for Projects and Organizations Which Advocate the Legalization and Regulation of Prostitution.* European Parliament, 2002.

Wiener, Antje. "Making Sense of the New Geography of Citizenship: Fragmented Citizenship in the European Union." *Theory and Society* 26 (1997): 529–60.

Williams, Andrew. *EU Human Rights Policies: A Study in Irony.* Oxford: Oxford University Press, 2004.

Wintemute, Robert. *Sexual Orientation and Human Rights: The United States Constitution, the European Convention, and the Canadian Charter.* Oxford: Clarendon Press, 1995.

Women Living Under Muslim Laws. *An International Network that Provides Information, Solidarity and Support for All Women Whose Lives Are Shaped, Conditioned or Governed by Laws and Customs Said to Derive from Islam* 2001–2007 [cited February 14, 2007]. Available from http://www.wluml.org/english/index.shtml.

Woodward, Alison. "European Gender Mainstreaming: Promises and Pitfalls of Transformative Policy." *Review of Policy Research* 20, no. 1 (2003): 65–88.

Zippel, Kathrin S. "Transnational Advocacy Networks and Policy Cycles in the European Union: The Case of Sexual Harassment." *Social Politics: International Studies in Gender, State & Society* 11, no. 1 (2004): 57–85.

———. *The Politics of Sexual Harassment: A Comparative Study of the United States, the European Union, and Germany.* Cambridge; New York: Cambridge University Press, 2006.

———. "Violence at Work? Framing Sexual Harassment in the European Union." In *Gender Issues and Women's Movements in the Enlarged European Union,* ed. Silke Roth. London, New York: Berghahn Books, 2007.

Cited Interviews

Angela Beausang, Former Chair of Sweden's National Battered Women's Association, interview concerning the Community's influence on Swedish policies pertaining to violence against women, Stockholm, May 19, 1999.

Sophie De Jonckheere, Policy Manager for the European Network Against Racism—ENAR, interview concerning the reach of EU equality policies concerning racism, Brussels, December 12, 2003.

Simon Duffin, Secretary for the Committee on Employment and Social Affairs, interview concerning violence against women and gender mainstreaming, July 28, 1999.

Anita Gradin, Former European Union Commissioner, phone interview concerning the Commission's approach to violence against women during her tenure, July 19, 1999.

Cécile Greboval, Policy Coordinator for the European Women's Lobby, interview concerning the Lobby's priorities and recent legislation, Brussels, December 12, 2003.

Agnés Hubert, Former Head of the Equal Opportunities Unit, interview concerning general developments in sexual equality policy in the EU with a focus on gender mainstreaming, Brussels, December 12, 2003.

Michèle Idels, Attorney and Assistant to Antoinette Fouque, Former Vice Chair of the Parliament's Committee on Women's Rights—CWR, interview concerning the Committee's history, Paris, November 29, 2005.

Kirsti Kolthoff, President of the European Women's Lobby—EWL, interview concerning the Lobby's challenges and current foci, Stockholm, November 18, 2005.

Malka Marcovich, President of Movement for the Abolition of Prostitution and Pornography and All Forms of Sexual Violence and Sexist Discrimination—MAPP, interview concerning the EU's positions on trafficking in women, Paris, December 8, 2003.

Anthony Simpson, Head of Justice and Home Affairs Task Force for DAPHNE, interview concerning the establishment of DAPHNE and funding procedures, Brussels, July 28, 1999.

Ailsa Spindler, Executive Director of the International Lesbian and Gay Association—ILGA-Europe, interview concerning the reach of equality policies for lesbians and gay men, Brussels, December 11, 2003.

Elvy Svennerstål, Head of Unit, Secretariat of the Parliament's Committee on Women Rights and Gender Equality, interview concerning the Committee, Brussels, July 28, 1999.

Index